On Modern German Literature

On Modern German Literature

PAUL KONRAD KURZ, S.J.

Volume I

English translation by
SISTER MARY FRANCES MCCARTHY

THE UNIVERSITY OF ALABAMA PRESS
University, Alabama

Table of Contents

1 Vicissitudes of the Modern Novel   3

2 Perspectives in Kafka Interpretation   30

3 Literature and Science   56

4 Literature and Theology Today   80

5 Hermann Broch's Trilogy *Die Schlafwandler*   105

6 *Hundejahre*   131

7 Doomed Existence   149

8 Skeletons of the Sayable—Demonstrations of a World   173

9 Journey into Dustlessness   194

Notes   216

Index   241

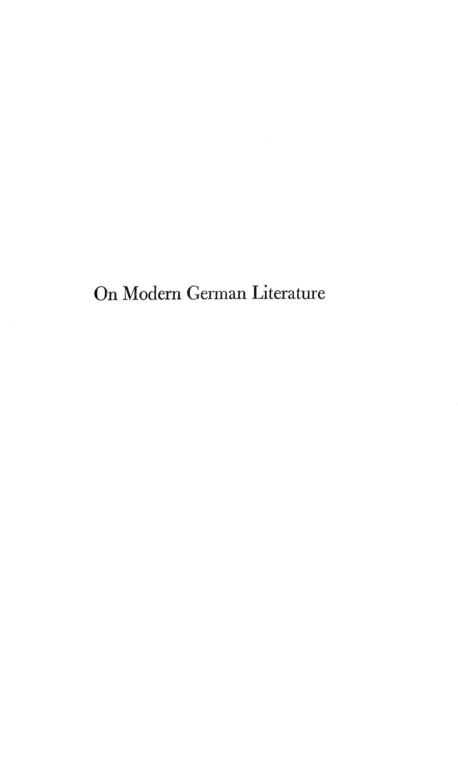

On Modern German Literature

1

Vicissitudes
of the Modern Novel

Most people encounter modern literature for the first time in the form of the novel. But the modern novel must surely disappoint readers whose expectations have been formed and nourished by the great novels of the nineteenth century, for it reveals less unity of structure than does the traditional or so-called classical novel. There are merely individual differentiations, narrative forms, which show to a greater or lesser degree the characteristics that we consider specifically "modern." Even more than the classical novel, the modern novel is a structure that is both ideal and typical; it is the result of literary philosophizing, comparing, and abstracting. Without the discovery of this ideal, typical structure of the modern novel, there could be neither the concept of genre (the discovery of the common element in a multiplicity of individual works), nor the awareness of an epoch. When we inquire about the "modern" novel, we are attempting to discover and to designate typical qualities, characteristic marks, common traits and tendencies in those novels of the present that—problematically, consciously, and formally—stand at the peak of their era; that is to say, in avant-garde structures that, in a normative way, give expression to the stylistic traits of the present. That this expression is to be found only in the artistic novel, not in the entertaining or light novel, needs hardly be stressed.

The Traditional Novel

Edward—for we shall give this name to a rich Baron in the prime of life—Edward had spent the most delightful hour of an April afternoon in his tree-nursery, grafting shoots, which he had recently received, into the stems of young trees. He had just finished this work and put his tools away in their box. He was regarding the completed task with satisfaction when the gardener entered, smiling indulgently at his master's absorbed interest.

"Have you seen my wife anywhere?" asked Edward as he prepared to leave.

"Over in the new park," answered the gardener. "The moss house that she's been making against the cliff opposite the castle will be finished today. Your Grace will be pleased. Everything has turned out quite well. There's an excellent view: below is the village, a little to the right is the church—you almost see over its spires—and opposite are the castle and the gardens."

These are the opening paragraphs of Goethe's novel, *Die Wahlverwandtschaften* [Elective Affinities], which he announced in Cotta's *Morgenblatt für gebildete Stände* [Morning Register for the Cultured Classes] on September 4, 1809. They reveal everything that we as readers expect the beginning of a novel to reveal: the "hero," the narrator, the action. Time appears in its normal guise, place in a recognizable garb. In dignified language and in a comfortable narrative tone, the words conjure up a scene that we find beautiful. The narrator has secured his vantage point and assures us of his superior knowledge. Like Zeus on Olympus, he surveys his kingdom, his characters, the course of the action. In a word, this is a "classical" novel.

The "hero" of this novel is called Edward. He is presented as "a rich Baron in the prime of life." The one who introduces him introduces himself with the majestic plural of royalty (*"we* shall call him Edward," he says). He is the narrator. He does not hurl the reader into the midst of the action or even compel him to reflect upon it. He does not isolate a single sentence from the action of the novel as does the modern author whose novel begins: "But Jacob has always crossed the tracks," so that the reader must ask himself, "Who is this Jacob?" "Who says this about him and what

4

does it mean?" The narrator in Goethe's novel is not like the narrator in Uwe Johnson's *Mutmassungen über Jakob* [Speculations about Jacob], who alienates the reader with his first sentence by presuming knowledge of a situation about which the reader knows nothing, thus making a riddle of it. The narrator of *Die Wahlverwandtschaften* takes the reader protectively by the hand and inspires him with confidence. Before he allows the conflict between husband and wife to develop, he depicts them first in peaceful harmony. And before he unfolds the action, he erects a stage for it, as much for the reader's sake as for the sake of the action itself. It is as if he said, "The action will take place here, in this environment and in this circumscribed area of the estate with its gardens, terraces, castle and church, cemetery and village." The thread of time is also carefully woven. It is "the most beautiful hour of an April afternoon." The Baron "was regarding his work with satisfaction"; the gardener was "smiling indulgently." After this universal contentment has been affirmed and the scene has been properly surveyed, the stage is set for the first conversation between husband and wife. A path leads past shrubbery and garden seat up to the favorite spot of the Baroness, the newly completed moss house. She awaits her husband there. The shrubbery is "attractive," the landscape like a cultivated park; the mood of the loving couple is "serene and happy." An incomparable idyll. The conversation can begin. The reader feels himself secure and, as it were, classically exalted. He is so enraptured that he scarcely notices that he himself is already in the midst of the scene, listening and watching. Soon he will be initiated into the very stirrings of the heart. "Hero" and plot are being created anew in his own breast. It is true that the reader will presently learn that the demon of passion has invaded the disciplined world of husband and wife. But the manner of its happening and the way it is told are elevating. The pure figure of the foster daughter Ottilie, who resolves the conflict, seems almost supernatural. The fate of these defenseless beings is gripping. The tragic outcome of this unsolvable dilemma brings its own peace. Marriage is sanctioned. Death is transfigured. The two lovers are glorified. Teller and tale, characters and language, freedom and fate; everything has been completed, perfected, ennobled. The end is unforgettable: "And so the lovers lie near to one another. Peace hovers over their resting-place; from the vaulting above, sympathetic angels look down upon them; and what a joyous moment that will be, when they at last awake again together." The harmony of the eternal shines through the earthly. Nothing wounds the sensibilities of the reader; his noblest feelings are aroused and approved.

Now that we have read the beginning and end of this typical classical novel, let us imagine a reader from another world, one who has been accustomed to read the pastoral, courtly, or picaresque novels of the Baroque Age and who, therefore, accepts the narrative technique and world view of the Baroque Age as normative for the novel as such. What would such a reader of the seventeenth century be compelled to think if *Die Wahlverwandtschaften* were suddenly recommended to him as a bestseller, or if all of Goethe's novels, from *Die Leiden des jungen Werther* [The Sorrows of Young Werther] to *Wilhelm Meisters Wanderjahre* [Wilhelm Meister's Travels] were stacked on the table in front of him? Doubtless he would be compelled to regard all that as disturbingly modern. This positively morbid psychologizing and youthful exaggeration of feeling in *Werther;* this questionable dissolution of form in the *Wanderjahre* with its tales, *novelle*, aphorisms, letters, excerpts from diaries, and philanthropic interpolations and pedagogical essays. This dubious absence of the outer world in the *Wahlverwandtschaften*. What kind of microcosm is this? No court ceremonies, no adventures, no wars, no travels to distant lands, not even a proper shepherd's play or a few real farces! Love in the *Wahlverwandtschaften* is not a harmless erotic game, but at once morbidly intense and unhealthily tragic. The emotional intensity of the characters and the noticeable lack of exterior action is suspiciously un-Baroque. We might continue our exercise in understanding the limitations imposed by history and the conditioning effect of custom on judgment by asking what an educated person from the Age of Enlightenment (for instance, Johann Christoph Gottsched) might have said to the tragic exaggeration of feeling in *Werther* or to the compulsively unfree love between Edward and Ottilie. How might a pious popular writer like Johann Fürchtegott Gellert have objected to the lack of Christian sentiment in Goethe's novels? Even better, we might

6

imagine to ourselves a literary critic who had learned his classical norms from Goethe's *Iphigenie,* or *Römische Elegien,* or *Hermann und Dorothea,* and who now proposes, under the aegis of the classical Goethe, to judge this late Goethe, in whose *West-Östlicher Divan* [East-West Divan], *Wanderjahre,* and *Faust II* the classical forms of lyric, epic, and drama have been dissolved. What has become of horizontal structure in the *Wanderjahre?* of the steadily progressive development of the "hero"? of the firm hand of the narrator? If Goethe himself cannot be measured with a single inflexible measuring rod, is it surprising that the *Wahlverwandtschaften,* written about 150 years after *Der abenteuerliche Simplicissimus teutsch* [The Adventurous Simplicissimus, the German], can no longer be judged correctly by Baroque standards? Is it surprising, to carry our inquiry one step farther, if we today, about 150 years after Goethe's "classical" novels, cannot really assess the modern novels of Kafka, Joyce, Musil, Grass, Walser, Johnson with norms derived from Goethe?

The Modern Novel

What makes the modern novel really modern? To the reader who has not been carefully prepared, the modern novel appears, at first, as an aggregate of restlessness, alienation, and disorientation in a world that he has learned to know and trust. Comfort and ease seem to have been relegated to the rubbish heap. What modern novel of any stature can be read after an evening out or recommended for relaxation? Many modern novels are problem novels. Reading them is like solving a puzzle; often enough, it is like sitting in a torture-chair. Their atmosphere seems too tense, their content repulsive. There is hardly a sentence to mankind from the Bible or from faith that they have not distorted, that might not have been dragged through the gutter of parody and the lower instincts. Men are shown as crass monsters, as run-of-the-mill also-rans, as successful administrators, as liars and debauchees, as torturers and abandoned victims. The world of this civilization seems as restricted as a concentration camp, as commercial as a billboard, inundated with sewage, soulless, expendable, uninhabitable, futile, and betrayed. The hard-won balance of our inner life is painfully stirred by the reading of such novels. Modern authors delight in tearing the last veils of soothing illusion from our hitherto peaceful eyes. Criticism of prosperity and literary sadism, pleasure and anger, demanding judgment and gratifying pandemonium are often hard to distinguish. Should we, as normally peaceful citizens, use modern air conditioners, travel on superhighways, and yet despise or at least ignore the modern novel? Such a gesture presumes knowledge. Knowledge almost always generates discrimination.

In contrast to the ancient and medieval epic, the modern form of the epic par excellence is the novel. The label "modern" as a designation for contemporary forms of literary expression is not new. In 1796, Fredrich Schlegel wrote an essay *Über das Studium der modernen Poesie* [On the Study of Modern Poetry], in which he attempted to assess "modern poetry" on its own terms, "to find the principle of its formation," to "understand by its own norms" poetry that by ancient classical norms would have seemed "lacking in character" and "anarchical." In fact, Schlegel contended, "unresolvable disharmony" and "colossal dissonance" have been detected even in the tragedies of Shakespeare. Is it not possible, then, that snap judgments about contemporary literature may reflect the existence of "aesthetic prejudices which are far more deeply rooted, more generally disseminated, and immeasurably more harmful than might appear at the first fleeting glance?" A generation later, in 1831, Heinrich Heine wrote angrily from Paris for the second printing of part two of his *Reisebilder* [Travel Pictures] about the "keen delight in pain that characterizes those modern lyrics which reveal no Catholic harmony of the emotions, but rather dissect them with Jacobinical inexorableness in the name of truth." Neither in the time of the young Friedrich Schlegel nor in that of the young Heinrich Heine had anyone found the *mot juste* for contemporary literature. In both generations, it was simply designated by the word "modern." From the same embarrassment and with the same inexactness, we speak today of the "modern" novel. Our task is, as Schlegel once said, to discover "the principle of its formation." The ancient and medieval epic was formally sustained by the verse. Even more, it was, of its very nature, sustained by a society whose members were conscious of being bound together by the same philosophy of life and the same attitude toward the world around them, by community in a world whose meaning might, it is true, be temporarily obscured, but was never called in question. For the "hero" of the Middle Ages, for Hartmann's "Erec" or for Wolfram's "Parzival," the meaning of life was both achieved and guaranteed when he had found his way to—or back to—the community. The epic structure of the modern age, the novel, is closely connected, both sociologically and psychologically, with the loss of a supporting community, of a comprehensive understanding of faith and of the world, with the individualization and isolation of the "hero." In the medieval epic—I am aware that I am generalizing toward an ideal type—the hero had only to seek out the community and prove himself by deeds. He knew in what direction to seek and in which virtues to prove himself. But the hero of the modern novel is no longer able to experience this meaningful wholeness of life. What, for the medieval hero, was simply a practical search for the meaning of life has become for the modern hero a theoretical search. With the passage of time, doctrine and education have afforded him consistently less and less preliminary orientation for life. The discovery of the meaning of life, the search for a possible horizon of safety in union with God and the world, is a problem for him. He is more and more frequently concerned not with proving himself, but with the problem of knowledge, of the critical discovery of fragmentary truth by means of personal experience and experiment. This experimental search for the meaning and entirety of life is responsible, in large measure, for the typical themes of the "classical" German *Bildungsroman* [psychological novel]. But here, too, there is no question of the firm belief, of the undisputed personal conviction, that meaning can be found. In other words, in the ancient and medieval epic there existed for the "hero" the "ideal" world of human society as the predetermined horizon to which he looked to find the meaningfulness of life. In the "classical" *Bildungsroman*, this fullness of meaning has not been predicated. But it can be sought for, found, and even established by the individual. He can set out with the inner certainty that there is a meaningful goal. On the other hand, the novel which is not merely recent, but specifically "modern," is, from the point of view of content, that structure in which the search for the meaning of existence no longer ends in discovery, in which the possibility of finding such a meaning is polemically denied, or—and this is the most modern form—in which the question of a meaningful whole is not even raised. The "classical," or perhaps better the traditional, novelist could assent, basically and totally, to the world. From this fact proceeded the assent of his "hero," which was confirmed in the course of the novel. The modern novelist and his characters have denounced any affirmation of the world that springs from the experiences of the past. They replace the unwavering "yes" of earlier times with an unwavering "no," or at least with an unwavering skepticism. In isolated instances, of course, life and affirmation of the world still appear possible; where and to what extent must be decided anew in each individual case. All the concurrence publicly displayed in the society of Prussia under the Wilhelms, in imperial Austria, in Nazi Germany, or in the postwar society of the *Wirtschaftswunder* has been more or less completely exposed in the modern novel as a deceptive illusion. The exhausting life of the average individual of today is not lived under the gilded dome of a refined society and a uniform belief. It is hemmed in by demands that are particularized, isolated, and often contradictory. How can a man find time for his soul when he is inextricably immersed in codes of behavior and traffic regulations that are all designed to serve the coming moment, or in fragments of news that are all concerned with the moment just past? How can he strive for wholeness when his entire life is taken up with the innumerable disconnected waves of his own associations and drives, with spasmodic stops and starts, with pills for poisons and for antidotes, with infinitesimal efforts to free himself and to burst the ever-present, anonymously controlled bonds that restrain him? That is why the modern novel is, to a large extent, a lament for a lost integrity, a criticism and a protest against the intolerable circumstances of life, an abysmal sadness before the powerlessness of the individual and the unattainableness of any ideal whatsoever, an unending reflection and inquiry about the smallest fragments of livable truth.

Far ahead of his time, Friedrich Schlegel contended in his *Kritische Fragmente* of 1797: "Novels are the Socratic dialogues of our age. In this liberal structure, practical wisdom has taken refuge from theoretical wisdom." The statement refers to the ideal and the typical. We need not ask ourselves how many novels either in our own time or in Schlegel's fall into this category. But there are undoubtedly many contemporary novels that express an occasionally Socratic uneasiness, a watchful questioning as to the present potentialities of life, a not completely un-Socratic irony on the part of the oppressed man of our day. Is it so surprising that both the beliefs and the protests of the novelist should change in a changed world? that most of the newer novelists show themselves skeptical of noble topics and seek, out of their own painful experience, the solid ground of the real?

Changes in the Structure of the Modern World

In Goethe's time, no one was writing genuine Simplicissimus-novels. In our time, no one is writing novels just like Goethe's. And this despite the fact that there have always been imitators and followers—whether rightly or wrongly we need not ask. Yet no one demands that his daughter dress herself and manage her kitchen exactly as his grandmother did. Why, then, should we censure a modern novelist because he no longer writes exactly like Grandfather Goethe or Great-Uncle Stifter, or even with Thomas Mann's sovereign mastery of inherited forms? It is no easier to turn back the wheels of literature than the famous wheels of history. All literary creativity is conditioned by the sum total of changes in the world; for the world, because it is the place where men live, is also the place where the literary artist experiences, sees, and produces. In its administration, traffic, society, and production plants, a modern metropolis has almost nothing in common with the Archduchy of Weimar, with the Vienna of the young Emperor Francis Joseph, or for that matter, with the Lübeck of the merchant's son Thomas Mann. Even the water and the air have changed. The air reeks of gasoline, the water of chlorine. Work on an impersonal assembly line or in the office of a modern business firm is far removed from Edward's work in the garden in the *Wahlverwandtschaften*. The average training of an intelligent young man of today has absolutely nothing in common with the amateurish observations of nature and the grandiose, almost legendary attempts, at once ideal and typical, of Heinrich Drendorf, the merchant's son in Stifter's *Nachsommer* [Indian Summer], to achieve self-knowledge. Machine-work on inorganic matter, fashions that change every season, films that change every week, fairs, meetings, deadlines and final deadlines, telephone and airplane lines, sirens and TV screens, biotics and antibiotics, spiraling salaries and prices, business worries, employment and housing markets, the belief that one can, by altering a few social premises and improving the unfavorable side effects, somehow remove suffering from the world and force happiness out of the test tube along with universal prosperity—these fundamental postulates, facts, and tenets of the post-agricultural industrial society have altered the structure of modern life and the collective attitude of mankind toward life.[1] Man, manipulated and managed, threatened by atoms and by economic crises; man, driven out of the last corners of safety and of nature[2] and delivered over to the mechanism of an almost totally contrived world; man, whose increasing familiarity with a technical world is making him ever more homeless within—this man no longer has the stuff of which harmonious men or truly ideal heroes are made. He has not even the strength for a great passion because his strength is never kept in reserve but is consumed too early. According to the testimony of sociologists, the average man of the modern industrial world has been deprived of most of the so-called primary realities of life. Even birth and death have changed for him;[3] they have become more standardized, more sterile, and, as the number of doctors and patients increases, ever more anonymous. Everyone bears his production and consumer numbers, the ends for which he can be used, on his back. Many simple terms have acquired another meaning. What was once a *homeland* is called on today's ID card a *place of residence*. *Day* connotes an eight-hour day, *week* a forty-two-hour week; *Sunday* a weekend, and *summer* vacation time. As such, these terms have penetrated modern consciousness. Everyone knows that the word *weekend* represents a very different reality from the *Sunday* of his grandfather's time. Awareness of time and place has changed unbelievably in the course of two generations. Today it takes less time to fly from Munich to New York than it took the mailcoach to travel from Munich to Bregenz. Astronauts are very different people from the officers of the Wars of Liberation. Whether things have changed for better or worse is a meaningless question in today's world. Certainly, almost everything has become different. Undeniably, truth is still truth, love is still love, family is still family, profession is still profession. But the conditions for truth and love, for family and profession have changed. The collective attitude of mankind toward faith, knowledge, feeling, and value has been altered, complicated, differentiated, shattered.

What, then, should the novelist do, who today, as in all other ages, must depict man in his world? Can he turn his gaze to a totally other man and a totally other world than the real one? Or should he not observe how this struggling, manipulated, exhausted, dissatisfied, pleasure-loving, impaled, exploited, and indestructible human being reacts to the impulses, demands and potentialities of life? He will do that with other linguistic tools than those of Goethe, Stifter, or Fontane, just as a competent skilled laborer uses other tools than those of the age of Goethe, or a laboratory assistant uses other instruments than those of the nineteenth century. The intellectual optics of the eye itself, its attitude and way of seeing objects, have been shifted from generation to generation, and these changes in the structure of the world and in the way of seeing the world have produced corresponding changes in the structure of the novel.

The Demise of the Hero

The traditional novel had its "hero." He ranged from the picaresque hero of the seventeenth century to the psychologically refined hero of the end of the nineteenth and the beginning of the twentieth century. He was called Simplicissimus, Robinson Crusoe, Werther, Agathon, Wilhelm Meister, David Copperfield, Green Henry, Raskolnikov, Karamazov, or *mutatis mutandis,* Madame Bovary, Rebecca, Effie Briest, Anna Karenina, and was still to be found in the works of Heinrich and Thomas Mann and of Werner Bergengruen, or as Veronica in the novel of Gertrud von Le Fort, or Mother Gisson in Hermann Broch's novel. In the years before and after World War I, however, the concept of hero began to disintegrate. It was no longer possible to speak, in the traditional sense, of the hero in the works of Kafka or Joyce, or in Broch's *Schlafwandler*-trilogy [The Sleepwalkers], or even in Rilke's *Malte Laurids Brigge*. The hero was becoming a synthetic or parabolic figure, a model phenotype, or the almost incomprehensible center of an exemplary self-consciousness, into whom the author poured all the experiential, perceptual, and cognitive awareness of his age.

How does the modern "character" differ from the traditional "hero"? The traditional hero can be described as an individual who affirms himself through his contacts with the world, who shows himself strong in his contacts with society, who takes his place in the world more or less effortlessly and as a matter of course. He is a character, a personality, a man made to order and shown to advantage against his background; he is superior as an adventurer, superior in his receptivity to culture or capacity for love, superior in passion or expiation, a man at once capable and capable of decision. He is no randomly selected mediocrity, no mere number masquerading as a man, no colorless functionary. The hero has a name and an origin. It is not by accident that the first chapter of *Der grüne Heinrich* [Green Henry] is entitled "In Praise of my Origins," that *Nachsommer* opens with the sentence, "My father was a merchant," that the *Buddenbrooks* is a genealogical novel, that Wilhelm Meister is called "Meister" [master]. All these heroes are heirs; even when they become criminals they become, each in his own way, masters. They have their personal identities. Often they are eccentrics; they are always vital personalities. They are uniquely powerful, unbroken, healthy. They bequeath their immortal name to posterity. They step before us with the same beauty and plasticity, the same tangible aliveness that we admire in Greek statues or in those portraits from the Renaissance to the nineteenth century, lifelike, organic figures, which the beholder does not have to vivify with his imagination, but which spring into life at his first glance. In much the same way, it belongs to the essence of the hero to spring into immediate life for the reader. The latter experiences in the person of the hero sensations of satisfaction, release, pleasure. He can yield himself to the illusion that, in the hero, he is meeting a bigger and stronger brother, the self of his wishes and dreams. He admires, sympathizes with, and respects this larger "thou" and stronger "I." Even when he must disapprove the conduct of Rebecca Sharp or Rodion Raskolnikov, he cannot refuse them his admiration and sympathetic allegiance, for his heart has communicated too deeply and too spontaneously with the heart of the hero. It belongs to the very nature of the hero that we are able to identify ourselves effortlessly with his strength, his ability, his passion, his good fortune, and his almost guiltless bad fortune.

It belongs to the disappointments of the traditional reader, on the other hand, that he so often finds in the contemporary novel, not a hero, but a very commonplace figure—incomprehensible, incapable of nobler instincts, suffocated by minutiae, banal, at odds with himself—in whom the reader is unwilling to recognize his own features. The traditional hero, whether adventurer, baron, lady in crinoline, or upper-class merchant, was an important individual. His counterpart in the modern novel is a timid, haunted, very obtuse, very disoriented, or very intellectual creature. Modern authors have said farewell to great world-conquering heroes—and with reason. For these heroes live on in weekly magazines, church newspapers, and cheap films, degraded beyond recognition as the heroes of second-rate literature, simpering virtue, or bedroom sexuality. In many places, the degraded hero has been raised to the status of "star." The "star" is the volume-controlled, image-controlled, spectacular, but less pretentious supermarket-edition of the erstwhile hero—a hero for an hour. He corresponds, perhaps, to a not too reprehensible and not too singular gadget that one might keep on hand for quick, light use. That there exist wise and brave men even in our day is something that no author of any stature will question. But the brave man no longer appears in the robe and mask of the "hero." The garb is no longer becoming. In fact, the role of the hero in our world has not been demythologized by the writer alone.[4] The modern world is not itself fashioned by superindividuals, but by teams, parties, groups. The independence and personal pathos of the individual have lost their foothold in the many complicated spheres of technical efficiency. Modern rules for abstract presentation, which have made of the earlier portrait "from life" a figure of wire and surface lighting, contribute their share to this undermining of the heroic personality. At best, a lifelike reproduction in the traditional sense is to be found today only in photography. Like the greater part of our technical world, the artist, too, finds his use of materials determined by strict laws of organization, composition, abstraction, montage. The *persona* of the modern novel no longer achieves the "beautiful" organic plasticity, the powerful fullness of life, and the harmonious smoothness of the "classical" hero. The classical hero is dead.

Both the critical author and the critical reader have known for a long time that the hero is not the man for our time. We cannot inquire here to what extent he was the man for former times, or, more exactly, corresponded to a concept of man that was, in comparison with our own, almost archaic and idealistic. It is enough to ascertain that he belonged to another psychological and sociological structure. Today the hero, wherever he appears, seems "novelistic." But the merely novelistic falsifies life. It is, of course, no accident that there are nearly always some readers whose contact with reality is faulty—young dreamers, who still demand the "hero." These same readers refuse to accept a character who expresses the distinctive and real properties of their time.

A short forty years ago, Edward Morgan Forster, novelist and critic, regarded the creation of "characters" as the duty and privilege of the novelist.[5] Kafka was already dead then, but still unknown. The leading person in both of his novels, *Der Prozess* [The Trial] and *Das Schloss* [The Castle], has neither character nor proper name. He is called simply "K," he has no ancestry and no recognizable countenance, and he has neither virtue nor passion as the nineteenth century understood them. The meaningless, uncommunicative initial manages, nonetheless, to communicate something quite meaningful that could not have been said of a "hero," but which corresponds to a very definite reality: this K is a random choice, a nothing of a man. He lacks the minimum requirement for human existence—a name. "Since the happy days of *Eugènie Grandet*, when the leading character of a novel was enthroned at the height of his power between the reader and the novelist—like a saint in the paintings of the primitives between the figures of the patrons—and was an object of veneration to both, he has steadily lost more and more of his attributes and privileges.

He was once richly garbed and endowed with every conceivable characteristic; he lacked nothing, whether silver buckles for his trousers or a swelling, replete with tiny veins, on the tip of his nose. Gradually, however, he has lost everything: the carefully built house, filled from cellar to attic with every conceivable object, even the most trivial; the estates and revenues; the clothes; the physique; the appearance, and even the most valuable of all possessions—his own unique character, which belongs to him alone. Often he has lost even his name." [6]

The estates, character, catalogue of virtues and decorations of the traditional hero can no longer encompass reality as modern man knows it. With the changed content, the mode of presentation has changed also. The man portrayed simply as a "figure" in a novel will have, from the point of view of both content and form, quite other features than the man who is designed and fitted to be the "hero." Present-day authors prefer to show aspects of man, the poverty of man, views from various vantage points, patterns of conditioning and response, observations, case histories and reports. Gantenbein in Max Frisch's novel *Mein Name sei Gantenbein* [My Name Is Gantenbein], Hans Schnier in Heinrich Böll's *Ansichten eines Clowns* [Views of a Clown], Anselm Kristlein in Martin Walser's *Halbzeit* [Half-time], Jacob and Achim in Uwe Johnson's *Mutmassungen über Jakob* [Speculations about Jacob] and *Das dritte Buch über Achim* [The Third Book about Achim] are such attempts at describing a case history and presenting an average character. They give much more evidence of abstraction and montage than do Robinson Crusoe or Wilhelm Meister.

The Demise of the Plot

"For most readers—and for the critics—a novel is, above all, a 'story.' A genuine novelist is one who understands 'how to tell a story.' The 'joy of narration' leads him from one end of his work to the other as the air carries the flying bird; it is, in a word, his element, his bliss, and his justification." "The novel tells a story. That is the foundation without which it cannot exist, the greatest common denominator for all novels." [7] In his book, *Die Sterb-*

lichkeit der Musen [The Mortality of the Muses], which appeared in German in 1958, Wladimir Weidlé writes: "Narration, the invention of characters, actions, and realms of phantasy, is the most unreflective, the most direct, and doubtless the earliest form in which art finds expression whenever she reveals herself in human speech and assumes a living form. But this art remains essentially the same whether it functions in a myth, a fairy tale, a legend, or in the more sophisticated forms of drama and epic. In our age, however, the fate of narration has become inextricably bound up with the fate of the novel, the universal form which can be made to serve every purpose, which, in the preceding century experienced its most successful and brilliant period, and which, for some time now, has been experiencing a crisis." [8] When reflection and philosophical analysis gain the ascendancy, plot, as Hegel foresaw, becomes an impossibility. In an age of growing self-consciousness, plot becomes a problem.

The plot runs like an unbroken red thread through the material of the subject matter, characters, and events. Meaningful distinctions have been made between *Geschichte* [story] and *Fabel* [plot]. A story is the narration of events in chronological order. It asks, "What happened then?" "The king died, and then the queen died" is the simplest form of a story. As a more intensively organized form, the same story is called a plot. Above and beyond the mere chronological order, it presents some causal relationship. It not only orders the events; it also interrelates them and binds them together. Our example would then read, "The king died, and then the queen died of grief." [9] That is a plot for a fairy tale. The novel *Die Wahlverwandtschaften* affords an example of a novelistic plot that is both simple and straightforward. It relates without intrigue or complication how the crisscrossing of love ended unhappily for one of the couples. Modern novels have nothing to equal the beautiful continuity of this plot, the spinning out of the narrative thread, the preparation of the conflict, and the denouement or tragic resolution of the conflict. But the critical author and the critical reader will be just as skeptical of the traditional plot as of the traditional hero. It is too "novelistic," too beautiful, and, despite all its apparent coincidences, too logical and smooth to hold the mirror up to real life. This blue-blooded, organic story is no longer credible. The traditional plot cannot capture the many-sidedness, the dissociation, the incoherence, the anonymity, the fortuitousness, the not so much linear as broad and flat contours of the modern experience of reality. "When a baby arrives in a novel," Edward Morgan Forster remarks ironically of the average plot, "it usually has the air of having been posted. It is delivered 'off'; one of the elderly characters goes and picks it up and shows it to the reader, after which it is usually laid in cold storage until it can talk or otherwise assist in the action." [10] Just as the hero is a *homo fictus*, a figure created by the author's imagination, so is the *fabula ficta* a beautiful, imaginative story, which constantly suggests to the reader that it has really taken place. Especially noteworthy is the "beautiful" role played by the love between man and woman, as though everyone needed only to think of love in order to be completely fulfilled and redeemed; as though there existed for every man, or more exactly, for every hero, the possibility of finding the perfect partner. Even Edward in the *Wahlverwandtschaften* knows, as a grown man, no other worry, task, or compulsion than his love for the innocent Ottilie. For our modern sensibilities that would be too simple and carefree to be credible. The earliest novelists resorted to abstract techniques in exactly the places where contemporary authors do not; they made the action linear by removing the conflict from the larger world around it and relating the crisis to a single simple source. Edward, in the *Wahlverwandtschaften*, is concerned with a single problem. With regard to all the other demands of reality, he seems to be quite free—which is surely an oversimplification, an abstraction, on the part of the author. The author limits himself to a single central problem. A modern author would doubtless place this problem in a far more complicated framework of consciousness and action, where it would, to be sure, lose something of its depth, its beautiful simplicity, and its tragedy. But the modern author would have understood it differently—which is to say nothing against Goethe's art, but rather this: the requirements of consciousness and narration have changed since Goethe's time.

Naturally, there are still some modern novels with linear plots. But they are mostly such as have been conjured up from the consciousness of the author and narrator. The plot is not there for its own sake and is not told for its own sake. What the novel is trying to say cannot, therefore, be relayed by a retelling of the plot. In the modern novel, the plot has rather the function of a bait that is to lure reality onto the hook. It is the fishing rod that the author draws through the great fishpond of daily life, with which he explores this corner and that, this ground and that. In other words, reality is no longer subordinated to plot; on the contrary, the plot must serve reality. In the final analysis it is not a question of the bait or the fishing rod, but of the catch. The plot as such, as this or that story, is no longer important. All that matters is that reality be captured. As an example of a contemporary novel in which the plot plays such a subordinate role, one might mention Martin Walser's not exactly epoch-making novel *Halbzeit* (1960). The title refers to the middle of the century, and the novel relates the economic rise of the no more than moderately intelligent Anselm Kristlein from door-to-door salesman to exalted advertising specialist for a business concern. With his plot, the narrator explores the sphere of reality and the stream of consciousness of a typically average man in our economic world as reflected in his business, marital, and extramarital relations. The action as such is uninteresting, without conflict or tension, exactly as uninteresting, flat, and tensionless as the life of an average businessman. But the author's concern is not with the action. His concern is to make visible on this level an average man with just these facets to his character, and hence a pattern of reality.

Already in the twenties and thirties, James Joyce and Virginia Woolf had dissolved their plots into a stream-of-consciousness technique and thus resolved the traditional plot. At the center of their novels is not a logically ordered happening, revealed in causal sequence, but the associations, recollections, exterior and interior phantasies, the reflexes of drives, imaginations, and thoughts, which convert the apparently causal logic of the world into the very different logic of human consciousness and reflect world events through the logic of consciousness. The stream-of-consciousness technique today is part of the stock-in-trade of every author. In contrast to the causal, linear structure of the traditional plot, this method makes possible the widening of the narrative thread into a narrative stream, an interiorizing of the action, and a reflecting of the logic of consciousness that all logicians and idealists find so uncomfortably autonomous. Narration by reproduction of the stream of consciousness is the last refinement of psychological and subjective narration. In contrast to such one-sidedly subjective narration, a group of novelists today—they are usually labeled as representatives of the *nouveau roman* (among the French writers: Alain Robbe-Grillet, Michel Butor, Nathalie Sarraute; among the Germans: Uwe Johnson, Peter Weiss, Otto F. Walter)—are striving to present a sphere of narration and reality that will be as objective as possible. They depict a novelistic happening that transcends the experience and consciousness of a single person in the novel. The actual description, the detail, the reporting of the true objective content of the situation, the change of narrative vantage point and perspectives, the admission of ignorance hold the foreground. What these authors have in common is the awareness of a supersubjective reality, a new recourse to objectivity. They are quite simply aware that no ordered and pondered consciousness disposes the reality that it is their task to present.

The actual act of narration is repressed, split, departmentalized, and endangered not only by thoughtful, analytical reflection (already a problem with Thomas Mann, Robert Musil, Hermann Broch) and by excessive use of the technique of association of ideas (the stream-of-consciousness novel), but also by excessive observation and description of detail (the so-called "new novel"). Without a minimum of action, there can be no novel.[11] Reflection can be carried so far that it becomes an obstacle to the plot and so to the novel. Walter Jens presents just such an obstacle in the dialogue of his uncompleted novel *Herr Meister* (1963). It is no accident that, since the death of the hero, the plot, too, has been losing its primacy. With the sacrifice of the plot and its usually dramatic structure, authors have also had to sacrifice an important, albeit usually only material, element of tension. The "what" of the narrative is becoming steadily less important. The "how" is becoming correspondingly more important.

The Demise of the Olympian Narrator

The traditional hero with his traditional plot is a creation of the author. Besides the hero and the plot, the author creates a third element, namely, the narrator. The narrator is not the author, but his creation. The narrator, not the author, narrates the novel. "A narrator is present in all narrative works, as much in the epic as in the fairy tale, in the *novella* as in the anecdote. Every father and mother know that they must become transformed when they tell their children a fairy story. They must give up the enlightened attitude of the adult and turn themselves into beings for whom the fictive world with all its wonders is a reality. The narrator believes in this world even when he is telling a prevaricated tale. In fact, he can lie only because he does believe. An author cannot lie. He can only write well or poorly. In all narrative literature, the narrator is never the author, whether known or unknown, but always a role invented by the author." [12] This role belongs inherently to the poetic world of the novel. The narrator stands as mediator between the reader and what is to be narrated. He can either remain completely outside the action, or maintain occasional points of contact with it, or, as first-person narrator, report his own fate. The narrator is always superior to his hero (also to himself as hero) and his plot. He has greater knowledge, a higher mode of perception. The traditional narrator sees, guides, and directs his characters as an Olympian god did his heroes— autocratically, surely, transcendently, infallibly. Because of his unfailing supervision of the action, this narrator has been called the "Olympian" narrator. His vantage point often appears to be not only spatially above the event, but also chronologically outside it. He gives the impression of omniscience. He knows the most secret impulses of his hero. The strength of a bear, the longing of love, the fragility of a linden leaf are all known to him. He foresees dangers, can explain and interpret them for the reader. He comments on the bravery, the passion, the inexperience, the emotional weakness of the hero. With sententious remarks, wise precepts, admonitions, warnings, and ironic counsel, he assures the reader of his superiority to hero and plot. A characteristic example of the superiority of the narrator is to be found in the

Wahlverwandtschaften. In the second chapter, the narrator comments on his hero, Edward:

Edward was unused to denying himself anything. From childhood on, the only and spoiled child of rich parents, who had persuaded him into an unusual, but highly advantageous marriage with a much older woman; pampered in every way by a wife who sought to reward his good behavior toward her with the greatest liberality; after her early death his own master; independent in his travels; master of every vicissitude and change; wanting nothing to excess, yet wanting much and many of what he wanted; frank, beneficent, upright, even brave upon occasion—what in all the world had ever been allowed to oppose his wishes? Until now, everything had gone as he had wanted it to; he had even succeeded in winning Charlotte, whom he had wooed with a stubborn, indeed with a romantic kind of fidelity; and now he found himself for the first time in his life contradicted, for the first time withstood ...

We do not intend to dwell here on the novelistic power of this hero, this enviably independent man, who meets his first opposition in his mature years, but on the autocratic commentary of the narrator. The narrator is likewise "present" in a first-person novel like *Die Leiden des jungen Werther.* His role as mediator is first revealed in his address to the reader:

Whatever I could find out about the story of poor Werther, I have assembled diligently, and I present it to you here with the knowledge that you will be grateful to me for it. To his mind and character you cannot deny your admiration and love, to his fate you cannot deny your tears. And you, good soul, who feel the same sorrow that he felt, draw consolation from his suffering and let this little book be your friend if, through destiny or your own fault, you can find no nearer one.

Thereafter, the first-person narrative begins in the form of a letter. The "I" of the narrator confronts us, however, in a twofold function: as the "hero," who is experiencing unhappiness in love, and as the narrator, who can report with superior awareness about himself and his circumstances. As hero, this "I" is immersed in the action. As narrator, he is superior to this blunt, real fate. If Werther-the-hero had had the lucid and superior knowledge of

Werther-the-narrator, he would never have reached for the pistol to end a life that seemed to him to offer no means of escape. In *Werther,* the "I" of the narrator also comments on the spiritual status of the "I" of the hero. Even in the first letter, Werther reflects sententiously on his sensitiveness: "*My friend, pains would be less among men if they didn't expend so much effort of the imagination in recalling past evil, rather than in enduring an indifferent present.*" Later, the "editor" turns directly to the reader to call his attention to the letters that belong to Werther's last days. These letters are not presented with a stream-of-consciousness technique, by which the narrator identifies himself completely with the consciousness of the hero. They reveal again the transcendence of the first-person narrator, who, it is true, knows exactly the condition of the first-person hero, but who is raised considerably above it. From above and from outside he looks into the heart of his hero and is able to sympathize with him, but he does not himself suffer the fate of poor Werther, nor does he pretend to be identical with him, his fate, or his exaggerated sensibility.

The all-knowing Olympian narrator, that narrator who presents his heroes as real people and his fictitious action as real action, who knows immediately the most secret impulses of his hero-creations, who gives them their measure of education, passion, talent, freedom, success, and tragedy, who can explain to the reader the whole *what, how,* and *why*—this narrator does not exist in the modern novel. The contemporary author refuses to create a narrator who is enthroned like Olympian Zeus above an action that purports to be real and to involve individual human beings. The narrator no longer presents himself as the omniscient narrator of a real and individual event. He no longer has the requisite naïveté about his own awareness. He cannot and will not make the ascent to a narrator's Olympus. He gives up the claim to indisputable authority. Because of this authority, the "Olympian" narrator has also been called the "authoritarian" narrator.[13] An authority does not stand on the same level as the men over whom he has authority. He is superior to them, at least in power, and also, in the classical sense, in morality and knowledge. The modern narrator has relinquished more and more of this autocratic and intellectual authority over the reality that he presents to the reader. Naturally, even the modern novel must be narrated, for "the death of the narrator is the death of the novel." [14] But the modern novel is narrated in a different way. And this difference in narrative technique has become more complicated.

The Increased Complications of Narration

In the traditional novel, happenings are told in order. The narrator constructs a situation for his hero, prepares the conflict, conducts the action to a happy or unhappy ending. The reader always knows how far the action has progressed and where he is. Such chronological narration does not exclude occasional additions from the childhood of the hero or supplements from his family history. In the modern novel, the harmonious course of the action by months, seasons, and years is not only considerably shortened, but a substantial part of the event is no longer told chronologically. There are novels in which the whole action requires less than twenty-four hours. *Ulysses* by James Joyce and *Der Tod des Vergil* [The Death of Vergil] by Broch are well-known examples. Into the course of such a day, however, is packed the whole sum of the experiences, recollections, associations, and knowledge of a lifetime. Time is compressed to the utmost limits. Intervals of past time are crowded into the minutely chronological time sequence of whatever narrative holds the foreground. Events with no directly causal relationship to one another can, through associations in the consciousness of the *persona* or the narrator, make their appearance simultaneously or side by side. This kind of presentation is especially difficult when the author's primary intention is to represent simultaneous events. For in that case many convoluted and interlaced scenes of action have to be depicted on different time levels. Böll's *Ansichten eines Clowns* allows preceding time spans to be seen with relative simplicity through the direct time of the action. This direct time of the action requires less than four hours: from the beginning of twilight to about ten o'clock at night on a single March day. But in these few hours, through memory, association, reflection, and telephone conversations, the clown reviews almost the whole course of his life and its principal persons and events. There is no question here of an episodic reviewing of past events as in the traditional novel, but of making the past a living and thematic part of the present through the consciousness of the novel *persona*. This more psychological than chronological and biological relationship of the modern *persona* to time, interrupted again and again by the narrator, complicates the structure of meaning in the novel. There is no real place for a developing hero and a straightforward one-level plot in this complicated relationship of *persona* to narrated time and of narrator to narrative time.[15]

The rejection of the Olympian vantage point of the narrator brings with it another difficulty for the reader. In Böll's *Ansichten eines Clowns*, all recollections and "views" [*Ansichten*] are filtered and blended by the clown's psychosomatic frame of mind. All the words that he thinks or utters are colored by the wounded, aggressive certainty of one who has been banished from human love and expelled from human society. The first-person narrator preserves to the very last sentence the vantage point and perspective of the ruined clown. They are implicit in his choice of character and situation—somewhat akin to the "point of departure" in philosophy. There is no longer an Olympian narrator who raises himself by sententious rationalizing and clever commentary above the limited perspective of his characters. For the reader, the first-person narrator is indistinguishable from the person of the clown. Many of the one-sided and bitter judgments of the clown would appear less offensive if reader and critic would be attentive to the narrative perspective and point of view. That is even more true of a satirically bizarre novel like Günter Grass' *The Tin Drum*. Obviously, it is no more than an invention and trick of the author that sets the narrative vantage point of the novel, in this case an intelligent, keenly observant brain, in the deformed body of a cretin. But once the author has, no doubt with tongue in cheek, chosen the perspective of a precocious rogue with the outward appearance of a three-year old who has cut himself off from society and is setting his life down on paper in a sanatorium and nursing home, much that is shocking and revolting in the novel will appear less shocking and more matter-of-course. With the abdication of the Olympian narrator, there is, to be sure, no one else to take the reader by the hand and say, "You mustn't take my revelations, my biting sarcasm, my malignancy, and obscenity so seriously. I'm just having a bit of fun with this impudent character whom I have created." The educated reader will have to realize for himself that the author, by this limitation of vantage point and perspective, has to some extent relativized his character and set him at a distance.

Even more difficult is the novel that shows an event from various perspectives, presenting it always in fragments that correspond to the knowledge and awareness of the narrating characters. Such a narrative, in which many narrators tell a portion of observed and interpretive knowledge, has as its goal the objectification of the structure of meaning in the novel as opposed to the static happening. Film fans know this presentation of multiple viewpoints from the Japanese film "Rashomon" (1950). The murder of a samurai is reported in sequence by his wife, by the murderer, by the ghost of the murdered man, and finally by a woodcutter who had had no part in it. As a witness outside and, therefore, above the action itself, he is able to expose the falsified reports of witnesses who are too personally concerned in their own cause. But what if no neutral witness is present? What if the structure of meaning is above all an interior one of the soul, which no omniscient narrator is willing to unravel, and which no "I" is able to unravel for himself? Then we have a novel like *Mutmassungen über Jakob* (1959) by Uwe Johnson. The novel is as unsatisfactory for the reader as a law case that the prosecuting attorney must dismiss for lack of proof. The narrative of Johnson's novel begins after the decisive event has occurred. On his return from the Federal Republic of Germany, Jacob Abs, a railroad worker in middle Germany, had met his death while taking his usual route across the railroad tracks to his place of work. The question that occupies the narrator is: Why did he meet death? Was it perhaps at once less and more than an accident? Was it the stumbling of a hunted animal? Was it because Jacob could not and would not be careful once he was convinced that there was no further possibility of a peaceful life? The narrator does not answer the question. He circles around it, approaching it from various angles until there arises from the interruptions, from report, dialogue, and interior monologue, a realm of reality—that realm of time and space in which Jacob Abs lived and died. The problem of the objective search for truth and reality from subjectively conditioned vantage points, perspectives, and fragments of knowledge reaches here the status of a valid technique for the novel.

This question as to the truth and meaning of what is to be narrated was posed at least a generation and a half ago in Kafka's fragmentary novel *Der Prozess* [The Trial]. Directly before his visionary gaze, K sees an unknown person bow from a window and stretch out his arms to him. *"Who was that?" he asks. "A friend? A good man? Someone sympathetic to me? Someone who wanted to help? Was it one man? Was it all men? Was help still possible? Were there avenues that had been forgotten? . . . Where was the judge, whom he had never seen? Where was the supreme court, which he had never reached?"* In like manner, the narrator in the novel *Mein Name sei Gantenbein* (1964) inquires about a dead man at the wheel of an automobile, whom he had mentioned earlier: *"Who was this man? Who could it have been?"* This question about identity combines with the experience of an unhappy marriage to form the springboard from which characters and narratives (it is not a linear plot) investigate the implications of a typical and real "case history" from everyday life, questioning and explaining without wanting or being able to give a single meaning to what, in the end, remains a puzzle. Although Max Frisch's novel is also told from several points of view instead of one, the realm of consciousness which he constructs is quite different from that in Johnson's novel.

The Olympian narrator of the traditional novel has abdicated. Is this, then, the death of the narrator? In the twenties and thirties, he hid himself, it is true, but only to emerge finally in a new guise. He concealed himself when he spoke through his characters by means of interior conversations and monologues. But for at least a decade now, he is once more in the forefront with a new technique of interrupting the narrative thread, shifting the narrative perspective, and creating an artistic montage of narrative fragments, dialogues, and monologues. By means of interior conversations and monologues i.e., speech existing only in the thoughts

28

of the characters the narrators of the twenties and thirties achieved the ultimate possibility in abolishing distance between characters and readers. They deliberately excluded themselves as mediators (which is not to say that they were no longer there). Most of the latest novels, on the contrary, are searching for a new orientation toward objectivity. One aspect of this objectification consists in their expressed statement: we merely narrate. What we present is not reality itself, but only fragments of reality, zones of reality reflected in narration. They expressly emphasize the distance from reality, the mediatory role of narration. They subvert the illusion of the plot.

Literary genres have always undergone changes of form. Each transformation, whether designated by a foreign term from classical antiquity as "metamorphosis," or more simply as "change of form," creates crises that can lead to destruction or renewal. Everything living experiences crises. No one today can predict with certainty whether the so-called crisis of the novel will prove to be its destruction. Most probably, what we are witnessing is merely the end of the traditional novel. Certainly the new novel, with the disappearance of the "hero," the linear plot, and the Olympian narrator, has become more complicated. But that, in a world that is itself becoming more and more complicated, need hardly surprise us. We may mourn for the beautiful simplicity and crystal clarity of the so-called "classical" novel. But we shall soon rank a whole series of contemporary novels as the classics of the twentieth century.

2

Perspectives in Kafka Interpretation

Though he had been known only to friends during his lifetime, Franz Kafka was honored soon after his death by such prominent authors as Hermann Hesse, Alfred Döblin, and Kurt Tucholsky. In the next three decades, he was raised to fame in the whole world of literature, first in France, then in the United States, and, after the war, in Germany and his native Prague. Last of all, he was recognized in East Berlin and in the lands under Communism. In the breadth and depth of his posthumous fame he surpassed even Hölderlin, and as the object of literary study and interpretation he stands in the first rank of German authors side by side with Thomas Mann and Bertolt Brecht.

When Kafka died of tuberculosis in 1924, people were content to see in him an offshoot of Expressionism, a pathological writer of horror stories. In time, however, his work came to exercise an irresistible, sometimes even vehement, fascination for men in a technological age, for the increasingly more confused operators of machines for use, abuse, and war. Was it the warning of a prophet? Did it affirm a universal experience? Did the phenotype speak, under its literal level, of that individual who clearly sees the changes, crises, losses, strengths, and tensions of the age? Did it present in a type the characteristic features of the epoch? Or was it "only" the frustrated bourgeois, the bachelor, the offbeat artist who spoke? Sphinx-like structures of pure "I" and "not-I" before the pyramids of a "not-society"?

During the thirties, Kafka was banned in Germany as a Jewish author of degenerate art. The complete edition of his works, begun in Berlin in 1935 by the Jewish publisher Salman Schocken, was continued in Prague. Emigré writers spread the work in the New World, whence the wave of Kafka enthusiasm returned to engulf old Europe. In 1947, Hermann Broch wrote from Princeton: "At the moment, Kafka is all the rage, but apparently none of the critic-boys has actually recognized the real greatness of Kafka: that a man with no artistic intention, not to mention literary intention, simply wrote down, as if under a dreamlike compulsion, what proved to be an exceedingly deep insight into reality; in his case, the primitive experience remained intact; yet even he found the writing of it an immoral blasphemy, otherwise he would never have ordered the burning of his manuscripts." [1] Kafka's name, like those of André Gide and Picasso, was "one of the watchwords, by which young intellectuals from Cambridge to Cairo, from Salzburg to San Francisco, were to be recognized," remarked Klaus Mann (1907–1949) in his biography, *The Turning Point*. He deplored the fashionable overtones in Kafka's posthumous fame and expressed the opinion that "one is almost ashamed to love an author who is praised (even if not always read or understood) by so many snobs and dilettantes." [2] Since the second edition of the *Collected Works* (New York and Frankfurt, 1950ff.), Kafka has become required reading for every aspiring man of letters. Alone during his lifetime, he found society after his death. Once labeled a pathological rebel, he has become an author to be studied in the schools; the outlaw has become a classic.[3] Adult education classes include him in their reading lists. The rear guard of the zealots for culture take instruction about *Das Urteil* [The Judgment] and *Vor dem Gesetz* [Before the Law]. The first dissertation about Kafka to be written in German appeared in Switzerland in 1941.[4] Today, the number of scholarly publications is astronomical. The *Kafka-Bibliography* compiled by R. Hemmerle (Munich, 1958) includes nearly 700 titles and references; that of Harry Järv (Malmö, 1961) includes nearly

31

5000. Heinz Politzer has added about 250 more titles in his new book on Kafka.[5]

What Kafka himself published fills a single volume. His not unequivocal request to his friend and executor, Max Brod, is well known: ". . . my last request: to burn completely and unread all diaries, manuscripts, letters either of my own or of others, sketches, etc. that are found in my literary legacy, as well as anything written or sketched that you yourself may have, or others from whom you may request it in my name." [6] It is Brod's service to have rescued and published the literary remains. The collected edition includes nine volumes, to date. But there is still need for a critical edition. The chief fault of the present edition lies in its lack of order, in its confusion and disjunction, and in the questionable titles that the editor has assigned to some of the manuscripts. The unfortunate arrangement of the edition is due in part to Brod's tactics of dispensing the works gradually; the occasional textual problems are the result of difficulty in reading the manuscripts and of Brod's interpretive decisions.

Among all the novelists of our century who have written in German, Kafka is the most enigmatic. Not only literary historians, but also philosophers and psychiatrists, theologians and satirists, sociologists and nationalists, bourgeoisie and Marxists have joined in explaining and deciphering him. Many a critic would like to draw the lion's share of the booty to his side, to see his own opinion confirmed by Kafka, and to debate with the author. Brod himself has left no doubts as to his interpretive will regarding Kafka's work. "What I emphasize and what, I believe, distinguishes my presentation of Kafka from others (e.g., Schoeps, Vietta, Stumpf), is the fact that I find his distinctive value in the positive, life-affirming, gently effective and, if one understands thereby a fully realized life, in the religious aspect of his work, not in the aversion to life, the despair, the 'tragic position.' " In *Franz Kafkas Glauben und Lehre* [Franz Kafka's Belief and Teaching], the supplement to the biography, Brod distinguishes expressly between the Kafka of the aphorisms (in the diaries) and the Kafka of the narrative works. "The Kafka of the aphorisms has recognized the indestructible in man; he has a positive, believing relationship to the metaphysical core of the world. He is a religious hero of the rank of a prophet, . . . essentially certain of heaven, of the transcendental. . . . The Kafka of the novels and *novelle* reveals erring man with all his terrors, in all his abandonment, . . . who has lost his connection with precisely that indestructible quality in man." [7] Therewith we have arrived at the first and basic interpretation of Kafka, that of Max Brod.

Religious Interpretations of Kafka

Brod's interpretation of Kafka is the most positive one of all. Its interpretation of the positive is to be understood within the framework of the Jewish religion. According to Brod, Kafka belongs "among the great renewers of the Jewish religion." "His monotheism," Brod writes, "was pure, and won in honest struggle with his conscience; he really lived what Kierkegaard describes as a 'transparent grounding of oneself upon God,' with all the intrepidity, danger, and suffering that arise from such a paradoxical relationship of the finite to the infinite." [8] Most literary historians are agreed today that Brod was, upon occasion, interested in "creating a Kafka after his own image," [9] a Zionist Kafka.

Hans Joachim Schoeps also interprets Kafka's work from the point of view of the Jewish religion, but his approach is predominantly negative. Schoeps is of the opinion "that it is a question of religious faith become recreant, in fact, of a theology of apostasy, of lack of holiness, in which Kafka sought despairingly for salvation. Only Jewish theology knows both the phenomenon of a genuine history of damnation, where the content of the history of salvation turns into its exact opposite, and the basic principle of revelation: that the law continues to govern even in the mode of absence." "What has been lost cannot, it is true, become the content of knowledge, but the direction in which one should seek is still visible." Schoeps considers Kafka's works the "source books of a negative religion," though there was "in Kafka's personal life" a "hope of the Messiah." [10] Among Catholic critics, the Frenchman Rochefort proposed a similar line of interpretation, but pursued it too far into the field of apologetics. Rochefort speaks of a religiosity of "negation" on the lowest level of the Judaeo-messianic tradition. Against his own will and "in spite of superhuman efforts, Kafka did not reach his goal, the absolute of negation: he could not find proof that the world was hostile and cold, the heavens empty, the law absent, and everything absurd. . . . He could not free himself of the hope that plagued and embittered him, . . . he had to recognize that there is something indestructible in man." Romano Guardini, in his introduction to Rochefort's book, made the important observation: "For Kafka, the personality of God has totally disappeared." [11]

Martin Buber's interpretation of Kafka occupies a position not identical to, but somewhere between, Brod's theologically positive and Schoep's negative interpretation. Buber's interpretation has its roots in a profound theological assessment of Judaism. "The Jew," he writes, "insofar as he has not been separated from the source—and this applies to the most exposed Jews, therefore also to a Kafka—is safe. Everything happens to him, but nothing can happen to him. He cannot, indeed, hide himself any longer 'in the shelter of Thy wings' (Psalm 61:5), for God conceals Himself from the age in which he lives, and not merely from the age but also from him, the most exposed son of this age; but by the fact of God's hiddenness in nature, about which he knows, the Jew is safe. . . . He [i.e., Kafka] describes from inner knowledge the world of the present time, he describes very exactly the sway of foul demons, with which the foreground is filled. . . . His unuttered but ever-present theme is the remoteness of the judge, the remoteness of the owner of the palace. . . . This is how the Jew is safe in the darkness—a quite different safety from that of the Christian." Buber is even of the opinion that one can recognize in Kafka the representative of a "Paulinism without Christ," that is, of a Paul who remains a Jew, who withstands the experience of demonism in his age and the absence of God without clinging, as did the Christian Paul, to the fullness of grace in a Redeemer and Mediator Who is both God and man. Into his interpretation of Kafka, Buber has put a good part of his own basic religious feeling and his theology of the age. He has not asked the basic questions: whether Kafka was competent to give expression to the Jewish faith, and whether he lived in a religious community that was, in fact, bound to the "source." The "safeness" of Kafka in the midst of the Jewish community seems, in view of Kafka's complicated ambivalence, his religious neutrality, and the brittle character of the religious fabric around him, to be something of an oversimplification.[12]

A quite different approach attempts "to place Kafka in the same category as the 'theology of crisis,' i.e., as the doctrinal tendency which sees an uncrossable abyss between God and man, between man and the good to be effected by human strength,"[13] that is, in the category of Kierkegaard (whom Kafka read for the first time in 1913 and again more extensively in 1917–1918) and as a parallel phenomenon to Protestant dialectical theology. This is essentially the interpretation supported, among Catholic literary critics, by Wilhelm Grenzmann.[14] As early as 1953, however, Theodor Adorno protested, and with reason, against the appropriation of Kafka by dialectical theology. Such an appropriation "founders not only because of the mythical character of the forces [in Kafka's work], which Benjamin has correctly treated, but also because the ambiguity and incomprehensibility of Kafka's work cannot be ascribed, as in *Furcht und Zittern* [Fear and Trembling], simply to the 'other' as such, but to men and their circumstances. It is that 'infinite qualitative difference,' predicated by both Barth and Kierkegaard, which is here eliminated: there is no real distinction at all between village and castle."[15]

In contrast to the above-mentioned interpretations, Günther Anders shows Kafka's nearness to the Calvinistic world view. "If there is any historical *credo*," he writes, "which Kafka's *credo* or *dubito* recalls to us, it is not the Jewish, but (apart from the agnostic) the Calvinistic one, which was, in a certain sense, also a secret *dubito*." The parallel is, as a matter of fact, astonishing. It concerns nonknowing in regard to the sovereign law and its power, the mercilessness of this law, and the reversal of the relationship between guilt and punishment through the fact that sin has been ordained and destined by the highest power. Even more: "In Calvinism as well as in Kafka's works, man not only has no opportunity of knowing whether he has been accepted or rejected, saved or damned; he does not even have the ability to prepare himself for acceptance. What Calvin calls asceticism, Kafka calls estrangement. *Voluptas*, which Calvin dismisses as the handiwork of the devil himself, Kafka regards as an unclassifiable residuum

35

in a realm of alienations." Anders sees the explanation of these spiritual parallels in the fact that for the Calvinist "faith is already, as it is for Kafka, a religious agnosticism, a religious skepticism." [16] Several thoughts present themselves, however, in regard to this attempt to determine Kafka's position. In the first place, Kafka is not a direct, though distant, spiritual descendant of Calvin, but a parallel phenomenon in the twentieth century. In the second place, Kafka never, either in the literary works or the diaries, envisages God with the same explicitness and vehement intent as does Calvin. God is not the same person for Kafka as for Calvin. Furthermore, Kafka's power-figures have many facets. They are only to a very small degree persons, it is true, but they exhibit the characteristics of several other levels of existence and value. Historical and sociological, as well as psychic and extremely anthropological, elements derived from the concept of God as Life Force mingle with the theological elements of their composition.

It is also difficult to dismiss the question of Kafka's proximity to the Gnostic view of the world. "The concentrated theme of evil and the devil in Kafka's aphorisms raises the question of the extent to which his self-doubt and rejection of the world approach the radicalism and dualism of Gnostic teachings." Günther Anders refers to Marcion, who saw in the Jewish God the demiurge responsible for evil. Erich Heller stresses Kafka's proximity to later Manichaeism with its "dualistic view of the world." Pongs, in this connection, places special emphasis on Aphorism No. 86 (H 49). [17] A parallel to the Gnostic concept of creation and the world can hardly be denied. To explain it, psychoanalysts point, not without reason, to the strong conflicts between the sensual and the spiritual in Kafka, to the lack of integration in his personality. It is neither contradictory nor surprising that the separation of body and spirit in a person like Kafka, whose temperament was basically (though in the broadest sense) religious and melancholy, should produce some similarity to the dualistic thinking of Manichaeism. Buber, it is true, rejects the interpretation of a Gnostic coincidence of creation and sinfulness in Kafka's thought. But they are very much closer to one another there than in Jewish or Christian theology. [18]

Brod himself refuted an extremely positive Catholic interpretation, which, so far as I can ascertain, has remained unique. It takes the extreme opposite position to a "nihilistic" interpretation, "which would rob Kafka of his intimate contact with the transcendental. The Catholic (and Christian) interpretation attempts," according to Brod, "to confine Kafka to the transcendental alone." It "understands properly the metaphysical content, but not the positive natural forces sublimely revered by Kafka." We can prescind here from Brod's misunderstanding of the Catholic viewpoint as a reduction of life to "the transcendental alone" and from his mystification of the "positive natural forces revered by Kafka." His argument is directed against Pierre Klossowski, who presents his "Catholic" view of Kafka in the foreword to the French translation of the diaries. Brod states correctly in opposition to Klossowski that Kafka "rejects the Christian teaching of a 'Mediator' (in the single person of the Messiah)." [19] The most recent Catholic interpretation, "Das Religiöse in der Dichtung Franz Kafkas" [The Religious Element in the Works of Franz Kafka], presents no clearly defined view. It links, somewhat vaguely, Kafka's "tragic position" (what does "tragic" mean? what could it mean in reference to Kafka?) with his "faith in the indestructible in man" (a word that also appears in Heidegger's later Afterword to *Was ist Metaphysik?*) and with "believing expectation," even "hope." [20] A more recent question of Christian theology has not been pursued, namely, whether and to what extent traces of a historical or mythical etiology are to be found in Kafka's literary and autobiographical works,[21] that is, traces of the interpretation of the past and present experience of man's salvation and damnation in mythical pictures and of a self-understanding that cannot occur without some contact with the Spirit of God.

Nearly all the religious interpretations that have been mentioned reduce Kafka too unequivocally to a common denominator or refer too explicitly and one-sidedly to the religious level. They give too little consideration to the complex psychological and sociological influences on the observant eye of Kafka, on his relationship, distorted from the beginning, to family, fellow man, self, and God. Wilhelm Emrich sees correctly that Kafka "makes a fundamental distinction between himself and Judaeo-Christian religiosity, yet is also definitely in contact with it: for him, there is no transcendental God, Who comes to meet man with threats and love as a 'totally other' Supreme Being. On the other hand, the 'indestructible' in man, his 'being,' is for Kafka a sphere completely withdrawn from the reach of earthly consciousness, feeling, or will, and thus presents a transcendency which, because it cannot penetrate the psychic, intellectual, or 'natural' region of man's mind, remains forever 'hidden' from him." [22] Like most other interpreters, Walter Muschg begins with the implicit assumption that Kafka's works treat of our Judaeo-Christian-Western "God," that it must be possible to discuss them in terms of a generally understood "God," a generally understood "life after death," and a generally understood "faith." He writes: "The way to life after death, to the certainty of redemption has been lost in his [i.e., Kafka's] case. God's throne is far beyond reach, the news of Him is doubtful and incomprehensible. . . . Faith can be experienced only as despair." [23] From the point of view of methodology, one should first inquire what these concepts, and such other keywords as "sin," "devil," "truth," "justice," "law," etc., mean in Kafka's notes and in what form they appear in his literary works. Only then should one attempt to establish a relationship between Kafka's statements and the world one knows oneself. And in doing so, one should make every effort to understand Kafka in his images and complex symbolic relationship, especially when he undertakes to remove the barriers into the unknown, the ambiguous, the anonymous; when he consciously breaks through all the usual conventions.

Surrealistic and Existentialist Interpretations

For the most part, the problem of Kafka's religious outlook has been of interest to interpreters only in German-speaking countries. French critics, on the other hand, have concentrated their attention on the surrealistic and existentialistic aspects of his work. The French surrealists belong, in fact, to the early discoverers of Kafka. By the end of the twenties, they had begun to admire his dreamlike construction of the surrealistic, and to regard his stories and novels as the documents of a nihilistic grotesquerie of unprecedented originality. Amid the fatalities and confusions of war, existentialist writers of the 1940s thought they had found their prophet in Kafka.[24] Had he not expressed in compelling images and episodes the comprehensive and anonymous threat of life, the inhuman legality of man, the all-enveloping clutches of a bureaucratic society? Whereas surrealists were more impressed by the form and artistry of Kafka's statement [*Aussage*], the existentialists were more impressed by its content: the nothingness, the hopelessness, the anonymity, the absurdity of human existence.[25] Today most interpreters are agreed that Kafka is neither a nihilistic prophet nor an existentialist saint as the French understood the terms. As early as 1953, Theodor Adorno took sharp, though perhaps too easy, issue with the oracles of existentialism: "Little of what is written about him [i.e., Kafka] is valid; most of it is existentialism. He is simply being made to fit into a predetermined mold of thought." [26]

At about the same time, Max Bense's book *Die Theorie Kafkas* made its appearance in Germany. Bense interpreted Kafka's work as existentialistic prose and as the epic parallel to Heidegger's fundamental ontology. "Kafka," he writes, "does not set down sentences that determine the thing [*das Seiende*], but sentences that interpret being [*Sein*]. In this sense, his prose follows a remarkable procedure of 'distortion' and 'concealment.' . . . Kafka's 'distortion' belongs in the same category as Heidegger's 'destruction.' It destroys the mold, the imitation, the mimesis; it is ambiguous only in terms of the classical concepts of being and sign. Understood properly from the point of view of fundamental ontology, it should be considered an explication for which, as in the case of everything which is a sign of something else, singleness of meaning is no longer a criterion." [27]

Even Emrich resisted such a positive classification and undifferentiated equation of Kafka with Heidegger. He is of the opinion "that, historically speaking, the same situation has found expression in both their works, but has been mastered in ways that are formally different for each of them—literary for the one, philosophical for the other. And yet," Emrich continues, "it is precisely the different language that betrays the divergence, the dividing cleft. Kafka . . . does not penetrate into the depths of root words," though he does, it may be added, penetrate into the depths of dream symbols and archetypal constellations. "In contrast to Heidegger, he never attempts to determine being itself linguistically or to express it directly. It remains, to an eminent degree, that which is empty, incomprehensible; that which, it is true, stands challengingly before our eyes, but which can itself nowhere be opened up, 'cleared.' For Kafka, therefore, being is not, as it is for Heidegger, something which was 'nearer' in prerational, half-mythical times than it is today; something which still 'existed' [*weste*] or dwelt in primitive linguistic forms, but has been replaced by the understanding thinking of western metaphysics. . . . Being no longer appears, in Kafka's work, as a hiding foundation [*bergender Grund*], which man can 'unhide' [*entbergen*] by destroying the limitations of representational thinking and opening himself to the horizon of all things [*Seiende*], thus entering into being [*Sein*]. . . . There arises in his work, in contrast to Heidegger's, an absolute emptiness which . . . threatens being [*das Sein*]." "Kafka's 'belief' in the 'indestructible,' in the 'being' in man which must be 'freed,' can, therefore, neither be totally identified with a religious belief that has appeared in history, nor be equated with modern Existentialism." [28]

Interpretation in Kafka's Native Czechoslovakia and Biographical Works

Peter Demetz, in his work *Kafka a Praha* (Prague, 1947), turned his attention from the religious and political trends in the interpretation of Kafka's works and emphasized instead the role of environment, even to the point of creating a legend around Kafka as a Czechoslovakian national hero. On the paternal side, Kafka belonged to a family of Czechoslovakian Jews of the provincial proletariat, on the maternal side, to a family of wealthy middle-class German Jews. "This origin separates him at once from the other writers of the 'Prague School': he was the only one who spoke and wrote an almost faultless Czechoslovakian; he was the only one who grew up in the midst of the Old City, on the edge of the Ghetto, which, at that time, was still an architectonic unity. Kafka never lost his close link with the Czechoslovakian people, never forgot this atmosphere of his youth."[29] Gustav Janouch reports a conversation in which Kafka said: "The dark corners, secret passages, blind windows, dirty courtyards, noisy taverns, and closed inns still live in us. We walk through the broad streets of the new city. But our steps are uncertain. We still tremble inwardly as we did in the old alleys of misery. Our heart is still unaware of the sanitary measures that have been taken. The unhealthy old Jewish city is far more real to us than the hygienic new city around us." [30] No one will deny that the atmosphere of Old Prague and the homelessness of the Germanized Jews of Prague have flowed, together with the juridical German of the Prague bureaucracy, into his work. But one cannot "explain" Kafka and his work simply in terms of local environment. *"Der Prozess* [The Trial] is no more exclusively a local story about Prague than it is an autobiographical self-analysis in which Franz Kafka punishes Josef K. for the misdeeds which he [Kafka] accuses himself of having committed. On the contrary, it is precisely the points of contact that undeniably exist between the novel and Kafka's life that reveal how great a distance the writer has placed between his experience and his creation." But it is certainly helpful to collect the biographical material and to evaluate it more carefully than was done in Brod's creditable first biography and in the first phase of Kafka criticism (to about 1950). A pioneering effort in this regard was Klaus Wagenbach's biography of Kafka's youth.[31]

Psychoanalytical and Psychological Interpretation

Kafka offers the psychologist, and more especially the psychoanalyst, an abundance of material. Everyone knows about his abyss of anxiety, his disagreement with his father's bourgeois stolidity and lack of aesthetic understanding; everyone knows about his broken engagements; about his social, professional, and religious misery; about his literary dream existence and his flight from what most men call reality. Freud's teaching was in the air then as Heidegger's is today. Kafka was strongly influenced by Freud's interpretation of dreams. For the years 1917–1918, diary entries afford conclusive evidence of his resistance: "psychology for the last time" (H 51); "nauseated by too much psychology" (H 72). He seems to have suspected that "the psychoanalytical illumination of the psyche means" nothing more than "the mastery of the world of the subconscious by a method which is limited and rational and that it therefore evokes a new falsification of the world of human truth and reality. The psychoanalytical possibility of getting a 'grip' on the subconscious leads to a technical manipulation of the psyche." [32] "I don't call it sickness," a later entry reads, "and I see a bungling error in the therapeutic side of psychoanalysis" (H335). For psychoanalysts of the strict school, Kafka must afford abundant proof of their theory of artistic creation from the subconscious, suppressed, unattained, unaccomplished. In 1931, in the journal *Imago*, edited by Freud, Hellmuth Kaiser interpreted Kafka's story *Die Verwandlung* [Metamorphosis] simply as a "struggle between father and son such as arises from the Oedipus complex." Along with the preconceived model of the Oedipus complex, he automatically introduced all the rest of Freud's terminological equipment into his interpretation of the work and spoke of "genital position," "regression into the anal phase," "Oedipus hatred," "castration acts," and more of the same. Such terms coarsen the story considerably, for they read into the allusions, and thus establish for the work, fixed meanings that are not really proper to them. When the father pelts his son Gregory, who now has the form of a beetle, with apples from the fruit bowl on the sideboard, that naturally reminds interpreters of the "meaning of the apple in the fall of man in the Bible." The only problem is: what have the apples here to do with the apple there? Important aspects of the story—Gregor's longing for the truer life; the course of his knowledge of self, knowledge of the world, and loss of personal identity; the subtle detachment of the narrator; the ironic portrayal of the family—all of these pass unnoticed. What is complex and particular in the story is concealed when it is subsumed under the simple formula of the Oedipus complex. The artistic form, the formative means used, and the ways of expressing aloofness and higher consciousness are not comprehended. Categories that have nothing to do with literature are applied too quickly and too exclusively to a text that apparently is thought to be nothing more than a "confession" of what is conveyed by the contents; a double misunderstanding. [33] Emrich is right in saying that Kafka "does not merely imitate, by way of 'inner monologue' or the so-called 'automatic dictates of the sub-conscious,' what takes place in the subconscious, as do the psycho-analytical association techniques of modern novelists. That is to say, he does not simply record dreams as they 'really' occur or could occur." [34]

Just as one-sided and oversimplified in another direction is Alexander Kuhr's explanation (1954) of Kafka's "imaginative fac-ulties, which propel the fictitious world of his dramatic tales out of the depths of his subconscious," out of his "absolute estrange-ment" in the world, his "schizophrenia" and his "tendency to de-stroy." The tales and novels are the products of a "compulsive neurotic," of one who "arrived too late, who cannot find the 'way' of being or cannot traverse it because the world confuses him with its traffic and trade." [35] That schizophrenia and compulsive neu-rosis as such produce no works of art is something that is never considered. About the possible presence of truth in Kafka's works, about their visionary quality despite the troubled source from which they emanate, about the specifically human and literary in the "non-arrival" which he portrays, about the "nevertheless" in what he leaves unresolved, about the attempt to get beneath ap-pearances—about these Kuhr asks no questions. Such a narrow interpretation of Kafka completely overlooks the fact that "for him all physical and mental illnesses were themselves rooted in one single sickness which is 'pre-conceived' in the 'essence' of man, . . . from which, in the last analysis, the flight into neurosis, etc., ema-nates. . . . Psychoanalytical illumination of the psyche, therefore, means for Kafka the mastery of the world of the subconscious by a method that is limited and rational, and evokes, in consequence, a new falsification of the world of human truth and reality." [36]

No one will deny that psychoanalysis and psychology can clarify some parts of Kafka's work. Kaiser and Kuhr, however, are one-sided psychoanalysts and, as such, completely unaware of any lit-erary criteria. As was to be expected, a number of literary critics, especially in the United States,[37] have used psychological findings to assist them in the interpretation of Kafka's works. The German-American Kurt Weinberg also works, in his comprehensive book on Kafka, from the vantage point of psychology, especially in his references to archetypal symbols and in his interpretation of archetypal metaphors and myths. His work is marked by an obstinate and rather exaggerated tendency to read Jewish and Christian interpretations into Kafka's images.[38] Pongs, in his somewhat problematical book about Kafka, pointed out the unusual "ambivalence" in Kafka's statements. This concept had been introduced into psychoanalysis by Bleuler in 1910 and adopted by his teacher Freud. "In contrast to schizophrenia, which is an unequivocal split in the psyche, ambivalence means a psychic condition somewhere in the middle, an oscillation between values," a "preliminary step toward schizophrenia." [39] Sokel, too, recognized the "principle of the split ego," the "ambivalence," the closeness to Freud's metaphysical and mythical world, and made it bear fruit in his literary criticism. It would seem that Adorno was right when he said, "Neither Freud nor Kafka ascribes any value to the possession of a soul." [40] Despite whatever traits they may have in common, Kafka "revolted against the father of psychoanalysis when he created dream symbols which are susceptible of the mythical, and when he undertook to restore faith, which Siegmund Freud had wanted to unmask as an illusion, to its original status." [41] "Psychoanalytical interpretations of Kafka are possible, even necessary, but they are meaningful only in terms of the themes more universally present in the works" [42] and with due regard for the literary form itself.

Sociological and Cultural Interpretations

One of the first interpretations of Kafka in German after World War II was that published by Hannah Arendt in the journal *Die Wandlung* and in the *Schriften der Wandlung*. She interpreted the novel *Der Prozess* primarily as "a criticism of the bureaucratic form of government in the pre-war administration of Austria" with its "hierarchy of officials" and its "bureaucratic apparatus." She finds that this is true also, though in another way, of the novel *Das Schloss*. "K comes to it [that is, to the government] voluntarily, as a stranger, and he wants to achieve a very definite purpose: he wants to settle down, to become a fellow-citizen, to build up his life and marry, to find work and to become a useful member of society. . . . Since his demands are none other than the inalienable rights of man, he cannot accept them as favors from the castle. . . . For the inhabitants of the town, K's strangeness is due not to the fact that he has been deprived of the essential things of life, but that he demands them." "Kafka's so-called prophecies were a sober analysis of basic structures that have today become apparent. . . . He had first to anticipate the destruction of the badly constructed world. Through this anticipated destruction, he conveyed the image (which was, for him, the highest aspect of man as a model of good will) of man as the *'fabricator mundi*,' the world-builder, who can put aside the faulty construction and build his world anew." She completely ignores the sin, complexes, distortions, subjectively conditioned contradictions and autobiographical insertions in the work and explicitly rejects any theological and psycho-therapeutic interpretation. Kafka's hero, she says, is "the prototype of the 'ordinary man' as an ideal for humanity." Kafka "wanted to construct a world in accord with human needs and human dignity, a world in which man's activity was self-determined and ruled by man's laws, not by mysterious forces which flow from above or below." Kafka and his heroes are, according to Hannah Arendt, objective critics of an historically concrete society and of a particular pattern of society.[43] There can be no doubt that this is a simple and, in the year 1946, a most impressive formula: only society is questionable, bad, or in need of reform; only the Kafkaesque hero is good in his struggle for freedom and human rights.

A few years later, Theodor Adorno, like Hannah Arendt an emigrant from the Third Reich, wrote one of the most pointed cultural and critical studies about and against Kafka to issue from the West. In 1953, years before the Marxist literary and cultural critics, he pilloried Kafka's "objectless subjectivity," the "absolutely subjective time and place" of his works; he noted the "depersonalization in areas of sex," and the "elimination of the concept of the soul." "The windowless monad proves to be a *'laterna magica*,' mother of all images, as in the case of Proust and Joyce." "The hermetic principle is that of a completely estranged subjectivity," which "has surrendered the power of discrimination." "The monstrosity, for which no contrast exists, becomes, as it did for Sade, the whole world, the norm." Not just society but "the world is revealed as absurd. . . . The central sphere of dependent beings turns into an inferno beneath the eyes of artificial angels. . . . The subject is objectified by renouncing ultimate acquiescence."[44]

Emrich, in 1958, was evidently untouched by Adorno's criticism. He recognized in Kafka's work not only an intentionally positive analysis of contemporary society but, in and through it, also an analysis of the contemporary world itself. "His so-called analysis of the world grew out of a very concrete insight into the structure of contemporary society." "The trappings of the world [of his novels] are the very concrete trappings of our world." "The genuine, humane utopia, which does not surpass reality, but unmasks it, has taken shape in Kafka's work. His work is the unique attempt, in a world that no longer knows any binding human charter and no longer follows any unconditional divine law, to reestablish the absolute responsibility of man." "Only when everything has been negated, life with its contradictions and conditions, as well as the absolute and mortally threatening claims [on man] . . . , only when man is no longer limited by anything preordained, only then can responsibility be transferred to him. . . . Formerly, man was the victim of his opponents. He subjected himself either to the necessities of life or to an absolute law. Now he is superior to both. But this is his true human position."

Kafka is for Emrich "in the strictest sense a moralist of modern European thought." He strove for the "destruction of the universal as the nineteenth century understood it" and for the reestablishment of "universal truth" and "universal morality." "The 'struggle' for the universally true is by no means a struggle for universal knowledge and understanding alone, but for universal love." "Kafka's struggle for full, inexpressible truth means the winning of a completely valid human existence." But if this new "reconciliation" is to take place, man must first, according to Kafka, "survive the absolute catastrophe." "By the fact that Kafka, on his own evidence (H 121), left the religious tradition and also rejected the traditional humanism that believed in the spiritual powers of man, in his so-called natural goodness, he opened up an unrestricted sphere in which 'being' and 'law,' unlimited existence and unrestricted ethical requirements coincide, in which the cleft between religion and humanism is nullified by the existence of a third sphere which, though unattainable and not reducible to a formula, has valid and unconditional claims upon man." Emrich regards Kafka's perception and morality as a new state of consciousness and a new revelation, as a possibility of self-redemption in this age.[45] A certain indebtedness to Hegel is clearly recognizable in Emrich himself. It should be noted that, without any methodological distinction, he adds to and incorporates into his interpretation, which is to a large extent inherent in the work, philosophical and ideological categories that are foreign to it.

Marxist Interpretation

"Unfortunately," wrote Helmut Richter (East Berlin) in 1962, "we cannot say that bourgeois literary criticism has succeeded in discovering the unique in Kafka's writings and in thus erecting a barrier against arbitrary and nonliterary interpretations." In 1952, Friedrich Beissner believed it possible to say unequivocally that Kafka "turned aside from the world of outer reality and discovered the inner man as the object of epic art, a world of no small dimensions and full of possibilities, and, moreover, a world whose unity and uniformity were indestructible." Against this view, Richter argued the exact opposite: "Beissner does not see that the interior life of man, even when it is actually the only object of Kafka's writings, can be nothing else than the reflection of the outer world and of the specific attitude of the subject to it." Here we encounter the basic principle of Marxist literary considerations, namely, that literature is first and always the reflection of social conditions, by which we are to understand society in the Marxist sense. Richter admits that Kafka was, for a long time, drawn into Marxist cultural politics and literary considerations only "as an example of bourgeois decadence."[46] As late as 1957, Paul Reimann had written in the *Weimarer Beiträge* [Weimar Contributions]: "The problem that Kafka poses is not only subjective, but objective; it proceeds from the inner contradictions of capitalistic society, and is well known to Marxists as the problem of the 'alienation,' the dissolution, and the dehumanizing of all human relations in the conditions of capitalism." According to Reimann, Kafka "is attacking in his works, and especially in his

47

greatest novel, *The Trial*, the basic questions of the capitalistic social order, of whose contradictions he was deeply aware, but without having seen a way to overcome them." For Reimann, Kafka's "pessimism" is a purely objective end-product. It "arises from the observation of serious social contradictions and of the human misery that they produce." "It was Kafka's goal as a writer," Reimann claims, "to track down the ultimate causes of the contradictions of bourgeois society. This attempt failed because Kafka's dialectic, which contains the brilliant beginnings of a real criticism, remained idealistic, and because he did not take one decisive factor into account—the active role of the masses." Richter, on the other hand, disassociates himself from such a narrow concept of "reality" and such a one-sided and simple view.[47]

Common to all the Marxist interpretations is a preponderant interest in the "problems of content." They confront literature with the criterion of their own consistent Marxist view of the world and look for a (scientific) "explanation" of the "phenomena" presented. K. Hermsdorf finds that "the statement of the inhumane character of imperialistic society in *Der Verschollene* [Lost without Trace; the novel is better known in English as *Amerika*] has been expressed with radical incisiveness." "Kafka's relatively few . . . criticisms of the contemporary scene . . . are intended as a criticism of the capitalistic system." In the two later novels, Hermsdorf admits, "the sharp protest against bureaucracy as such, which is expressed in the works, is directed against an abstract bureaucracy which exists only as an allegory—and thus loses the character of a protest directly intended as social criticism." "Kafka's antirational world-view," Hermsdorf realizes correctly, "is at the same time 'hyperrational' . . . . When Kafka places the narrative event to a considerable extent outside the law of causality (that is, as Marxists understand the law of causality), he presumes, whether intentionally or not, the existence of a transcendent sphere, a super-reality, which, it is true, never takes shape, but which is consistently and latently present in the world-view of the novel. It would be possible to call this form of Kafkaesque irrationality a latent fideism without content. It is a hidden belief in hope and a redeemer," which Hermsdorf, of course, believes ". . . is no way a belief in God." He recognizes, rightly I think, Kafka's extreme subjectivity (whether he interprets it rightly is another question). The "subjective *I* . . . becomes the crucial, almost the exclusive organ of the whole concept of reality, a medium, through which all objective being is filtered and, in the process, subjectified. . . . His estrangement becomes an alienation of all things. . . . But since this prominent subjective *I* has shape, is a relatively concrete and therefore objective figure, the subject appears at the same time as the object, as the object of contemplation." [48] Such a statement is a needed corrective for those Western interpreters who regard Kafka too exclusively as the revelation par excellence of human existence in this age.

We can disregard here Richter's problematical division of Kafka's work into consecutive creative periods that merge into one another. He is of the opinion that "Kafka turned from the loneliness of an unfulfilled life to the knowledge and conquest of the world around him. . . .The tragic end of his heroes and his growing perception of reality enabled Kafka to devote greater attention to the social conditions which he had thus far neglected. He discovers in them so many contradictions, antitheses, and dangers that he is no longer able to advance as a justified claim the subjection of the individual to the stipulations of a given society. . . . It is subjectively and objectively impossible to survive in the bourgeois world and to establish a meaningful existence in it." "In his last creative period, Kafka built his works around the difficult theme of an artistic gift divorced from life. He shows how unsatisfactory and morally untenable is any way of life which isolates man from his social milieu. . . . This knowledge includes a self-criticism of Kafka himself, on which his testamentary dispositions—in which he ordered the destruction of his literary remains—are a striking commentary." [49] The younger Marxist critics seem totally to have missed the fact that what Kafka questioned was not only human existence in this concretely experienced society (which in the Prague of his time was not merely, and not even predominantly, a capitalistically conditioned and misformed society), but, over and above that, human existence as such. In the Marxist view, Kafka's lack of logic is at the same time an increment of logic that completely surpasses every superficial view of man, Western capitalistic as well as Eastern Marxist.[50] For Georg Lukács, too, Kafka belongs (with Proust, Joyce, Musil, Benn, and others) to the avant-gardist literature of the West which is, in its entirety, a decadent product of the capitalistic world. "The world of present-day capitalism viewed as hell and the powerlessness of everything human in the face of this power of the underworld produces the content of Kafka's works." Kafka's "realism of detail" is converted "into a disavowal of the reality of this world." His works show a "universality of distortion" and a *credo* of meaninglessness." [51] Lukács, to be sure, overlooks the fact that for Kafka "reality" and, therefore, also the "reality" that is contradictory and questionable, nowhere corresponds to that circumscribed and standarized concept of reality that is peculiar to Marxism. Further, what Lukács declares to be a "*credo*" was for Kafka at best only a way of regarding the world, of comprehending or not comprehending; it was by no means an ideology or an ideological formula or system.

Considerations of Form and Structural Analysis

Actually, every interpretation of a literary text, even of one so idiosyncratic and difficult as Kafka's, must originate in a consideration of form. The more literary the text, the less can one compose his statement about it in the direct way of logic and form a preconceived conceptual system, that is, without investigation of the images and their interrelationship, of the particular perspective and total structure of the work. However one may designate the mode in which a literary text is present, there is, for a literary work, no intrinsic value that is not contained in "construction," "form," or "structure." For that reason, all interpretations, to the extent that they do not, at least implicitly, focus on construction, miss the message that has been incorporated into the work. "Most faulty judgments about Kafka are due to the use of heterogeneous methods," states Dieter Hasselblatt. "At the beginning of serious research into Kafka's works, just as at the beginning of any piece of research, there must be rejection," warns Heinz Politzer, "the rejection, namely, of the all too facile direct translation of Kafka's symbolic language into whatever language happens to be currently in vogue, whether it be the jargon of existentialist philosophy, of the theology of crisis, or of psychoanalysis." Martin Walser formed the impression in 1951, when he was working on Kafka, that "Kafka is too often misused by nonliterary commentators in support of all possible theories. And, in fact, an enormous number of articles appeared in those years that isolated one or another feature of Kafka's work from the context, incorporated it directly into that time and reality, and exploited it for a small excursus into cultural criticism." Wilhelm Emrich expressed the opinion in 1954: "Basically, it is not yet possible to speak of Kafka's literary work. That will be possible only when his structure is known and the inner arrangement of its parts has been elucidated. His ambiguous and apparently hermetically sealed work compels the literary historian to enter into the labyrinth of these writings and to let himself be guided solely by the directives given him by the work and its creator." [52] In and around 1950, there occurred a break in research about Kafka. The philosophical aspects, which had been, for the most part, wrung from Kafka's work by a political and supposedly logical direct approach, began to receive less emphasis—at least, they were no longer isolated by a faulty methodology. As a counterbalance and perhaps, too, as the sign of a more critical awareness of the task at hand, aesthetic questions advanced into the foreground.

Beissner's pupil, Martin Walser, was one of the first critics to undertake a "description" of Kafka's narrative "form." He analyzed the elements of narration and the perspective of the narrator;[53] he observed the functionalism of persons, times, and places and the nonempirical form given them; he recognized, among other things, the category to which Kafka's "heroes" belong and their dispute with the rest of the world; the role of the spectator in the events of the story; the "disturbance" with which the novels and many of the stories begin; the relationship of the individual parts of the novel to the novel as a whole; the impossibility of a psychological development, etc. In an important article in 1952, Clemens Heselhaus had applied the concepts of "anti-fairytale," "anti-novel," and "parable" to "Kafka's narrative forms" and had revealed consistent elements in his structure.[54] Emrich himself, in his book on Kafka (1958), showed that Kafka's narrative technique lies "beyond allegory and symbol," as Goethe understood the terms.

"Whereas Goethe's poetic view and use of symbolism disclose the true nature of things and reveal the universal primeval phenomenon, Kafka's view and his use of poetic devices have precisely the effect of destroying the truth, even the reality of man and thing. . . . His works . . . possess the character of a parable for which aesthetics and poetics have not yet coined a name. . . . Their structure is disclosed only in the interchange between the individual images and the universal intention." In a later article, Emrich inquired into the particular nature of "Franz Kafka's world of images."[55] Heinrich Politzer does not claim with the same certainty that it is possible to make an unequivocal interpretation of Kafka's figurative and aphoristic language. By means of a short narrative work *Gibs auf* [Give It Up], he shows the difficulty of making a positive interpretation; for the interpretation will vary according to whether one considers the twelve-and-a-half printed lines to be story, anecdote, aphorism, allegory, or exegetical commentary. He demonstrates impressively what a psychological, a religious, or an existentialist interpretation can accept or reject without thereby coming into conflict with the individual text. "Kafka's parables," Politzer remarks, "have not only 'many levels,' but also 'many meanings'; they are, so to speak, the 'Rorschach tests of literature.' " More strongly than other authors, he concentrated on the figure of the "bachelor" as basic to Kafka's works. He designated Kafka's fundamental narrative form as the "paradoxical parable."[56] Sokel recognizes in the work the "split" and "rifts of the ego," the sexually atrophied women characters, the number of those who have or lay claim to "power" among Kafka's basic characters, "ambivalence" as a basic principle of both characters and background, "tragic ambivalence," and "tragic irony."[57] Hillmann, too, in the third part of his work on Kafka inquires into the genres of narration and examines the "structure of the work": sentence structures, forms of gesture and mimicry, of image and perspective.[58]

Hasselblatt begins his study with an examination of the "parables." He finds the principle of "discussion and admission" with "progressive involvement" and "destructive development" [de-velopment], as well as the "non-final" in Kafka's narration, and he is energetically on his guard not to measure Kafka against or by classical categories.[59] The same new methodological attention and care that Klaus Wagenbach (1958) bestowed on biographical details has also been accorded literary structure and linguistic form. Thus a new stage has been reached in research into Kafka's works. The years when writers capitalized on Kafka for political, cultural, or journalistic purposes are past. The partly subconcious appropriation of Kafka to support one's own conviction, whether of the absurdity of one's own world or that of others, is no longer thought to suffice.

This attempt to survey the very varied interpretations and interpretational directions in critical works on Kafka has shown, I hope, the positions occupied by different interpreters, shed some light on their various points of departure or vantage and on their methodological procedures, and offered some orientation for understanding the newer literature about Kafka. Nearly every tendency in literature, interpretation, and cultural politics in our time, the extremely traditional as well as the extremely revolutionary, has tested itself on Kafka. Just as the history of critical studies of Shakespeare's works has developed into a history of English philology and literary criticism, so do critical studies of Kafka's works reflect the literary tendencies and methods of the present time. The greater or lesser failure of the various methodologies to disclose the essence of Kafka's work can be ascribed to ideological, isolating, structural, or traditional misunderstandings. Common to all of them is their precipitate, unsuitable, *a priori* attack on the basis of prejudiced and predetermined criteria. Ideological prejudice and exclusiveness permit the appropriation of the literary work by a given philosophical system or conceptual program and by no other. The misunderstanding that isolates consists in removing a single aspect of the greater whole and then beginning (more or less expressly) to explain it as if it were the whole. Psychologists and sociologists, as well as the biographical interpreters of the older school, almost always resort to this invalid type of isolation. The will to "explain" is common to all of them. They strive to reveal, in the shortest way possible, the "causes" and the literary "content"; they fail to understand the text from a structural point of view. What they overlook is the fact that literature is neither information, nor a direct communication in standardized images, nor a direct description of one's own life or one's own world. They ignore the sculptured and patterned structure formed by the process of artistic creation. Even where the structure is basically known, as it is to professional literary historians, there still lurks, when one is dealing with Kafka, the possibility of misunderstanding the tradition within which he wrote. If one measures Kafka's literary garment with measuring rods derived from the "classical" Goethe or from "classical" Expressionism, one finds either that this garment is too short or that it is not the right garment at all. Most of those who undertake formal or structural analyses are at least on the way to measuring it properly. "Description of form," interpretations based on what is immanent in the work itself, the so-called "non-evaluating" criticism may be, at first, a mere exactness of method. But if method is raised above the status of method and made the only acceptable literary "philosophy" or the dominant tenet of literary criticism, then it exceeds its competence and comes to take pleasure in aestheticism. The Eastern interpreters have an advantage over the Western ones in that they inquire explicitly into the relationship of Kafka's message to the reality of the world as they themselves understand and interpret it. They do not divorce literature from the rest of their thinking but express their allegiance to an order and (as they see it) a wholeness of life. Whoever (even though not in the same way as in Marxist lands) believes in the possibility of a critically founded realization of the world and in a firmly committed truth, will try to establish some kind of relationship between his structural analysis and interpretation of the individual work and his own understanding of the world: between his interpretation and what he and a larger, it might even be a very large, community recognize as truth, perhaps only incompletely but never relatively or individualistically. Yet the attempt to establish a relationship between the literary message and one's own understanding of the world must always be a second step. The fact that every thinking man brings his own preconceptions and his own range of experience to the text will be harmful only if he adheres uncritically to his preconception, not really opening himself to the text but merely subjecting it to his own fixed idea.

Literary criticism is not a simple, horizontal activity. A literary work of art contains many levels of meaning. Psychological, sociological, philosophical, or theological interpretations, when they proceed in isolation, encompass only one aspect, one level of meaning, and this leads to distortion.[60] Whether each text has a single peak of meaning, or whether several possible peaks of meaning can be juxtaposed and interlaced in such a way that they are all equally meaningful, or, at least, in such a way that their arrangement does not compel recognition of only one of them—that is a basic literary question and one that is not limited to the criticism of Kafka alone. In the case of Kafka, the answers of interpreters and critics range from existential singleness of meaning (Emrich), over sphinx-like multiplicity of meaning (Politzer) and fundamental ambivalence (Pongs, Sokel), to the ambiguity of abstract forms and even to the meaninglessness of the absurd. Grotesque alienation, disconnected dream elements, unexpected omission of necessary realistic details, and voluntary failure to report the stream-of-consciousness make it difficult to discern Kafka's literary pattern without ambiguity. Since modern parabolic narration does not clearly reveal the relationships between the literary pattern and the possibly real event, a multiplicity of interpretations present themselves when one attempts a "concrete" application. Not the least of the dialectical tensions in Kafka's work is that between "the clarity of statement in each individual sentence and the increasing lack of clarity in the whole; between the most extreme ambiguity of context and the precision of linguistic expression modeled on Johann Peter Hebel or Heinrich Kleist (two of Kafka's favorite authors)." Kafka himself, in his comment on the Prometheus legend, pointed out four versions of totally different meaning: "The legend attempts to explain the unexplainable. Since it has its foundation in truth, it must end in the unexplainable." Loss of tradition, inability to decide, apprehension of the inapprehensible, astonishment before the mystery? Kafka's capitulation before the impossibility of determining possible meaning? or constantly renewed sallies against anxiety and toward moments of confidence? "If one had to name an author," wrote W. H. Auden, "who was as important for our age as Dante, Shakespeare, and Goethe were for theirs, Kafka would head the list." [61]

3

Literature and Science

The Discussion in England

The last essay of the late Aldous Huxley[1] deals with the tension between literature and science. It was written against the background of the controversy in England between Charles P. Snow and Frank R. Leavis. In the Rede Lecture of 1959, Snow, who was first a physicist, then a novelist, and in the last war Director of Technical Personnel in the Ministry of Labor, advanced the thesis of the two separate cultures: the intellectual and literary as opposed to the strictly scholarly, or more exactly scientific, culture. This thesis was certainly not new, but it became a theme of primary importance in England, where it aroused wide discussion, in which the literary critic Lionel Trilling and the atomic physicist Robert Oppenheimer took part. Snow, the initiator of the controversy, placed the responsibility for the gulf, which had been clearly recognizable since the turn of the century, on those educated in the humanistic tradition and gifted with literary creativity, who, on the one hand, were scarcely aware of developments in the natural sciences and, on the other, accorded no recognition to scientists or those engaged in laboratory work. For this accusation, Snow was attacked by Frank R. Leavis, a respected professor of literature at Cambridge, in the Richmond Lecture of 1962. Snow, said Leavis, imagines that he possesses both cultures, but he possesses neither the true scientific nor the true literary mentality. In presenting his thesis, he is comparing things that are not comparable. Ignorance, for instance, of the Second Law of Thermodynamics is not on the same plane as ignorance of the works of Shakespeare. But neither Snow nor Leavis attempted to say what the relationship between the two cultures actually is, or what it could become with some thought and mutual tolerance. Aldous Huxley was a cultivated, many-sided author and a keen critic of the cultural scene. Obviously he had both the background and the training to ask the right questions and to establish the proper perspective in the struggle between the two views. He was a grandson of Thomas Henry Huxley (1825–1895), the naturalist and staunch defender of the theory of evolution, and a grandnephew of Matthew Arnold (1822–1888), the writer, critic, and school inspector. Moreover, he was a brother of the biologist Julian Huxley.

Huxley's questions read: "What is the function of literature, what its psychology, what the nature of literary language? And how do its function, psychology, and language differ from the function, psychology and language of science? What, in the past, has been the relationship between literature and science? What is it now? What might it be in the future? What would it be profitable, artistically speaking, for a twentieth-century man of letters to do about twentieth-century science?"[2]

Object, Method, and Goal of Science and Literature

Every intellectual discipline can be described in terms of its object, of the viewpoint from which that object is considered, and of the method by which it is presented. "In the present context, science may be defined as a device for investigating, ordering and communicating the more public of human experiences. Less systematically, literature also deals with such public experiences. Its main concern, however, is with man's more private experiences, and with the interactions between the private worlds of sentient, self-conscious individuals and the public universes of 'ob-

57

jective reality,' logic, social conventions, and the accumulated information currently available." [3]

The object of the natural sciences is nature circumscribed by natural laws—concrete, objective, logical, general, calculable nature; that of literature, on the other hand, is the specifically human individual person, composed of body and soul, limited by his social milieu, and gifted with freedom, and the personal world of the society in which he lives. Over all literature, as over all the other arts, stands the sentence from Alexander Pope's *Essay on Man* (1773): "The proper study of mankind is man." Both natural scientists and literary artists observe their object and present their observations. But they do it in different ways, from different vantage points and viewpoints, with different eyes and different perspectives, and for a different end. The scientist is interested, above all, in explaining a single property according to theoretical principles. He prepares the object of his investigation, introduces it into the constellation of his experiment, establishes the most ideal conditions possible for observing a particular behavorial pattern, a possible reaction, or a measurable, and therefore demonstrable, property. He abstracts and dissects his object, repeats his experiment under conditions that are as similar as possible. The literary artist, on the contrary, looks at the concrete and complex whole, at the multiplicity and involvement of its properties, its milieu, its historical development, and its personal decisions; at the intractable and often antagonistic nature of man with its rationalism and irrationalism, its matter and spirit. He knows about the uniqueness of the person, the irretrievability of the situation. He wants neither to reduce his object to a single level of meaning nor to isolate it from its surroundings, but to observe the play and counterplay of behavioral patterns and decisions in a world of multifarious and unlimitable tensions. "The world with which literature deals is the world in which human beings are born and live and finally die; the world in which they love and hate, in which they experience triumph and humiliation, hope, and despair; the world of sufferings and enjoyments, of madness and common sense, of silliness, cunning, and wisdom; the world of social pressures and individual impulses, of reason against passion, of instincts and conventions, of shared language and unsharable feeling and sensation;

58

of innate differences and the rules, the roles, the solemn or absurd rituals imposed by the prevailing culture. Every human being is aware of this multifarious world and . . . by analogy with himself, he can guess where other people stand, what they feel and how they are likely to behave." [4]

The literary artist has to interpret rather than analyze his object, look at it rather than dissect it experimentally part by part, present it rather than explain it. His mental vision is not enlightened by *ratio* alone. He is capable of figurative and structural perception, of emphatic, intuitive, often mythical and mystic vision. His interpretation is frequently based on a preconceived (which does not mean unfounded) estimation of the world. Every artistic presentation of one part of the world contains a certain view of the whole world. The individual scientist investigates and observes only parts of nature. The more exact his individual observations have been, the greater is the danger that he will lose sight of the whole, in fact, must lose sight of it in order to concentrate wholly on his individual observation. The literary artist is always, in one way or another, engaged with the whole of mankind.

Huxley designates the method and goal of the natural sciences as "nomothetic," that is, "they seek to establish explanatory laws" that are as universally valid and as unequivocal as possible. "Literature is . . . 'ideographic'; its concern is not with regularities and explanatory laws, but with descriptions of appearances and the discerned qualities of objects perceived as wholes, with judgments, comparisons and discriminations, with 'inscapes' . . ." [5] A science seeks to erect a system of knowledge, to coordinate a series of concepts in such a way that, with their help, an aspect or a part of the world will be explained according to regular laws. Thus every science wants to have "its own frame of reference." "For Science in its totality, the ultimate goal is the creation of a monistic system in which—on the symbolic level and in terms of the inferred components of invisibility and intangibly fine structure—the world's enormous multiplicity is reduced to something like unity . . . and simplified into a single rational order. . . . The man of letters [on the contrary] . . . accepts the uniqueness of events, accepts the diversity and manifoldness of the world, . . . the radical incomprehensibility . . . of . . . unconceptualized existence . . ." [6] He gives form to that which cannot be grasped either mechanically, electrically, or optically; to that which cannot be established conceptually; to the vacillating, the undetermined, the only partially determined, the too quickly determined; to the valid and the invalid; the grotesque and the absurd; to the claims of truth and of masked deceit. He wants neither to create a system of knowledge nor to force the world through the retort. Yet he does want to discover and to reveal. He wants, for example, to reveal the spirit of the age, the forms of society, the relationship of individual and society; of tradition, convention, and freedom; of reason and passion; of appearance and actuality in the life of the individual and of society. He wants to reveal the conditions of progress, of freedom, of human dignity; to show profit and loss in the *condition humaine*, the perils of being human. He wants to make the claims of truth visible; to expose the forms of deceit; to diagnose the sicknesses of the age, of the nation, of social groups; to denounce the unjust strongholds of might; to call attention to contradictions;[7] to remind man repeatedly that he is man. Huxley includes within the scope of the writer an area of observation and inquiry which certain literary groups, in Germany and elsewhere, would gladly dispense with: the area concerned with the metaphysical nature and transcendental potentiality of man. "Who are we? What is our destiny? How can the often frightful ways of God be justified?" [8] A theodicy, then, in a modern anthropodicy. Huxley's psychologically colored transcendence and predilection for myth seem to us just as questionable as his so-called "infused contemplation," [9] with its shades of the Orient, of Buddhism, of Gnosticism—and even of drugs! He fails to recognize the authenticity of Christianity and the historical structure of Christian existence. But he sees correctly that the man of letters must burst the seams of the scientific horizontality of the modern world, that he must reveal to civilized man, entangled in the horizontal planes of life, the verticality of religion.

The Difference of Language

Science and literature are distinct, then, even in their objects, but above all in their formal viewpoints, in their methods of searching for truth, and in their goals. They are also distinct in their methods of presentation and in their language. Literature does not present its findings conceptually, or graphically, or photographically. Its presentation is through the plastic structure of the word. The literary artist tries to present an animated reflection of man's world in dialogue and plot, in narrative, evocation, and image, in simile and suggestive metaphor. All this reflection and visualization can take place only through the medium of speech. Even the scientist, despite "electron microscopes, cyclotrons, and electronic brains," despite all his mathematical, physical, and chemical symbols and formulas, must use human speech when he wishes to formulate his observations and findings. But he will use a technical language, an unambiguous jargon, freed as far as possible from human subjectivity and emotion. Word and sentence will be simplified, exactly defined, and unequivocal to the point of allowing only a "single interpretation." Speech is not presented here for its own sake, but merely as a means for the presentation of something else. It is used in a purely functional manner. Comprehension is already present before the process of verbal presentation begins.

It is different with literary language. In it, meaning appears for the first time in word and image, in linguistic form. Comprehension and presentation—what is presented and the medium through which it is presented—are here much more closely connected; they affect each other and penetrate one another mutually. What is comprehended is identical with the poetic word by which it is expressed, and the poetic word is identical with that which is comprehended, with that which is nowhere present except in the poetic word. "The purified language of literary art is not the means to something else; it is an end in itself," insofar as "significance and beauty" are in it, and insofar as it makes human existence real and gives form, content, and meaning to intellectual being.[10] The literary artist puts the rough and worn common language of men through a creative process of purification and renewal. He takes the overused, misused, and abused words and sentences, which the world around him has hardened into clichés and filled with poison, and breaks them up, melts them down, re-forms them, and coins them anew. One might compare this literary processing of language to the melting down of old metals or to the purifying of healthful, natural water. "Donner un sens plus pur aux mots de la tribu" [11]—this is the linguistic task of the man of letters. Just as healthful, natural water absorbs a certain amount of waste water, decomposes it, removes the poison, purifies it, and restores it to the household of nature, so can the language of literature capture the worn and abused language of every day, the jargon, the clichés, the slogans, the hyperboles, filter them, break them up, form the words anew from their linguistic elements, and restore them with new life to the world of man. Since literary language presents the world of man, it cannot be broken into horizontal segments and anchored in concepts. It must present its complete object in all his diversity, with all his wealth of relationships, and in his concrete, dynamic, and living individuality. That is why the literary word has many levels and often many meanings. It has bearings in depth and space that the conceptual word does not have. Its exactness often consists in the fact that it has no sharp delimitations, but is open on all sides, just as man himself has no sharp delimitations but is open on all sides to historical, social, and cosmic relationships. The literary word neither can nor may have the clearcut distinctions of conceptual language, because, like concrete and individual man, it is incommensurable and almost infinitely related to the universe around it. For that reason, it can almost never claim the unambiguousness of chemical formulas or of metropolitan traffic regulations. If even the paragraphs of a law book, despite all efforts at exactitude, cannot be sharply defined but still remain open to a multiplicity of interpretations, how much more true is this of man himself. Added to this is the fact that literary language must express both the finite and the infinite, the fixed and the variable. If, in its own way, it repeatedly abstracts, reduces, and simplifies, it must, nonetheless, depict everflowing life with its complicatedly conscious and unconscious imaginings, rational and irrational impulses, associations, thoughts and images, drives and decisions, influences from within and without—and the interrelationships and interpenetrations of all of these. What is unthinkable in scientific language is necessary in literary language. That is why undertones and overtones, even dissonances and static, and an almost endless chain of reminiscences and images vibrate in it, as they do in the language and deeds of man himself. "Even if logic is the prerequisite for scientific language, in which singleness of meaning and precision of inference are essential," said Werner Heisenberg, "it is no adequate description of living speech, which has at its disposal so many richer means of expression. Not only does the spoken word evoke in our minds a particular movement, which is fully known to us and which we might designate as the meaning of the word, but it causes to emerge from the half-darkness of our consciousness those many secondary meanings and associations that, though we are hardly aware of them, may be essential to the meaning of the sentence we have heard. . . . Therefore poets, especially, have often protested against exaggerated emphasis on the logical structure of language and have pointed with justice to these other structures"—to the logic of literature as opposed to the horizontal and one-sided logic of science—"which form the basis of the specifically artistic use of language. . . . If, in the sciences, we must make the logical structure of language the basis of our thinking, at least we should not be oblivious to its other, richer, possibilities." [12]

A History of the Encounter between Science and Literature

As yet, no one has written the definitive history of the segregation and integration of science and literature. Huxley himself did not do so even for English literature. When knowledge about nature had not yet been separated from verbal imagery and from a personally constructed myth, as, for instance, in Hesiod's *Works and Days,* there was no opposition between science and literature. Yet even Socrates, by his ethical questioning, expressed his dissatisfaction with knowledge about nature alone and opposed to it the idea of knowledge about man. "Now nature is on one side, man with his culture on the other. The problem of whether it is more important to know nature or the nature of man stands, therefore, at the very beginning of Western thought." [13] As their heritage from Aristotle, Stoics and Epicureans retained the division of the world into nature and spirit and, with it, the gulf between "physics" on the one side and "ethics" on the other. In Neoplatonism, nature was degraded as "physics." The Christian Middle Ages raised the status of nature, which they regarded as being as much God's creation as was spirit, and thus gave rise to a new wholeness. But the new and really decisive step toward modern science occurred during the Renaissance (Leonardo da Vinci, Copernicus, Giordano Bruno, Galileo), when man turned away from Aristotelian cosmology and medieval Scholastic philosophy and toward experiment and exact observation of nature. The modern dichotomy between science and the arts has existed since that time. It was intensified and rendered acute in the course of the nineteenth century.[14]

Once, in the sixteenth and seventeenth centuries, a lyric poet like John Donne could, without undue difficulty, incorporate his increased knowledge of the natural history of the world (not the impact of the cosmic system) into his lyrics. As long as man's new discoveries and his broadened understanding of the world were met with entities that could be seen or at least imagined, which could be understood without any special prerequisites, the poet, like every other man, was able to appropriate them to himself. He could also transfer them to his poetry. Thus Goethe, with his great interest in new ideas, appropriated the scientific title *De attractionibus electivis* from the Swede Torbern Bergman and used it creatively as the title of his novel *Die Wahlverwandtschaften* [Elective Affinities] in 1809. The observation that certain chemical substances are attracted to one another by a kind of natural necessity and that they strive toward union offered him both a simile and an explanation for that compulsive "choice" [*Wahl*] in human beings that takes precedence over freedom. He attempted to encompass in lyric verses, in which he even anticipated the concept of evolution, his new scientific findings about the metamorphosis of plants and animals. Some decades later in England, while composing the poem "In Memoriam" (published 1850), the lyric poet Alfred Tennyson became interested in Charles Lyell's *Principles of Geology* (1830–1833) and his exciting ideas about the evolution of the earth. By the middle of the century, in fact, "even a poet could understand the Darwinian hypothesis in its primitive form—could understand and rejoice, if he were a freethinker, over its antitheological implications or, if he were an orthodox Christian, react indignantly or with nostalgic tears to what *The Origin of Species* had done to Noah's ark and the first chapter of Genesis. Today the picture, once so beautifully clear, has had to incorporate into itself all the complexities of modern genetics, modern biochemistry, even modern biosociology. Science has become an affair of specialists. Incapable any longer of understanding what it is all about, the man of letters, we are told, has no choice but to ignore contemporary science altogether."[15] In Germany, Arno Holz and other naturalistic writers toward the end of the century were extreme Darwinists. The young Franz Kafka was not only a Darwinist but also a follower of Ernst Haeckel. The general scientific tendencies of the age were, so to speak, in the air.

For English-speaking countries, Huxley made the comment: "Of the better poems written since 1921, the great majority do not so much as hint at the most important fact of contemporary history—the accelerating progress of science and technology. Insofar as they affect the social, economic and political situation in which individuals find themselves, some of the consequences of progressive science receive attention from the poets; but science as a growing corpus of information, science as a system of concepts operationally defined, even science as a necessary element in the formulation of a tenable philosophy of nature and man, science, in a word, as science, is hardly ever mentioned." [16] The question is whether "science as a system of operationally defined concepts," as it is currently understood, has any place at all in poetry, and whether it can produce anything more than a few didactic poems. The presentation of science as such, that is, in its own sphere, to a broader public is certainly not the task of literature but of modern technical manuals and other means of communication. It is my opinion that science and literature can have a common meeting place only insofar as science comes into contact with man and with human society; insofar as it influences, revolutionizes, and imperils human consciousness—*total* human consciousness; insofar as it decisively reshapes the world of man, his thinking, feeling, and willing. In the sphere of the novel, Huxley might have pointed to his own disillusioned anti-utopias—*Brave New World* (1932) and *Ape and Essence* (1948)—for the presentation of the unsalutary changes in human consciousness and the disastrous influences wrought on men by the findings of science. Signs of a change in consciousness and awareness as well as in the interpretation of facts are discernible almost everywhere in the modern novel. In German-speaking countries, for instance, Robert Musil described, in the first chapter of his novel *Der Mann ohne Eigenschaften* [The Man without Qualities], a "beautiful August day of the year 1913" in technical phrases drawn from meteorology: "barometric minimum" and "maximum," isotheres" and "isotherms." Readers were repelled by this deviation from the usual concept of the beautiful and by the loss of feeling. At the same time, from the beginning of the thirties, Hermann Broch had been steadily asking himself what consequences the "theory of relativity" might have for the narrator of a modern novel.[17] In general, it can be said that the theory of relativity can be expected to alter the consciousness of the narrator, the narration itself, and the events narrated, only to the extent that human consciousness itself has been altered by the theory of relativity and its consequences—whether rightly or wrongly understood. As was to be expected, writers and authors manifested the greatest interest in the observations, findings, and hypotheses of the psychoanalysts. It is well known to what an extent young Franz Kafka was influenced by the scientifically oriented findings of psychoanalysis. The "stream-of-consciousness" novel, with its juxtaposition of many currents of thought, belongs, since the time of James Joyce and Virginia Woolf, among the narrative forms possible at the present time; the ability to manipulate the stream of consciousness is one of the prerequisites of modern narration.

Huxley is of the opinion that lyric and tragedy offer little scope for the inclusion of science. The lyric poets seem, in fact, to have had the strongest disinclination for the rising sciences. Blake and Keats, two prominent lyricists of English romanticism, shunned Isaac Newton. Wordsworth, on the contrary, held him in high esteem, though his lyrical penchant for nature had almost nothing in common with the Newtonian observations of nature. For Rilke, the greatest of the German lyric poets of the twentieth century, science played no role. Even before World War I, however, young Gottfried Benn was incorporating medical vocabulary and ideas into his early poems. Oddly enough, they are almost completely absent from the poems of his middle and late years. The literary genre of tragedy has been rendered well-nigh impossible by the scientifically causal determination of events and by the psychological dismemberment of consciousness. The modern trend toward demythologizing and strict inquiry into the historical course of a personal or social "catastrophe" has likewise contributed to this situation. Where man is confronted only by himself, a "tragedy" may still be possible, though all comedy seems to become "tragicomedy." Drama cannot, and in the natural order of things need not, treat of scientific themes. It presents human conflicts. They arise when scientific results enter the realm of human society, whether the scientific findings contradict the traditional views of society (as in Brecht's *Leben des Galilei*, 1943) or are misused for political purposes (as in Dürrenmatt's *Die Physiker*, 1961) or are politically "betrayed" (as in the recent play by R. Kipphardt, *In der Sache J. R. Oppenheimer*, 1964). Many social and human conflicts are conceivable in these areas. They occur wherever an attempt is made to segregate or integrate the scientifically known and the merely human.

The stricter form of the essay, if one includes it among the literary genres, affords a direct possibility for the encounter of scientific content and literary form. The essay appeared as an independent literary form at about the same time that science was beginning to separate itself from the humanities, that is, during the Renaissance (Montaigne, Francis Bacon). It plays an important role within the modern novel, as, for instance, in the works of Hermann Broch, Robert Musil, and even Thomas Mann. The narrator reveals himself as thinker, knower, observer; as the expert, who expresses himself about an area in which he is competent or about his scientifically determined personal observations.

Huxley felt that there was far too little incorporation of scientific findings and content into modern literature. From the point of view of content and theme, that may be so. But the literary man's way of thinking and seeing, the temper of his mental outlook does, nonetheless, show that he is coming closer to the scientist's attitude toward the object of his investigation. It is no accident that the very title of Franz Kafka's earliest work, *"Beschreibung eines Kampfes"* [Description of a Struggle] (1904–1905), reveals it as the attempt to describe methodically the inner and outer condition of a complicated and immature man. The concept of "description" became significant for Kafka under the influence of the teachings of Ernst Mach and the experimental and inductive psychology of Franz Brentano. The second part of the above-mentioned story is, against all tradition, labeled "proof": "a proof that it is impossible to live." That is a new narrative attitude for an author to adopt toward the world that he is to observe and portray. Since the fifties, the efforts of the authors of the *nouveau roman* have been going much further. Uwe Johnson's novels, *Mutmassungen über Jakob* [Speculations about Jacob] and *Das dritte Buch über Achim* [The Third Book about Achim], show clearly this critical, scientifically influenced awareness on the part of the younger writers. Men of letters are becoming increasingly concerned about preserving a critical distance from the object to be observed and described, about the avoidance of all possible subjectivity, about conscious knowledge, about their own position within the sphere of reality that is under observation. They illuminate their object from all sides, show critically to what distortion a one-sided contemplation may lead, prescribe cold observation instead of a feeling of identification with the object, change the position and perspective of observation, force what is factual, psychic, and emotional through the filter of reflection, analysis, and criticism, and thus prevent our direct concurrence with what has been presented.

In contrast to the English romanticists, the early romantic writers in Germany had introduced the concept of "experiment" into literary work. "A good physical experiment can serve as the model of an inner experiment and is itself, besides, a good inner, subjective experiment." "To experiment with images and concepts and with the possibilities of presenting them in a way analogous to that of physical experimentation." [18] These fragments from Novalis refer to the cognitive experiment with the object and the formal experiment of linguistic presentation. Emile Zola's programmatic work of 1880, *Le Roman expérimental*, did not refer to an experiment with a new form of novel, but with a new method of evolving the action of the novel from the premises of experience and philosophy. "For Zola, the consciousness of the writer was a kind of test tube in which a chain reaction was set in motion according to strict scientific laws. The protocol of this reaction yielded the action of the novel. These two married persons with this particular heredity, united at this particular time, must in the end kill one another in this particular way as determined by the teachings of heredity and the theory of environment." [19] In the chapter "*Symposion oder Gespräch über die Erlösung*" [Symposium or a Conversation about Redemption] in his trilogy *Die Schlafwandler* [The Sleepwalkers] (1929–1932), Hermann Broch transfers some of his main characters into an experimental situation. His purpose is not to demonstrate, as Zola did, the naturalistic principle of determinism; he wants, in the shortest way possible and in a model situation erected by himself, to demonstrate and allow free play to the thoughts, trials, and struggles of his characters. Beda Allemann has shown "that experimental traits and the will to artistic experiment are recognizable in all spheres of modern literature, that, in fact, the reference to this experimental character of modern literature has for some time now belonged among the commonplaces of literary criticism." [20] That an unsuccessful linguistic experiment is not a work of art is self-evident. That an author like Alfred Andersch should resist the thoughtless transference of the concept of experiment into the realm of literature is a healthy reaction against the vague and the merely modish. In the present context, there has been an effort to point out not merely the points of contact in the content of literary and scientific works, but also the increasing proximity of the two disciplines in method, in the observation of their object, and in the preparation of their product.

The Depoetizing of the World and the Self-Knowledge of the Modern Author

"Science sometimes builds new bridges between universes of discourse and experience hitherto regarded as separate and heterogeneous. But science also breaks down old bridges and opens gulfs between universes that, traditionally, had been connected. Blake and Keats, as we have seen, detested Sir Isaac Newton because he had cut the old connection between the stars and the heavenly host, between rainbows and Iris, and even between rainbows and

Noah's Ark, rainbows and Jehovah,—had cut the connections and thereby de-poetized man's world and robbed it of meaning." [21] Scientific thinking and mythically interpreted experience, science and the humanities, science and supernatural faith, immanence and transcendence, world and God—all these have been separated. The world that appears to man's senses has been put more and more often under the microscope, dissected, analyzed, measured, objectified, planned, rebuilt, and misbuilt. The world as nature—as the natural, created, and hereditary living space of man—is being driven further and further into the background. The world projected by the scientist, the artificially reconstructed, technically produced world, is looming larger and larger, this world of tracks and wires, glass and cement, pills, formulas, aggregates, traffic lights, and windshields. Closely linked to this reconstruction of the world are the processes of demythologizing, deanthropomorphizing, denaturalizing. Typical of the development of this world is the substitution of city-lyrics for nature-lyrics by the German Expressionists and, in more recent times, the substitution of test-tube-lyrics for city-lyrics.

We can illustrate the loss of the old natural and mythical world by two examples. The moon, having become the goal and already the landing place of rockets, no longer serves as the subject of tender lyrics. Goethe's immortal lyric to the moon is not even conceivable today:

> Füllest wieder Busch und Tal
> Still mit Nebelglanz,
> Lösest endlich auch einmal
> Meine Seele ganz;
> Breitest über mein Gefild
> Lindernd deinen Blick,
> Wie des Freundes Auge mild
> Über mein Geschick." [22]

This free transferral of mood and sentiment to the friendly moon, the awakening of a spiritual and poetic mood by reference to earth's companion, her great and friendly neighbor, no longer even occurs to a poet, to an "enlightened" man. Such a sentiment and awakening are no longer possible. The moon is no longer the

trusted, mysteriously silent friend of man. It is a satellite that ro-
tates around the earth on a constantly narrowing elliptical course
at a mean distance of about 238,857 miles and about whose climatic
conditions, mountains, and reflection of the sun man is somewhat
informed. But human feelings? At the best, feelings of inquiry
and conquest, that is, modern scientific feelings of the objective,
"matter of fact" kind, not poetic and personal feelings.

From time immemorial, another favorite subject of lyric poetry
has been the nightingale. In England there are at least as many
lyrics about nightingales as there are in Germany about the moon.
But the nightingale, too, has lost its tender lyric nature since the
animal psychologists have discovered that the cock nightingale
(not Philomel) sings "not in pain, not in passion, not in ecstasy,
but simply in order to proclaim to other cock nightingales that
he has staked out a territory and is prepared to defend it against
all comers." Nothing remains of love's nightly longing and lament
since man has discovered through scientific observation that the
cock sings "because, like all the other members of his species, he
has the kind of digestive system that makes him want to feed every
four or five hours throughout the twenty-four. Between cater-
pillars, during these feeding times, he warns his rivals . . . to keep
off his private property." [23] Like the philosopher and the man
in the street, the poet must learn today that things signify themselves first. Inappropriate transferrals of feeling, unconsidered hyperboles of thought, naïve anthropomorphizing of the world are
no longer permissible. "In an age of science the world can no
longer be looked at as a set of symbols, standing for things outside the world. *Alles Vergaengliche ist NICHT ein Gleichnis*," [24]
at least not in the idealistic *a priori* sense of a Plato. Unconsidered
allegorizing and exaggeration create today the impression of a
flight from the harder realities of the uncompromisingly real.
Such a flight makes everything that was previously believed about
reality no longer quite believable.

In the preface to the second edition of the "Lyrical Ballads" in
1801, Wordsworth describes poetry as the "spontaneous overflow
of powerful feelings." It would be difficult to find a definition less
suited to the greater part of contemporary poetry. Feelings, especially the feelings that affirm the world, have been, in almost

every case, skeptically and critically withdrawn. The intellect is sent ahead to reconnoiter, take soundings, spy. Feelings are suspect, are consciously subdued. This world can no longer evoke a spontaneous affirmation. The withdrawal of feeling is at the same time the protection of a self whose deductions about the world have given it a different orientation. A spontaneously experienced unity between poet and world no longer exists. For the poet and artist, there remains almost no other reaction to the world than a gradual and partial affirmation, brought about by the painful process of observation and reflection, criticism and abstraction. It is doubtful whether the new synthesis, which Huxley proposes as the ideal— a synthesis, for example, of the ornithological truth about the nightingale and a mythologically constructed human projection— is possible for the literature of our generation. A generation that has experienced the shock of emotional disillusionment, the results of an inappropriate projection of the emotions, and the rejection of their own, naïvely spontaneous trustfulness can scarcely be expected to produce, in the next breath, a new "yes" to the world, a sympathy now critically filtered, a sentiment—consciously differentiated by scientific means—of new trust and psychic contact, a sense of inclusion in the inner, meaningful world of men. Perhaps a relationship on a scientific basis will be possible between man and nature in the next generation, for man will no longer experience the shock, but will have accepted science as a matter of course, and will know the limits of the scientific viewpoint and the extent to which science can be conquered. The process of demythologizing nature will, at first, proceed as before. For the rest, Kafka has already shown that the secondary, administered, bureaucratic world is susceptible of both myth and poetry.

Poets do not speak today of a "divine instinct" that guides them, of "inspiration," of "enthusiasm," of the "spontaneous overflow of powerful feelings." Poetry is, for the most part, no longer "inspired"—at least no one speaks of it as such. It no longer "originates"; it is "made." For that reason, the German classical idea of the "organism" is seldom used in the interpretation of or as a norm for the modern literary work. The modern artistic entity no longer aspires to imitate an organic entity. It is no longer to be understood simply as "mimesis." The *poiesis*, the *making*, has become more important. The literary work of art is a "piece," a "piece of work," an entity made as technical products are made. Modern writers think of themselves as "chemists," who mix poems out of linguistic elements (W. H. Auden), or as "literary engineers" (Valéry, Enzensberger). Louis MacNeice wrote in 1948: "Literature is a precision instrument for showing how man reacts to life." [25] The writer no longer wants to act as guide to the rarefied heights of a harmonious life that has no existence in reality and is radically misunderstood by a sleepy and uninterested bourgeoisie. He lays no claim to an authority that transcends his own observation, the world of characters that he has presented, the word he has formulated. Even he is engaged, although he must keep the scope of the whole work in mind, with partial questions, which, admittedly, are not so much quantitative in nature as humanly, historically, and socially qualitative. It never occurs to him to present a whole— the road to maturity, for example, as portrayed in the "classical" German psychological novel [*Bildungsroman*]. In intensive preliminary inquiry, he concerns himself not only with the formal side of presentation but with the processes of observing and approaching the object to be presented—processes that are at once presupposed by the linguistic form and contained in it. The recently deceased T. S. Eliot has given us Valéry's concept of the poet: "He is no longer the disheveled madman who writes a whole poem in the course of one feverish night; he is a cool scientist, almost an algebraist . . . comparable to the mathematical physicist, or else to the biologist or chemist . . . , the austere, bespectacled man in a white coat. . . . The ivory tower has been fitted up as a laboratory—a solitary laboratory." [26] These and similar comparisons are not intended to degrade the poet of times past or to deny that new problems in regard to both his profession and his task confront the laboratory-poet of today. When, for example, society as a whole recognizes no generally binding truth, then the writer in such a society cannot be guided by a generally binding "norm" of truth. Truth is for him—and in this, too, he is like the scientist—only that understanding of reality which he himself has discovered, or can discover, through "experience." "Tradition" is for him a word as meaningful and problematical as it is for the man in a chemical laboratory. It may be taken for granted here that a concept of reality whose sole criterion is the "experiment" is a great loss to humanity. It seems important for our understanding of the relationship between modern literature and science that we realize how much the self-understanding of modern writers is expressed in scientific and technical language. The modern author is no longer primarily a man imbued with feelings of oneness with the "gods" or the cosmos or nature. On the contrary, he must discipline himself to approach his "object," to observe it critically, to present his findings both objectively and poetically. Occasional extreme outbursts of phantasy merely show the effect of such strong discipline, the swing of the pendulum into an area that is less demanding and not so predetermined by the object to be presented—an area of primitive and self-determining creative freedom.

Preservation and Recovery of the Human Element in a Scientifically Understood and Technically Constructed World

Enthusiastically, though not without reservations, Wordsworth, in 1801, anticipated the future covenant between poet and scientist. "If the labours of Men of science," he wrote, "should ever create any material revolution, direct or indirect, in our condition, and in the impressions which we habitually receive, the Poet will sleep then no more than at present; he will be ready to follow the steps of the Men of science, not only in those general indirect effects, but he will be at his side, carrying sensations into the midst of the objects of science itself. The remotest discoveries of the Chemist, the Botanist, or Mineralogist, will be as proper objects of the Poet's art as any upon which it can be employed, if the time should ever come when these things shall be familiar to us, and the relations under which they are contemplated by the followers of these respective sciences shall be manifestly and palpably material to us as enjoying and suffering beings. If the time should ever come when what is now called science, thus familiarized to men, shall be ready to put on, as it were, a form of flesh and blood, the Poet will lend his divine spirit to aid the transfiguration, and will welcome the Being thus produced as a dear and genuine inmate of the household of man." [27] Wordsworth's ability to envisage the developments of science was obviously limited. Some of the most important discoveries of the newer physics, for instance the structure of the atom or the nature of electromagnetic waves, are simply not apprehensible by the senses. They cannot "put on a form of flesh and blood." When the realms of representation, of what can be described in words or at least conceived by the imagination, have been left behind, literature and art can no longer function representationally.[28] To this must be added the fact that the "divine spirit" of the poet is not even needed for the scientific and, in its wake, the technical transformation of the world. Science and technology can change the world without any help from the poet.

Wordsworth was totally unaware of the threatening and rapidly advancing banishment of man from the "paradise" of nature, of the increasingly spiritual homelessness of modern man, of the attempt to reconstruct the world of man as scientifically as possible—and, certainly, of the steadily increasing political threat to nations from the instruments of superpower, the so-called ABC weapons, that science has made possible.[29] He was unaware of the increasing inner estrangement from the world that accompanies man's increasing scientific familiarity with it. Convinced that the poet "is the rock of defence for human nature, an upholder and preserver," [30] one who sympathizes with all that exists, Wordsworth did not know to what extent man is at the disposal of the world he has conquered by science, how it directs him as if he were an objective potential, disregards his last possession, his freedom, and regards him as a small functioning part of an immense scientific, technical, and economic piece of equipment. To the scientific belief in progress, in a unilateral process that reduces everything to the realm of science and makes no distinction between theory and practice, the man of letters cannot but refuse his unreserved assent, his uncritical acceptance, because this process encroaches upon man's rights, because this paradoxically practical utopian belief imperils man, however many pain-killing drugs and work-lightening gadgets he may invent.

Nevertheless, the man of letters must be as conversant as possible with the scientific mind and attitude. "Literature cannot be spared the necessity of adapting itself to the scientific world view, and a part of its present irrelevance is due to the fact that it is so slow in doing so," wrote Robert Musil in 1927.[31] Henceforth only pseudopoets can cling to their ancestral emotions, their dim idylls, their allegedly unimpaired fortress. For the most part, it is their language that betrays their lack of alertness toward reality. They do not live in the real world that oppresses man from all sides. Modern man, unless he wants to withdraw to the last recesses of bush, island, or dream, can no longer accept or reject the scientifically and technically altered world. It is simply there. He is born into it. And just as the individual person, the family, the religious community, and the nation live in this world and must prove themselves precisely as person, family, religious community, and nation, so must the literary artist prove himself according to the demands of this world, its criteria, its conditions, its elimination of free time, its media of communication, its language. Science will influence him not only by its attitude toward the world, but also by its consciously objectifying and critically observant way of thinking and of seeing everything from its own standpoint. The omniscient author, for example, whose ideal view of persons, things, and events was so much taken for granted in the traditional novel, is no longer conceivable today. Such a way of narrating would no longer be acceptable. It is based on presuppositions about knowledge that science and the scientifically limited, partial, object-bound way of regarding the world—both long since absorbed into the general consciousness—can no longer recognize as being in accord with reality and hence true. The idealistic concept of "omniscience" and the idealistic subjection of the world to its dominion no longer correspond to the structure of our knowledge or to the true demands of the world.

If the contemporary writer should be conversant with the scientific attitude toward the world and the scientific way of viewing the world, this does not mean that science as such, its conceptuality, its formulas, its specialized areas of compartmentalized knowledge, its systems, is to become the object of literature so that literature may prove its relevance to reality, its up-to-dateness. From the literary point of view, that would be poetic materialism; from the scientific point of view, an education of the masses.

But this latter—certainly, a necessity—is, as we have already said, being carried out by the so-called technical manuals and mass media of communication. The man of letters does not have to become the handyman and aide of science. In the first place, he cannot, "because the advance information that readers have gained from instruction through other media makes direct instruction through novels, lyrics, or dramas automatically unnecessary." [32] In the second place, he should not be permitted to attempt it. If he does, his words will "settle" on the level of information and instruction, of the merely useful and objective. That would, perhaps, excuse him, but it would also disarm him; he would be rendered *a priori* harmless to society, degraded to the state of "fellow traveler" and "yes man."

The real theme of literature and literary culture is man. But, in 1970, that does not mean the man of 1770. Even the manner of looking at things is different now (which does not mean that it is better or worse, though to demand, even implicitly, the retention of the vision of 1770 would be to demand that it be worse, for it would mean the inability to grasp the phenomena, and therefore the reality, of the modern world as it is.) To the writer and poet "it is a question of showing the substance of man in a world that has sacrificed all poetic charm and has, in consequence, until now eluded the grasp of literature; that is, the world of science. The Russian Revolution may have been assimilated into the poetic consciousness, but the second industrial revolution has not been; in fact, poetry has as yet scarcely crossed the threshold beyond which the modern age begins; that hazardous enterprise lies before it." [33] It would be difficult to conceive of a more intensive and pressing theme for the conflict that is present in a thousand variations in modern life than that of the struggle of man with his scientifically and technically changed and changing world. Just as a preacher, for instance, by becoming acquainted with the method and content of modern Biblical exegesis, can bring considerable clarity to the understanding of the Bible that he had, perhaps, earlier learned and accepted, so must the poet be as open as possible to changes in the method and content of modern consciousness, especially as it is fostered by science. It is hardly necessary to prove that he must, in the process, observe certain

77

definite professional limits, that he cannot himself become a scientific research scholar.

The real theme and the real scope of the poet is man and man's world in the here and now. But the man of today is also that man whom the factual and partial findings of science have left unnoticed; that man who is more than a number of molecules, chromosomes, cells, electric charges, circulatory and digestive organs; more than a sum of attitudes, expectations, and reactions; that "citizen of the republic" who does not simply wear a production and consumer code on his back; that man who, it is true, needs science, but to whom science can give only the surface facts and no information at all about his total orientation as man, about his spiritual horizon, which surpasses and penetrates the material world. Werner Heisenberg gives a summary description of the multitude with its unreserved confidence in the scientific bid for power: "With the apparently limitless extension of its material power, mankind is in the position of a captain whose ship is so strongly constructed of steel and iron that the magnetic needle of his compass points only to the iron mass of his ship, not to the north. With such a ship, he can reach no goal, but merely ride around in circles, exposed to the wind and the current." [34] In a world predominantly guided by its scientific and material *credo*, the writer, as the guardian of human values, will stress the importance of the intellect and the person, perhaps even help to rediscover and reconquer them. In this scientific and technical world, which is almost always preoccupied with isolated questions and partial systems, he is responsible for the larger horizon of man and its relation to the whole. The problem of the poet's responsibility for knowing the whole scheme of things is one that Hermann Broch saw very clearly. In his essay, *Geschichtsgesetz und Willensfreiheit* [Free Will and the Law of History], which belongs among his studies of mass psychology, he wrote: "The talent for arousing participation, a gift and talent which is proper in the highest degree to the religious intelligence, is almost totally lacking in the purely rational [we might interpolate "the purely scientific"] intelligence. Above all, it is not, in contrast to religious intelligence, a centralized intelligence, that is, it is not ordered around a central truth from which the organon of knowledge and hence of culture is to be grasped as a unit, at least in its essential unifying principles; rather it is a web, which possesses in each of its points an unchanging significance and importance, so that the appearance of unity, without which there is no participation, no illumination of the dusk . . . , and finally even no wisdom, is rendered utterly impossible." [35]

The responsible writer, who is both aware of the scientific mind and attitude and cognizant of the value of the person and the basic orientation of personal life, will always be man's defender, guardian, and admonisher. Wherever the scientifically oriented world draws man objectively and superfically into its material world of observation and schedule, wherever shortsighted utilization of scientific claims imperils man and his society, the writer will rise up as the critic and corrector of public consciousness. Whence he derives his better knowledge, his more critical experience, his more comprehensive and structured truth, in what manner he is, as citizen and critic of this world, at the same time immersed in the scientific superficiality and imperiled consciousness of the world that he is to portray—these problems of the search for truth and its discovery cannot be touched upon here. The inquiry about the larger horizon will be formulated differently by the philosophically, theologically, and historically educated writer than by one who merely calls upon his own experience, whether present or buried in memory; it will be formulated differently, too, by the Christian writer than by the expressly non-Christian one. For their part, leading men of science have already declared: "Even in science, the object of research is no longer nature as such, but nature as delivered over to human questioning; thus here, too, man once more confronts himself." [36]

4

Literature
and Theology Today

The combating of pagan attacks is not the sole justification
for literary studies. With this important thesis, which he does not
attempt to prove, Saint Jerome concludes Epistle 57, "On the Best
Manner of Translating." As early as the turn of the fifth century,
this Father of the Church considered a purely apologetical attitude toward secular literature an antiquated one for the Christian.
Nearly a thousand years later, toward the end of the Middle Ages,
Giovanni del Vergilio at the University of Bologna composed an
epitaph for Dante, which began as follows: "Theologus Dantes,
nullius dogmatis expers . . ." ("the theologian Dante, stranger to
no knowledge . . .").[1] Such an epitaph would never occur to a
eulogist today; indeed it could not occur to him, not even if he
understood the word *dogma* not in its narrow conceptual meaning,
but as theological knowledge in the broadest sense of the term. To
be theologically informed is not one of the aspirations of contemporary literature.

Literature and theology today: it might appear presumptuous
to try to confine within the limits of a single essay a theme so
comprehensive and important and, at the same time, so amorphous.
Literature and theology, which in the earlier stages of human
consciousness were so close to each other, which in their mythic

and mythological beginnings were indeed one, have since developed in different directions. Both have arrived today at a high level of reflection and critical self-examination. More emphatically than ever before, they inquire today about their own nature, their understanding and experience of the world. Yet never in the history of Western thought have theology and literature confronted each other as independent partners. Most theologians, though not always for the same reasons, set small value on literature; most literary men set a correspondingly low value on theology. It is not difficult to advance reasons for this mutual distrust and lack of esteem. One has the impression that each side would accuse the other of shutting out a part of reality, of ignoring and despising it. Each side believes, and thinks that it can prove on historical grounds, that the other has repeatedly laid claim to a position of understanding and authority in public life that is far in excess of the premises on which its claim is based. Theology, at any event, would like to subordinate literature to itself, take possession of its content, and catalogue its predications as quickly and effortlessly as possible under its own familiar headings. Ecclesiastical circles are inclined either to reject the utterances of literature as expeditiously as possible or to harness them as expeditiously as possible to their own wagon. But literature cries for freedom. It distrusts these coachmen; today it distrusts ecclesiastical bell-ringers even more than those who beat the drums of politics or promise the blessings of prosperity. Literature, for its part, if I may be permitted a generality, is no longer ready to accept theologically binding truths about heaven or hell. It is inspired by the truth of personal and individual experience.

Distrust and antipathy between literature and theology arise, to no small extent, from their mutual lack of knowledge about each other. What tormented the writers (and artists in general) in the so-called Decade of Expressionism, before and after World War I, caused almost no anxiety at all to the theologians of those years. No theologian even read what the secular authors were writing with prophetic alertness and, if not with the greatest skill, at least with diagnostic and prognostic relevance about the insecurity of man in their time. Nothing similar is to be found in the writings of contemporary theologians. They were encouraged by their hierarchy to adhere to the teachings of Thomas Aquinas rather than to observe changes in the consciousness of their fellow men.[2] On the other hand, there are indications at present that literary writers are disregarding the efforts of the most recent Church Council to arrive at an understanding of the world today. Ignorance of others, disdain for their efforts, entrenchment behind bastions and polemics have always been easier than conversing over the wall.

Vatican Council II has imposed upon the Christian the duty of dialogue with this other world. Dialogue in all directions is intended to break down long-established fronts and make Christians at last aware of the presence of that other, who, even when he reflects an opposing viewpoint, is not always motivated by bad will. *The Pastoral Constitution on the Church in the Modern World* is constantly aware of the difficulties of dialogue between the purely secular and the Christian view of the world. But it expresses the opinion that these difficulties "can stimulate the mind to a more accurate and penetrating grasp of the faith. For recent studies and findings of science, history, and philosophy raise new questions which influence life and demand new theological investigations." And, it continues, "literature and the arts are also, in their own way, of great importance to the life of the Church." The reason follows: "For they strive to probe the unique nature of man, his problems, and his experiences as he struggles to know and perfect both himself and the world. They are preoccupied with revealing man's place in history and in the world, with illustrating his miseries and joys, his needs and strengths, and with foreshadowing a better life for him. Thus they are able to elevate human life as it is expressed in manifold forms, depending on time and place. Efforts must therefore be made so that those who practice these arts can feel that the Church gives recognition to them in their activities, and so that, enjoying an orderly freedom, they can establish smoother relations with the Christian community." [3]

Artists and writers today undoubtedly do not have the immediate impression that they would be understood by the leading intellectual representatives of Christianity, that is, by its theologians. It is not probable that theologians will, in the near future, come to a closer understanding of men of letters, or that writers and theologians will appear together on television. Nor is it likely that professional theologians will even read secular authors. Both sides have too much to do. Both are producing books as never before. They speak and write a different language. Literary conventions meet without theologians; theological conventions, without men of letters.

Basically, there have always been difficulties between theology and liturgy, between literature and theology, between secular experience and theological directives. In a period when literary art belonged more or less expressly to the ecclesiastical sphere of consciousness, differences could be reconciled wherever the two spheres seemed to meet. But today, the greater part of literature and literary life takes place outside the ecclesiastical sphere. In their own way, art and literature today have completed that specifically modern emancipation of thought from the sanctuary of faith which is taking place on every level of human existence. "The Atheism of the Enlightenment first clearly formulated the idea of opposition to a theologically defined realm," Helmut Heissenbüttel notes in his recently published "13 Hypotheses about Literature and Science as Comparable Activities." [4] Before discussing the relationship, opposition, and juxtaposition of literature and theology, it will be well to consider some basic concepts. What do we mean by "literature"? by "theology"? What does "today" mean as applied to both?

The Area of Concepts

"In the instant when the apparently so clearly defined word 'literature' is no longer intended and understood in the sense of an empty collective term, it loses its unambiguous connotation. Literature per se has as little actual existence as society per se or man per se." Thus begins an article in *Rowohlts Deutsche Enzyklopädie*.[5] Literature is not simply a matter of evaluation, of current popular taste, of group formulations, of consultation, or of entrance into a literary Valhalla. Literature is different, even ambiguous, in different lands and in different times, not only because there are changes of emphasis in the course of history, but because there are differences of evaluation even at the same time or in the same place. What is the meaning, then, of "this ominous word 'literature,' this obligingly comprehensive name for an apparently clear object?" asked Ingeborg Bachmann in the winter semester of 1959–1960 from the newly founded chair of poetry at the University of Frankfurt.

The word itself has a long history. In Christian usage during Saint Jerome's lifetime, the word *literatura* was used to distinguish heathen secular literature from Christian biblical *scriptura*. The word was introduced into German by the Humanists, at first with the original Latin meaning of "alphabet," "instruction in reading or language," and finally in reference to literature in general. Until the eighteenth century, because only cultured persons could write, it continued to refer to a cultured manner and art. Not until the second half of the eighteenth century was it limited to aesthetic literature, the so-called belles-lettres. The restriction to "aesthetic" literature is deceiving. Today the word literature is applied both in the generally comprehensive sense (i.e., to all the written transmissions of the human intellect, even to professional writings of a technical kind) and in the narrower sense that is pertinent to the present discussion. In this narrower sense, the word signifies works of linguistically artistic quality. It makes no difference whether one prefers to attribute this artistic quality to a divine or to a human spirit, to regard it as dependent upon creative genius or upon technical ability, to refer to it as intuitive and contemplative activity or as activity of the rational and critical intellect. In the traditional sense, literature emphasizes contemplative creativity, the conception of an image, the infusion of thought, the sublime and ennobling tone of the literary work of art; it requires depth, harmony, human feeling, familiarity; in a word, it is classical. But literature does not really care whether it originates in divine inspiration, in human feeling, or in contemplation of the whole; whether it is sublime and harmonious; whether its mood is ennobling. It cares only that the work be well constructed, that the word be expressed clearly and with stylistic effect, that the word exist primarily as word, the verse as verse, the narrative as narrative. Contemporary literature would rather become once more the product of an *"ars poetica"* than rely upon an uncontrollable creative process. The question as to whether great literature is necessarily poetical, and the other

84

question as to whether—and, if so, why—our age is an age of prosaic rather than poetical literature, we shall leave unanswered. Walter Benjamin's *Städtebilder* [City Pictures], Jürgen Becker's *Felder* [Fields], Heinrich Böll's *Brief an einen jungen Katholiken* are prosaic literature. Martin Walser's *Halbzeit* [Half-time], Uwe Johnson's *Zwei Ansichten* [Two Views], Max Frisch's *Mein Name sei Gantenbein* [My Name Is Gantenbein], Helmut Heissenbüttel's *Texte* [Texts], and Peter Weiss' *Die Ermittlung* [The Inquiry] are all prosaic literature. Rolf Hochhuth's *Stellvertreter* [The Deputy] does not consistently achieve the rank of literature, that is, of a linguistic construct that is self-contained by virtue of its language. In Hans Magnus Enzensberger's verses, there is more prosaic than poetical literature; in some of Ingeborg Bachmann's poems and in many of Nelly Sachs' verses, there is more poetical than prosaic literature. "Poor Bertold Brecht" wrote both prosaic and poetical literature of the highest order. Even Schiller, Klopstock, Luther, Gottfried von Strassburg, Germany's leading minnesinger Walther von der Vogelweide, and the master craftsman Hartmann von Aue wrote prosaic literature.[6]

For some time now, literary historians and critics have been giving their attention to the works of literature. They are not quite so superfluous as many would like to believe. They bring literature to the public and the public to literature. They belong to literature. They write literature about literature.

It is obviously impossible today to overlook a third area of literary activity, the literary industry. There are literary exchanges, literary markets, literary brokers, literary lobbyists. Publishing houses have commercial newspapers, salesmen, and advertising departments. Literary groups and literary conventions cannot entirely escape the literary industry. Market prices and literary quality are not always identical, nor do they have to be. But it is certain that our approach to literature and our attitude toward it are determined today, more than we may care to admit, by the literary market.

Even more difficult and indefinite than the concept of "literature" is the concept of "today." It is an addition to the concept of either literature or theology that both qualifies and links them. We are familiar with the idea of today's date, today's mail, today's news. But the "today" of literature and theology is not the "today" of daily living. It is rather the "today" that dates from the most recent caesura in intellectual pursuits, the "today" of a decade, perhaps of a generation. But is not this "today" half buried in "yesterday"? Does the "today" of literature begin around 1910? at the end of the twenties? after 1945? or not until the fifties? In my opinion, the question cannot be answered with a simple either/ or. Contemporary literature is inconceivable without the rise and fall of Expressionism, even when it is most distant from it. And there are new trends in the form and content of German literature in the fifties that do not simply abolish the "tabula rasa" of the caesura of 1945.

A purely chronological definition of "today" is of little worth. Conversely, a more qualitative definition need not say anything about the rank of literature or theology as such, as if the literature and theology of today were in any event better than those of yesterday. All that can be said with certainty is that today's literature and theology cannot and should not be those of yesterday. In literature, those who are closest to "today" are called the avant-gardists; in theology, the progressists. Both terms are labels for quick use in an age when definitive allocations are difficult. Perhaps it would be better to make use of a more neutral terminology. In literature, the word "phenotype," which Gottfried Benn transferred to literature from the field of genetics, suggests itself. The phenotype is that particularity, in any given era, that gives clearest expression to the characteristic traits of the age; it is the artistic type that realizes and presents with its changes, increases, and decreases the basic core of existence in a given era. Today's literature, then, must be defined as something more than the merely chronologically contemporary; it is that literature which presents in a literary fashion today's awareness of an exemplarily alert man, his intellectual experiences and his drives, the good and bad tendencies of the age, its specific problems.[7]

Theology, too, encounters the historical "today." Both literature and theology share equally the world of today. They want to understand it, to explain it. They must prove themselves in their encounter with it. It is given to them. The "world of today" is farther ahead of theology than it is of literature. Theology is a "theology of today" only to the extent that its methods and themes are relevant to the "world of today." Its partner is not merely the God who revealed himself in a historical past, but also, just as certainly, the recipient of this revelation, mankind in its "today." Only recently has theology begun to respond to this imperative in a way recognizable to the man on the street. There is no need here to enter into a discussion of the linguistic and conceptual history of theology. It is sufficient to recall that theology has been given, since the Middle Ages, the comprehensive meaning of a science of faith and a corresponding responsibility toward the totality of revelation and the faith and understanding that are ordered to it. It is the task of theology not only to establish the objective content of faith by a study of its sources, that is, of revelation, and to show it in its historical continuity, development, interpretation, and presence, but also to disclose its existential and existentialist significance for man and for man's understanding of the world and of himself. For theology is not knowledge unconnected with time, it is not a mere systematization outside historical reality.

The today of theology can be determined from several standpoints. One might, for instance, say what has just been said of literature: theology is a theology of today insofar as it takes the world of today seriously, understands it, takes its point of view, and does so in such a way that the world can draw from the contact with reality and the interpretation of life provided by theology firm and believable conclusions about the reality of the salvation that became incarnate in Christ and is now operative in the world. Then it would be possible to describe "theology today" more on its own terms, i.e., according to its present directions and tendencies, its hermeneutic and exegetical efforts, its modern ecclesiology, its eschatological reflections, its incorporation of evolutionary findings into theological thought, the new accentuation of the personal instead of the former objective and factual thinking in regard to the theology of the sacraments, the intensive new understanding of history and of the world, the increasingly serious attitude toward the Christian in the world and the individual conscience, the awareness of the existential and existentialist condition of man, a new concept of the word, an altogether new dynamic.

It is a theology that no longer claims an *a priori* knowledge of everything, no longer argues dispassionately from a position of idealistic certainty, has abandoned static definitions, admits to a certain poverty of contact, and seeks a new dialogue with the world; a theology that is not in every respect a closed system, erects no barriers to the advent of new forms of knowledge, and does not try to conceal or reveal the world by a theologically relevant *Summa*. "Theology," as Pope John XXIII once said, "is not an archaeological museum." It admits, for instance, that the classical doctrine of transubstantiation as based on Aristotelian principles is not the only plausible reason for the possibility of the Eucharist. It admits that the traditional notions of substance, nature, or natural law, as founded by the scholastics, are subject to criticism. Theology has once more become a science of inquiry. It has burst out of its syllabus-ghetto and no longer regards natural science, the transformation of society, and technology per se as its principal opponents. Its manner of thinking is no longer static and material. Properly speaking, we have once more a realistic theology, a flexible theology, not predominantly representational or narrowly oriented toward the past but open to what lies ahead.

Finally, it would be possible to determine the nature of "theology today" from the point of view of the official church (a determination not possible in the case of literature) and to say: "Theology today" is that theology for which the Second Vatican Council prepared the way and by which it comes into contact with the world. To this extent, theology today has a visible historical caesura of a kind not found in other disciplines and forms of world understanding. To quote once more from *The Pastoral Constitution on the Church in the Modern World*: ". . . recent studies and findings of science, history, and philosophy raise new questions which influence life and demand new theological investigations. . . . In pastoral care, appropriate use must be made not only of theological principles, but also of the findings of the secular sciences, especially of psychology and sociology. Thus the faithful can be brought to live the faith in a more thorough and mature way. . . . May the faithful, therefore, live in very close union with the men of their time. Let them strive to understand perfectly their way of thinking and feeling, as expressed in their

culture. . . . Theological inquiry should seek a profound understanding of revealed truth without neglecting close contact with
its own times." [8] A theology that achieves this attitude and openness to the world can be called a "theology of today." Just as
the term literature is not limited to the affairs of the author, but
refers to the whole realm of literature, so too, and to an even
greater extent, the term "theology" is not limited to the labors and
scholarliness of its professors, but to a whole ecclesiastical realm,
in which the child who is making his first Communion, the pastor
in the village church, and the scientist who is also a Christian each
shares in his own way.

On the History of Theology and Literature

"Once, in antiquity and in the Middle Ages, the world was
whole; despite outer conflicts, there was still a world unity." So
Heine wrote, not without melancholy, in the *Reisebilder* [Travel
Pictures] of 1829. What he said was basically a repetition of the
opinion of his former academic teacher, August Wilhelm Schlegel. He also affirmed in his own way the medieval unity of faith,
doctrine, and literature so beloved of the romanticists. "Although
the epic poetry of the Middle Ages was divided into a religious
and a profane poetry," he wrote in *The Romantic School* in 1832,
"nonetheless both branches were, in their essence, completely
Christian . . . the whole life of the times with all its Christian
philosophy and aspirations was reflected in the profane poetry." [9]
This view of the Middle Ages has become a commonplace in
cultural history since the Romantic Period and still has wide acceptance. The unity between literature and theological thought in
that far-off time seems self-evident to those of us who learned
in school Walther von der Vogelweide's famous poem: "Ich saz
ûf eime steine" [I sat on a stone], that great synthesis of "êre"
=*honestum;* that is, social life), "varnde guot" (=*utile;* that is,
worldly possessions), and "gotes hulde, der zweier übergulde"
(=*summum bonum;* that is, theological grace, supernatural salvation, which surpasses the other two). We have forgotten Walther's
predicament as he juxtaposed the three "goods" ("deheinen rât
kond ich gegeben") [I could find no counsel], and we have re-

membered only his idealistic striving toward wholeness. There is, of course, in the Middle Ages the dream of Parzival, the explicit striving for "God's favor and that of the world." Hartmann von Aue seeks this, too, in his epics; and we cannot overlook the fairy tale quality and the dreamlike idealism—the modern expression would be utopianism—of this world that is sought and established in harmony. But the experience of "zwîvel" [doubt], the dichotomy, the indecision, the lack of certainty, which both Hartmann von Aue and Wolfram von Eschenbach portrayed and of which Walther von der Vogelweide was aware, seem more basic and realistic to us. In *Tristan und Isolde*, it is not the idyllic reconciliation of a Parzival to which Gottfried von Strassburg has given form but the tragic breakaway from the world of society and from the grace of God.

The thesis, usually only implicitly present and accepted without proof, that there existed a beautiful unity between literature and theology in the Middle Ages, can be viewed from another angle. Jean de Meun, who revised and continued the *Roman de la Rose* in the second half of the thirteenth century, tried to raise the status of writers in the society of his time and to establish their position more firmly. What nobles are by birth, he said, poets are by spirit. Thus he defended the concept, which had been emanating from Paris since the twelfth century, that literature, wisdom, and scholarship are of equal importance. But precisely this equality was contested by Scholastic writers. The way to a disdain for poetry had been paved by Hugh of St. Victor. He distinguished two basic classes of literature: first, the philosophical textbooks; second, the *appendentia*, i.e., everything else. To the latter category belongs poetry (*huiusmodi sunt omnia poetarum carmina*). Its products consist of "rhetorical amplification, mannered obscurity, and random eclecticism." [10] The conclusion to be drawn is, of course, that poetry is not really necessary. One should read it only occasionally, and then for recreation. Thomas Aquinas, in the *Summa Theologica* (I, 1, 9), accords poetry the first place among the educational disciplines. His teacher, Albertus Magnus, had said: "the pursuit of poetry is the lowest of the philosophical pursuits" (*poeticus modus est infirmior inter modos philosophiae*). This attitude was generally accepted among the Scholastics, as

Ernst Robert Curtius has shown. Scholasticism "produced no poetics and no theory of art. . . . Scholasticism had come out of
twelfth-century dialectics. It maintains the latter's opposition to
the 'auctores,' rhetoric and poetry. . . . It eliminates the philosophical justification of poetry from Aristotelianism. Hence it necessarily arrives at the opposite pole from the poetics and poetry. . .
of a Dante." [11] In general, the problem of the poet's mode of existence was experienced also by the poets of the Middle Ages:
"How can the poet fit into society? What is his function in the
nation, the state, the school, the church? In the Middle Ages there
was yet no concept of an autonomous 'culture.' " [12] What theologian of that period, or in later centuries, could have shown the
poet his role, or the author the justification of his existence in a
world that was, and was expected to remain, the property of
theology? When one considers that Scholastic theology has, until
most recent times, stamped and controlled the whole spectrum of
Catholic theology, one will realize that the relationship between
"theology and literature today" is troubled by problems of long
standing.

One fact, at least, is indispensable for our understanding of the
medieval poet and his literature: he could not fail to be aware of
God, and he never lost his awareness of God's creative role. He
did not question the transcendent place of what, in modern terminology, might be called the "Archimedean point" (Kafka).

The gradual reorientation and transformation of Western consciousness that began in the fourteenth and fifteenth centuries, was
completed in the sixteenth and seventeenth, and finally encompassed all spheres of thought and penetrated all forms of life—
this process of emancipation and secularization—did not originate
with the literary authors. It was not literature that created, or
even introduced, the modern crisis of faith, though it did, indeed,
contribute its share to the formulation of this new consciousness
and hence indirectly to the crisis of faith. But, then as now, the
task of literature is merely to formulate what is more or less in
the air. It would be as unjust to blame literature per se for the
fact that some Humanists were in the vanguard of the intellectual
current as to blame it for the fact that some angry young men at
the end of the nineteenth century ended their works with pseudo-

classical clichés. It was to be expected that the writings of both groups would irritate those who would not, in any event, have wanted to think or to learn for themselves.

We are accustomed to think as uninhibitedly about the Baroque Era as about the Middle Ages. Its religious achievements in art and literature, especially its intensive efforts to reconcile God and world, faith and consciousness, are to some extent known. But in that age, in which the bourgeois life of the city was beginning to create a new ethical way of life, the unity of the religious conception of world and life was irrevocably lost, though it may have persisted in the consciousness of some few. The real forced its way into the forefront; sinful man, who, theologically speaking, had never become totally Christian, discovered the world anew and realized his own potentialities in action. "The beginning of this important process," wrote the literary critic Paul Hankamer (died 1945), "is to be sought in the seventeenth century wherever secular reality was no longer regarded, as it had been during the Reformation, as a prerogative of the middle-class, but as an entity with sovereign rights, which could establish its jurisdiction over the moral struggles of man. However, there is no question here of a new heathen or atheistic philosophy of life for the masses alone, but only of an actual, though still implicit, lack of a religious motivation for the kind of moral activity that the middle-class citizen was beginning to consider his own and to justify within his own sphere of activity. The middle-class citizen is (still) devout; but practical life and religion are two almost mutually exclusive spheres. . . . The emancipation of secular literature from Opitz to Hofmannswaldau was made possible only by an attitude toward life which had already begun to separate the two spheres, even if still unconsciously, and which no longer had recourse to a religiously determined totality of existence." [13]

There exist, in Christian circles, singularly undifferentiated and untried judgments about whole eras. Thus the basic content of Baroque literature is thought to be unequivocally Christian. But, to mention only one example, were "*fortuna*" and "*vanitas*," the two main figures in the literature of the Thirty Years War, specifically Christian? Did they express the essential message of the Gospel? Can they be understood by norms derived from the

Gospel? Are there, in point of fact, many concepts that, in confrontation with a world visited by pestilence, division, plunder, and war, can make the Gospel message visible in a literary form? A reference to contemporary dramas about martyrs is not quite to the point. For the martyr, despite the witness that he bears in time of conflict, can offer no answer to this world that is crying out for a solution and answer to its questions. He knows "only" the validity of his faith, the course of transcendence. But this leaves the man whose conflict is totally of this world alone in his perplexity.

There is no need to prove that the so-called Enlightenment furthered the process of the separation of reason and faith, secularism and Gospel, or that Herder, Goethe, and Schiller were sons of the Enlightenment. For more than two generations, Christian teachers, reviewers, and readers have, with an unreflecting assurance that is almost totally incomprehensible to us today, regarded this enlightened classicism as *the* literary, *the* exemplary, *the* valid. Whence does a Christian critic, theologian, or reader derive the right to label Goethe and Schiller as exemplary and to protest, in the name of Christianity, against Kafka, Brecht, and Frisch? Is it the fault of the younger writers that they are, by now, the great-grandsons of the Enlightenment? that they are somewhat further removed from the Gospel of the Middle Ages? that they have fallen somewhat more deeply into the funnel of reason—which can only mean into the mills of perplexity? Enlightenment, however one may define it, is even today a process of becoming aware and of extending the range of one's awareness, and it still entails the discovery of freedom. Romanticism, which at first sought to extend the range of awareness even to the universal, soon degenerated into an attempt to link, isolate, mingle, and combine the parts, and so moved backwards into history. It shattered the beautiful classical view of the world as a harmonious whole. Any theologian or literary critic who hopes to distinguish between secular forms that were historically necessary at the beginning of the nineteenth and even into the twentieth century and forms that were non-Christian, half-Christian, and anti-Christian will have to formulate his question with extreme care. The answer will almost never be a simple one; often it will be ambiguous. Ambivalence, not the clear-cut distinction between good and evil, but their interpenetration and fragmentation, is the keynote.

In the history of ideas, almost all modern and contemporary literature stems from the Enlightenment. Only the individual phases and the tendencies within the phases are different. Today, it is not belief that is enlightened, but doubt. If we can judge by what we read, the vehicle of an almost universal optimism about the best of all possible worlds, or one capable of becoming the best, has fallen into the opposite rut of an almost universal conviction that this is the worst and most hopeless of worlds. Instead of the former exaltation, a worldwide depression governs today's literature. It is possible to distinguish three currents of thought that are fundamentally those of the Enlightenment: a Humanistic, a Marxist, and a Christian. The Humanistic Enlightenment extends from the Liberal Party to the Humanistic Union. The Marxist one has an Eastern dictatorial and a Western idealistic form. Tendencies in the Christian Enlightenment extend, always in a different manner, from dialectical theology and the theology of demythologizing to the advanced position of Vatican Council II. The Humanistic and Marxist Enlightenments have brought more breadth to their understanding of literature than can be predicated of the Christian Enlightenment. A large part of Group 47 belongs to the Humanistic Enlightenment. The Marxist Enlightenment flourishes across the Elbe and across the Rhine. It would be necessary to search for a Christian Enlightenment in our region. It is, of necessity, the most difficult. It is common to all forms of literary Enlightenment that they are antiutopian and nonconformist.

Besides the literary currents mentioned above, there also exists today a kind of literary vagrancy that is nothing but protest: forms of social estrangement that place no heavy burdens upon themselves. Dada and many of the Surrealists were moving in that direction, as are the beatniks and their German cousins, the "Ultimisten." [14] But protest is not of necessity unjustified and negative. Some writers whom we must take seriously are of the opinion that "people who are too fastidious (and among them we ourselves) need a little shock, a little Ionesco, or some beatnik yowling if we are not to lose our appetites completely." [15] But all protest must prove itself in forms that are human. The particular character of art as play, the mark of its freedom and its higher spirit, expresses itself now almost entirely in the satire or parody, which sounds a bitter, angry, or strenuously intellectual note. Satire and parody are forms of protest. Upon close observation, all contemporary literary currents reveal themselves as combinations of Enlightenment and protest. There can be no immediate objection to that, for Christian protest is also possible.

Contradictions and Misunderstandings of Literature and Theology

The demands of literature have increased in the twentieth century in direct proportion to the growth of Enlightenment and protest. Goethe's admission in the thirteenth book of *Dichtung und Wahrheit* [Poetry and Truth] is to be regarded rather as the humility and detachment of a wise man than as pretentiousness: "True poetry can be recognized by the fact that, like a secular Gospel, it can free us, by internal cheerfulness and external comfort, from the burdens that press upon us." [16] In the year 1813, when he wrote these lines, Goethe did not think of art and literature as Promethean weapons for changing the world, but as a means of making visible the order on which the world is founded, a basically natural and accessible order dating from the decades of the French Revolution. And therein lies, however much we may agree with it, the problematical character of his statement. Present-day writers, more often than not, come forward with a vehement demand for the true and the political, with a moral demand to be seen and heard, not with the modest offer of a "secular Gospel," as Goethe understood it, but with the anger of a prophet and the Cassius Clay attitude of a boxer.

Since modern life is so cramped, no one will demand of the modern author the detachment that Goethe had achieved in his later years, or the playfulness of the Rococo. The answers to the questions of life either directly or indirectly given by the institutions and public media of communication in our society compel

the writer of today to strenuous intellectual deliberation. Where
literature—it is immaterial whether in its own name or in the name
of science or in an impure admixture of both—rejects the message
of revelation, it must of necessity come into conflict with theology.
One of the most recent formulations of a literary attitude in the
spirit of the Enlightenment reads as follows: "Literature and science are comparable in two of their fundamental attitudes: (1)
they no longer admit that proof or reason can exist in revelation,
myth, empathy, higher insight, and so on, but only in experience,
on the principle that experience is accessible to everyone; (2) they
attempt to shed light without prejudice, insofar as that is possible,
on the living space and living conditions of man as well as on the
laws of nature and of the world in which man lives; that is, within
the intellectual function that is common to both of them, they
establish goals for themselves that, when they have been attained,
are always recognized as being temporary. . . . Progress on a scale
that is deliberately infinite makes literature and science the two
parallel activities of the human enlightenment, and does so on the
basis of their emergence from the closed framework of the theological interpretation of the world in which they had their origin.
All earlier literature and sciences (ancient, Far Eastern, etc.) still
rest upon a final mythical or theological foundation and are, therefore, comparable only in respect to this foundation, and not in
respect to their autonomy." [17] That is the Humanistic Enlightenment: a tremendous literary ambition, which would no longer
occur to most of the natural sciences (because they are account-
able only to themselves for their premises). It accepts only personal experience as valid, and is incapable of distinguishing a
theological form expressed in mystical images from the closed
theological domain of a particular period or from the revelation
that has been definitely imparted to mankind. The impossibility
of uniting a literary demand so formulated and so understood with
the demands of theology is obvious. It is the antinomy of this
stupendous demand of literature.

" 'The people need poetry as much as bread'—Simone Weil once
wrote this touching sentence—a wish, really," Ingeborg Bachmann comments, and continues: "Poetry as much as bread? This
bread would have to be crunched between the teeth and reawaken

hunger before it stilled it. And this poetry will have to be sharp with understanding and bitter with longing if it is to penetrate man's sleep." [18]

The word bread reminds us of Jesus, the man of Nazareth. One day, after some not very successful attempts to make Himself known and to win men to Himself, He communicated to His startled countrymen the tremendous news: "I am the Bread of Life. . . . I am the Living Bread, which has come down from heaven. If anyone eat of this bread he shall live forever" (John 6:48, 51). His hearers were shocked. The world exploded in their brains. The provocation was complete. On another occasion, in contradistinction to the Jewish form of humanity, the Torah, with its circumscription of Yahweh by the word and letter of the law, He pointed to His own person and teaching: "I am the way, and the truth, and the life" (John 14:6). There is, then, no monopoly. One may find bread in the Gospel and bread in literature; provocation in the Gospel and provocation in literature; truth in the Gospel and truth in literature. If one recalls that other word about the truth which makes you free (John 8:32), then there is a call to freedom in the Gospel and a call to freedom in literature. And if one recalls Saint Paul's warning against sleep (Romans 13:11; Eph. 5:14), and Ingeborg Bachmann's message and Günther Eich's poem: "Wake up, for your dreams are bad," then one can say that there is also a warning against sleep in the Gospel and a warning against sleep in literature. But we must ask ourselves first if we can, without more ado, equate our own position with that of the Gospel and designate the position of others as "literature," that is, as being without or against the Gospel. Then we must ask ourselves if "bread," "truth," "life," "freedom," and other basic words do not sometimes refer to the same concept and occupy the same existentialist plane. Thirdly, we must ask ourselves if theology and literature, when they use the same word to designate what is different in content and form, can talk to each other at all, if misunderstanding—and misunderstanding of each other—will not of necessity creep in. As long as each side brings only the one-sided certainty of its own position, but no readiness or ability to understand the word of the other with any degree of formal rightness, then there is no possibility of dialogue. This kind of antithesis can be called an antithesis of speech and understanding. It is of a complex nature, for a formal misunderstanding is added to the misunderstanding of content and intention, and conditions them to a large extent. As Goethe has already pointed out in his maxims and reflections: "Everyone sees the material before him; only he finds the content who has something to add to it, and the form is a mystery to most."

A fairly exact understanding of form has always been difficult to achieve. Today's literary forms are, in many respects, different from those of yesterday. For the most part, they are more difficult. Much of the misunderstanding or lack of understanding for present-day literature arises from the inappropriate expectations of the reader. Theologians are readers too. And Christians in the theological domain are readers. Theological institutions of learning have not as yet introduced lectures and seminars for the discussion of form. Only in very recent years, and then only through the works of liberal critics from outside, have theologians become aware of the linguistic forms of the Bible.

Christians and theologians judge literature in their own way. Prepossessions based exclusively on notions about past literary epochs or derived uncritically from personal taste cause repeated disappointments about the literature of today. A good proportion of the norms they use and of their half-conscious basic attitudes spring not so much from the Gospel as from their preconceived expectations. Some of their expectations and disappointments might be mentioned. They expect harmlessness, for example, and find harmfulness. They look forward to a nice straightforward story and find a complicated and fragmented field of consciousness. They want entertainment and meet provocation. They are looking for a kind of self-affirmation and are pitilessly queried. They expect the portrayal of the world with which they are familiar, and they find strangeness. They desire what is clear and open and they stumble across mystery and alienation. They expect human feeling and they find a positively mathematical intellectualism. "Human feeling?" asked Gottfried Benn provocatively, "Personally, I don't have any." [19] They search for the positive, the sublime, or at least for something that will help them to live, and they find the negative, the banal, the depressing, the apparently destructive. They look for the advent of harmony, of the beautiful, and of the beautiful whole. And they find the dissonant, the ugly, the fragmentary, the disillusionment of the real. Perhaps they prefer the tragic view of life, but they meet the grotesque at every turn. They want to be soothed and they are frightened; they want to enjoy and they are challenged. Theological writers, when they discuss a work of art, are still inclined to speak idealistically about "beauty," "harmonious splendor," transcendence, the reflection of the eternal.[20] They seem not to have grasped the fact that beauty and harmony, as they understand them, are not, and cannot be, of primary importance. Of primary importance are the demands of reality and formal structure and the forms by which the truth that has been recognized can be incorporated into literature.

Evidence of the preconceived expectations of readers can be found in the issues of Catholic periodicals for about the past two generations. In 1920, Friedrich Muckermann, for instance, one of the most intelligent and theologically trained of the Catholic literary critics of the twenties, wrote as follows in the periodical *Der Gral* [The Grail] about an anthology of Expressionist lyrics, *Menschheitsdämmerung* [The Twilight of Humanity]: "A glance at the mystique of Expressionism, as it is revealed in the tendencies of *Menschheitsdämmerung*, may make clear how poison ventures to invade the holiness of our souls even in the forms of pious hymns and mystic dreams, what an abyss of mire, foulness, and godlessness often shows itself beneath the most harmless and shining blanket of flowers." "After the rejection of the supernatural and purely spiritual beauty that is so beautifully reflected in our image of the world and that somehow spiritualizes all beauty, it is quite natural that the sensuous elements in the objects of beauty should gain a strong ascendancy, that the new God, the reproductive urge, should become the soul of the new beauty and should draw luminous art completely into its dark spheres." [21] So general and idealistic a judgment astonishes us today. As foil to the "mire, foulness, and godlessness," the same issue offers a "monkish" poem by Richard von Schaukal, in which Christian sentiments are "blissfully fluted." At best, that is new romanticism, well-intentioned but weak and unreal. The objective lack of truth in the style of many of the verses that *Der Gral* published as morally and exemplarily Christian is, we think today, in grotesque contrast to their pretensions. Is there not in a poem so scandalous for pious ears as Gottfried Benn's "Kleine Aster" [Little Aster], the frigid tale of the autopsy of a "drowned truck-driver," more thought, more reality, and more truth than in innumerable sentimentally written and piously printed Christian verses? The anthology *Menschheitsdämmerung* is not nearly so annoying to us of a later generation as are the pretensions and sentimental clichés of many of the poems in *Der Gral*.[22]

Today we are farther removed than ever from a harmonious classicism or a simple Christianity in literature. Walter Höllerer remarked correctly in "Nach der Menschheitsdämmerung" [After the Twilight of Humanity] that present-day poetry "achieves artistic expression [only when] the awareness that suffering defines the boundaries of this art has penetrated into the very form of the poem." [23]

A too-ready moral intervention and the demands that moral theology makes upon literary works have also had their share in arousing tension between author and theologian. Once, authors were afraid of the theological censor. Now they are more likely to find him comic, sometimes annoying, especially when they have the not-unfounded impression that the censor has not understood their message because he has had no access to their form. Besides lack of understanding for the form, this moral intervention also conceals a new lack of understanding for the theory. Most theologians are too little aware that they are arguing from the level of abstraction and from the horizon of the ideal, whereas, in the events narrated, the authors find themselves in the situation of the existentialist, that is, of the non-idealistic, of the threateningly concrete and the individually real. For the most part, they lay no claim, in their productions, to the morally normative or to the exemplary.

Necessity and Possibility of an Encounter

No one will deny that theology and literature should come nearer to one another. It is not simply that writers need theologians.

Theologians also need writers—and not merely on the external grounds that the recipient of theology, the Christian in the world, reads the writers of today. Theologians, as interpreters, guardians, and announcers of the historically imparted word of God, need contact with the living language and with creative linguistic forms. They need, too, to see reflected in literature the way in which the world of today is being understood, queried, revealed, and criticized. It would probably be possible to demonstrate in every period of the modern era that writers have shown a more luminous and alert sense of the world's understanding of itself than have the theologians.

Most of the leading authors of today are outside the theological sphere. Thus they will not come to the theologians. The theologians and theologically trained literary critics will first have to prove to the writers that they are capable of literary dialogue. And there are other prerequisites. The theologians will have to take seriously literature's claim that it understands the world. They will have to realize that writers possess an often astonishing sensitivity for the perception of reality. They will have to understand, too, that their Scholastic and metaphysical concept of beauty is of little value for an understanding of the phenomenon of today's literature (or yesterday's). "It is to the credit of modern artists that they have the courage of unreserved dedication to reality as it is at any given moment. The subjective truthfulness involved in acceding to that which is, has become the distinguishing principle of modern artistic style. The virtuosity of the late bourgeois era has had to give way to an ethos of intellectual hardness and honesty." This observation was formulated by a Protestant theologian.[24] Readers and critics from the sphere of theology will have to be more on their guard than they were formerly against inappropriate expectations from literature and will have to reconstruct their judgments accordingly. They will learn to understand the literary language of forms as well as changes in stylistic tone and literary genres. *The Tin Drum* by Günter Grass, for example, is not the same as a psychological novel by Goethe, or a society novel by Fontane, or a *Simplicissimus* novel by Grimmelshausen. It is a nonconformist parody of a psychological novel and a Gargantuan rogue novel with all the symbols reversed.

Theologians will have to learn about morality of form as well as morality of content. A properly formed sentence, a well-made poem, a well-constructed novel or play (even though not in the classical sense) are, above all, human achievements. They are more likely to contain an effective morality than are the badly constructed works fitted out with Christian phrases to make them inoffensive to theological ears. "The tension in which Christian existence finds itself is determined by quite different poles than in the case of aestheticism. . . . Courage before the unknown, manly uprightness, and sympathy—thus can we describe the artist's new concept. He wants to speak the truth, which he understands chiefly as exactness—and that is largely a question of style." [25] Writers experience a moral obligation not only to form but also to the reality that they are to observe. Ingeborg Bachmann has said: "It is possible to speak of a compulsive drive, which at the moment I am not able to identify except as a moral drive that is above all morality, an impulse to thought that is not primarily concerned with direction, a thought that seeks to understand and hopes to reach something with and through speech. Let us call it reality." [26]

It would seem that theologians possess today more of the prerequisites that will make possible an encounter with secular literature. They no longer write theological *summae* because they know that it is impossible today to arrange the world under neat subheadings. They recognize the claims of inquiry, of the historical and interpretational detail, of methodical awareness, of open probabilities. The idea of a great and harmonious whole and of perfect uniformity, in which God and the world would have their places for centuries to come, no longer occurs to them. Hence it will not be difficult for them to concede that writers, too, have problems of observation, of view, of detail, of fragmentation, as well as the awareness of the relativity of their own standards of observation, interpretation, and presentation. What is today known as the *nouveau roman* reflects, among other things, a turning toward the objective, toward exact description that must render a strict account of itself, not the subjective outline of a beautiful story issuing from the Olympian predetermination of an author who is at once seer and owner of all he surveys.

Theologians are in a better position today than in former times to allow profane literature the necessary amount of freedom, for they have a better understanding of human freedom itself. Vatican Council II begins its declaration of human freedom with the words: "A sense of the dignity of the human person has been impressing itself more and more deeply upon the consciousness of contemporary man. And the demand is increasingly made that men should act on their own judgment, enjoying and making use of a responsible freedom, not driven by coercion but motivated by a sense of duty. . . . This demand for freedom in human society chiefly regards the quest for the values proper to the human spirit." [27] No one will doubt that literature is concerned with the spiritual, and specifically with the human, values of man. Whoever grants man the right to a responsible discernment in matters of conscience in the religious sphere can and must grant men of letters the right to follow their consciences in recognizing what can be experienced and portraying what is real.

Even their own new understanding of the world should help theologians to allow writers the freedom of the world as the locale of their experiences and presentations. They recognize and admit: "The world of today has become worldly, and unless everything is deceiving us, the end of the process is not yet in sight." "All the anxious efforts [of Christians] to protect themselves against the world presuppose, more or less as a matter of course, that the worldliness of the world as such is something basically contrary to the Christian understanding of the world and must therefore be totally overcome by the Christian." We no longer live in the numinous world of the Greeks, or in the alien framework of the world that the Renaissance had from antiquity, or in the natural world as earlier centuries understood the term, but in a world that is eminently and historically man-made, a "humanized" [humanisiert] world. And it is the problems of precisely this world of and for man that are presented in literature. The theologians claim, in fact, that "the worldliness of the world, as it originated in the modern process of secularization and as it confronts us today in a universally heightened form, has its origins basically (though not, it is true, in its individual historical appearances) in Christianity. It was originally a Christian phenomenon; hence it produced, in our world situation, the intrinsically historical sovereignty of

the 'hour of Christ.' " [28] Even the acknowledgment by theologians
of the existence of a pluralistic world and the provisionally formulated theory of the "anonymous Christian" [29] in this world could
contribute to a spirit of openness toward the literature of today
and to the lessening of the antithesis between sacral Christianity
and profane literature.[30] It is a world of today that is common to
both theology and literature, a world that can show itself to both
and that they can interpret from different viewpoints and under
different aspects. Literature and theology are concentrating with
an unprecedented intensity upon this world of man. That is their
chance. It shows their vitality. It should make dialogue possible.

5

Hermann Broch's Trilogy
Die Schlafwandler:
Contemporary Criticism
and Novel of Redemption

When Hermann Broch died in New Haven in 1951, his novels, especially *Der Tod des Vergil* [The Death of Vergil], were just beginning to become known to a larger public. Like Musil and Kafka, like Joyce and Gide, Broch realized the significance of the present-day novel. He was himself a phenotype of his age. With brilliant awareness, he probed its characteristic features. He diagnosed it and gave it expression. He demanded that authors of rank make "the totality of their presentation of the world an instrument for the philosophical probing of existence." He made the "will to cognition" a condition of literature and imposed upon it as a duty the will "to absolute cognition." In the essay, "James Joyce and the Present" (1932–1936), he wrote: "It belongs, no doubt, to the essence of the bourgeois world view, or, more correctly, to the philistine, which is older than the bourgeois and likely to survive it, to regard the work of art as a means of enjoyment, as a purely aesthetic creation whose ultimate ideal is derived from the inartistic. Perhaps such a depravation of the artistic is at the same time a symptom of the deterioration of a given culture, the return of ethical strictness the sign of a new form of culture. It is a turning aside from the pathos of the tragic to the painfully comic situation of the creature and to the discernment of its existence, from a theatrical setting to that higher reality which is rooted in the inner being of man. . . . It is almost as if art had first to proceed through all the infernal regions of *l'art pour l'art* before it could bring itself to the extraordinary task of subduing everything aesthetic to the power of the ethical." [1] Broch demanded not only the "epistemological novel instead of the (merely) psychological" [2] but also the ethical work of art.

Hermann Broch, critic, moral philosopher, thinker, and writer, was born in 1886 as the son of a Jewish textile worker in Vienna. Thomas Mann was then eleven, Robert Musil six, James Joyce and Virginia Woolf were four; Franz Kafka was three years older than Broch, and Gottfried Benn of the same age. After finishing secondary school, Broch attended the School of Technology in Vienna and the School of Textiles in Mühlhausen in Alsace. At the age of twenty, he made an educational trip to America. When he was twenty-two, he entered the family business, which he conducted until he renounced the world of industry in 1927 to resume the study of philosophy and mathematics, which had interested him in his youth, and to devote himself to literature. He worked on his first novel *Die Schlafwandler* [The Sleepwalkers] from 1928 until the beginning of 1932. After long revision, especially of part 3, it was published in 1931–1932 by the Rheinverlag [Rhine Publishing Company] of Zürich, which, in 1930, had also published the German translation of Joyce's *Ulysses* (first English edition: Paris, 1922). Thomas Mann's *Der Zauberberg* [The Magic Mountain] had appeared in 1924, the year in which Kafka died. The last part of Marcel Proust's *À la Recherche du Temps perdu* was printed posthumously in 1927. Two years later Alfred Döblin's *Berlin-Alexanderplatz* was published. In 1930–1932, at the same time as *Die Schlafwandler*, parts 1 and 2 of Robert Musil's *Der Mann ohne Eigenschaften* [The Man without Qualities] were being edited.

Summary of Contents

Die Schlafwandler presents criticism of the contemporary scene in the form of a trilogy.[3] The three parts are entitled: *1888: Pase-*

now, or Romanticism; 1903: Esch, or Anarchy; 1918: Huguenau, or Objectivity. Together, they present a chronicle of the Wilhelmine era, not a tableau of Wilhelmine society. They present neither consecutive calendar years nor a comprehensive picture of society. The calendar years in the titles of the three parts of the trilogy designate the beginning, middle, and end of the reign of William II. Three typically inadequate forms of existence and three attitudes toward life are exemplified in the Prussian officer Pasenow, the industrial Philistine Esch, and the enterprising deserter Huguenau.

The scene of the first part of the trilogy is the country estate of the aristocratic Prussian landowner von Pasenow and the Berlin of his younger son, First Lieutenant Joachim von Pasenow. The Pasenows live in a world of fixed conventions and fashionable superficiality. Both father and son are completely uninterested in politics. Their intellectual horizon is limited to the management of the family property and the preservation of the "honor" due their social status. "Order" stands at the peak of their ethical materialism; "honor" has become the *summum bonum* of their empty and formalistic ethic. The "uniform" is the symbol and guarantee of this "order"; the duel is the ritual observance of this "honor," and to it Pasenow's eldest son is sacrificed. In order to replace him as heir to the ancestral estate and to enter into a socially acceptable marriage with Elisabeth, daughter of a neighboring family, Joachim von Pasenow doffs his uniform and repudiates Ruzena, the girl from the Casino. Joachim's more perceptive friend and ironic adviser is Eduard von Bertrand, who is a successful salesman, a convinced and disillusioning nonromantic, an aesthete with a taste for the absolute. Caught in inaccessible loneliness, Bertrand had quickly understood the emptiness of this world of uniforms and had removed his own. In the minds of the Pasenows, a "civilian" belongs to a lower level of humanity.

Whatever in the novel might thus far appear as "a Fontane-atmosphere" or as "naturalistic romanticism," [4] is shattered in two noteworthy conversations between Bertrand and Elisabeth. Bertrand can, it is true, warn Elisabeth of the emptiness of a marriage for convention. But his icily Mephistophelean world of thought cannot help her. The fourth and last chapter in the first part of the novel contains only four and a half printed lines. Joachim and Elisabeth have married. But they do not love each other. "Nevertheless, after about eighteen months of marriage, they had their first child. It really happened. How it came about need not be told. From the materials provided here for the building of character, the reader can work it out for himself" (p. 170). The time for the comfortable "telling of little stories" is past. The story has reached its conclusion when the historically pertinent elements of time have been indicated, not when the fates of the characters have been fulfilled in all their private fortuitousness.[5]

The second part of the novel presents characters from the amorphous world of the lower levels of society in the industrial cities of the Rhineland. The bookkeeper Esch, falsely accused of a bookkeeping mistake, is dismissed from a firm in Cologne. Bookkeeping mistakes and unjust dismissals develop in Esch's mind into symbols for the anarchical state of the world. He finds employment in the warehouses of the Middle Rhine Joint-Stock Company, whose president—it is now the year 1903—is Eduard von Bertrand. Esch never gets a glimpse of the president. From fragmentary pieces drawn, sometimes irrationally, from his own consciousness, he constructs an exaggerated image that gradually transforms Bertrand into a fixed caricature of the corrupt and inaccessible executive. Esch makes him responsible for the disorder that he himself has experienced in the world. Under circumstances that resemble those of a sleepwalker in a dream, the lowly Esch becomes aware of the monstrous anarchy in the world of big business and the pursuit of pleasure. He rejects this world. Totally lacking in experience, he lets himself be persuaded into financing wrestling matches for women. Through his attraction for Mother Hentjen, the order-loving, inflexibly domineering widow and owner of a tavern in Cologne, Esch is able to give up his anarchical sexual relationships. His lonely thoughts and dreams begin to center compulsively around "order," around a "new life" and "redemption." The narrator reports a sleepwalking visit of Esch's to the guilt-laden Bertrand of his imagination. The dream conversation in the latter's dream castle reflects Esch's inner awareness of guilt and loneliness, his longing for expiation, order, and redemption. Esch accuses Bertrand of homosexuality. Bertrand eludes

the accusation by suicide. After the impetuous Esch has conclud-
ed a legal marriage with Mother Hentjen, he is compelled to admit
with disappointment "that there can never be fulfillment in real
life" (p. 363). At the end of this part, too, the narrator abandons
the narrative thread to the reader. "Esch now found a position as
chief bookkeeper in a large industrial concern in his native Luxem-
bourg, and for this his wife admired him more than ever. They
went hand in hand and loved one another. Sometimes he still beat
her, but he did it less and less frequently and, finally, not at all"
(p. 366).

The principal characters of the first part of the novel were presented in moderately distinct silhouette and clarity. In the second
part, the characters are "sometimes too sharply defined" (Esch
himself); "sometimes reduced to indistinction" (e.g., Martin Geyring, secretary of the trade union, Ilona from the variety show, and
Mother Hentjen toward the end of this part of the novel); "sometimes disintegrate into a completely dreamlike state, as do the two
Bertrands, and stand on the very edge of reality." [6]

The third part of the novel begins with the desertion of the
Alsatian, Huguenau, from the German Army early in the year
1918. Huguenau, in civil life a textile salesman, leaves the Belgian
front and settles in a small town in the Moselle district. There he
meets the titular heroes of the first two parts of the novel. Esch
has established himself as owner and editor of the local newspaper,
the *Kur-Trier Messenger*. Major von Pasenow, the Joachim of
Part I, is town commandant of the same small town. Pasenow, still
with his old penchant for the military, the patriotic, and the romantic; Esch, risen in social status and now a respectably ordinary
citizen; Huguenau, with his single-minded concern for his own
advantage—all three appear on the same stage. Huguenau forms a
partnership with Esch. His brisk activity outwits both Esch and
Pasenow, who seek their salvation in a common Bible hour. In the
confusion at the end of the war, Huguenau, now successful, runs
his bayonet into Esch's back. The deserter and murderer procures
an authorized military permit and returns to his native Alsace. His
rise to municipal office is indicated in the "Epilogue."

The inner axis of the whole novel is the "disintegration of former values," [7] which is demonstrated in all the characters. The com-

plicated structure of the third part of the novel is composed in levels that run parallel to the main action: the episode of the "military hospital," the study of Hanna Wendling, and the grotesquely real account of the shellshocked militiaman Gödicke. They all reflect the loss of a center of meaning and the abyss of loneliness. Contrapuntally to these stories of deterioration, a newly introduced narrator, "Bertrand Müller, Dr. phil.—" not to be identified with the Bertrand of the first part, though he is, perhaps, his ethically purified, intellectual brother—relates the "Story of the Salvation Army Girl in Berlin." The same narrator reflects upon the historical and philosophical background and makes essayistic comment on the "collapse of values" that is everywhere present in this era. How is "the era" portrayed?

Portrayal and Criticism of the Era

In the classical and romantic novel, time is simply there. It surrounds the hero as inevitably as does the air. It accompanies him like a cheerful brook, or carries him on the back of its mighty current. Time is primarily the time of nature, of sunrises and sunsets, of successive years of life, and of happy fulfillments that, in the end, ripen almost of their own accord. In the modern novel, the relationship of man to time has changed. It can no longer be taken for granted; it has become problematical. To a large extent, time, like space, has lost its secure character. Man is far more aware now of the fact that he is conditioned and imperiled by time. The process has been reversed, and it is now man who establishes time. Time is no longer understood, at least not primarily, as the time of nature, but as a dimension to be established, formed, molded, or lost by human discernment and freedom.

There is no attempt in *Die Schlafwandler*, as there is, for instance, in the works of Marcel Proust, to seek and regain time through the instrumentality of memory; nor is the novel primarily an attempt, as are those of James Joyce and Virginia Woolf, to portray the inner stream of consciousness. In *Der Zauberberg*, Thomas Mann diagnosed the loss of human awareness of time as a new sickness befalling all mankind. The characters in Broch's *Die Schlafwandler* have not lost their awareness of time. In various ways, they imagine themselves in sure possession of it, as does a sleepwalker; they move forward with time in a kind of obscure certainty; they neither criticize nor question it, although it is far from being something to be used unreflectively. The "sleepwalkers" fail to realize the significance of the present hour. If, like the smalltowner Esch, they feel themselves troubled, they can attribute their uneasiness only to their own forebodings; they have fallen prey to their own irrational powers. Once the public as a whole has lost its regard for norms and ordinances, the individual, too, will cease to respect them. The object of Broch's diagnosis is twofold: first, to show that the individual's lack of awareness of the time in which he lives, though apparently ordered, has in reality lost its relationship to being; second, to point out that man has ceased to believe in the present as a time with meaning and a promise of security. For a modern novel of any importance, such a theme is unusual and even, one might say, unique. Robert Musil limited himself in *Der Mann ohne Eigenschaften* to a satirical criticism of royal and imperial Austria as it actually existed. He allowed his hero Ulrich to seek "salvation" in a privately incestuous, erotically mythical escapade. There is no search in *Der Mann ohne Eigenschaften* for a historical and metaphysical meaning to life that would be binding on all. Even the moment of fulfillment, once it has been sought and found, proves to be insufficient. Toward the end of Broch's novel, on the other hand, hope appears as a principle capable of supporting and transforming the world. For Broch, the investigation of the phenomenon of time includes an investigation of the time of values and of salvation. In this sense, he is perceptibly "unmodern." What is particularly manifest in the individual characters of *The Sleepwalkers* is the outer and inner stringency of the age, for the novel reveals neither personal liberty nor ideal freedom, neither an extreme case nor a series of extreme cases, but only the very real subjection of average people to their age and its stipulations. For this reason, *The Sleepwalkers* may be regarded as a novel of contemporary criticism of its epoch. A French review of the novel in 1932 employed the subtitle "Apocalypse du Temps présent," a revelation of the present time.[8]

The novel of contemporary criticism had its inception in Germany with Immermann's *Die Epigonen* [The Epigones], which was published in 1836 and was little more than a helpless presentation of the "peculiar illness" of the contemporary age: "We are, to compress the whole misery into a single word, Epigones, and we bear the burden that clings to all inheritors and successors." [9] A romantic feudal attitude toward life still prevails in the novel, but its mood has obviously succumbed to the prevailing illness of the time. The forces that point to the future are either not recognized or are rejected with hostility. The writers of Young Germany [*Jungdeutschland*] were then pitting their "idea of the new age" against that of the old romantic feudal age. It was they who developed the novel of contemporary criticism, for example, Laube's novel *Das junge Europa* [Young Europe, 1833–1837] and, especially, Gutzkow's novel *Die Ritter vom Geist* [The Knights of the Spirit]. The spirit of the Young Germans, a combination of imaginative romanticism and revolutionary utopianism, prevented their making a quiet, objective diagnosis of their time, just as their lack of artistic sensibility prevented their finding its proper literary expression.

A novel of contemporary criticism must relate its own narrated and critically illumined time to real historical time. Novalis' *Heinrich von Ofterdingen* or Stifter's *Nachsommer* [Indian Summer] stand in a place that is almost timeless in its relation to historical time, whereas Eichendorff's *Ahnung und Gegenwart* [Presentiment and Present] indicates the historical relationship. The idealistic novel requires no historical chronology within the world that it presents. The realistic novel of later decades uses historical chronology, for the most part, as a fictive means of increasing the impression of reality and actuality. The novel of contemporary criticism requires historically recognizable and datable reality as the object of its criticism. However fictive his characters and events, the author of the novel of contemporary criticism must relate his criticism to some historically real time. In this sense, the dates given in Flaubert's *L'Education sentimentale*, in Thomas Mann's *Die Buddenbrooks*, or in Robert Musil's *Der Mann ohne Eigenschaften* are more than just instruments of fiction.

In the very titles of each part of *Die Schlafwandler*, a calendar year is indicated; the first part of the novel begins with the words, "In the year 1888 . . ."; the second part begins with the date,

"March 2, 1903 . . ."; the third begins, after a brief introduction, with the spring of 1918. The first two calendar years could have been moved a few years backwards or forwards without detriment. It is only in the third part that a single historical event is introduced into the plot itself. The years 1888 and 1903 are intended, both really and symbolically, as, respectively, the first year of the reign of the last German Kaiser and the exact middle between this beginning and catastrophe. In accordance with this symbolism, old Mr. von Pasenow is presented even on the first page of the novel as a man who "wore a Kaiser William I beard." It is clear, in the second part of the novel, that the wheel of history has continued to turn, for it presents the milieu of industrial employment, socialist agitations, and the vaudeville-type entertainment to be found in large cities. In the third part of the novel, the historical events of the era are combined with the action of the novel and related to it. The era is easily recognizable from the portrayal. All three parts of the novel begin in the spring and end in the fall. This necessitates the introduction of narrative techniques for omitting or telescoping time and the organization of time into large segments. The seasons as such play no part in the novel because the characters no longer experience any real link with nature. Nevertheless, the springs and wintry autumns do acquire a symbolic character. The dated November days of the year 1918, for instance, mark not only the time of year, but also the political collapse. All three years are referred, by means of a particular character in the novel, to a particular idea. "Romanticism," "Anarchy," and "Objectivity" characterize the years 1888, 1903, and 1918. Pasenow, Esch, and Huguenau are presented as the exemplary products and exponents of their era. The symptoms of its illness are evident in them. The historically oriented reader might wish, perhaps, to reserve the title "Anarchy" for the year 1918, especially since the end of the war appears in the Huguenau-novel as a dissolution of order. But the author recognizes the roots of this dissolution in the false "romanticism" of 1888 and in the anarchical state that existed, if one looked deeply, beneath the outer appearances of order. The end of the war merely shattered the last illusion of order. It made apparent the inner lack of structure and the metaphysical lawlessness that had long been present.[10] For that matter, it is far more exact to think of romanticism, anarchy, and objectivity as being juxtaposed and interrelated than as existing in chronological sequence. The technique of the novel lets this principle of simultaneity become visible in part 3 in the meeting of Pasenow, Esch, and Huguenau, and in the tapestry-like interweaving of the many threads of simultaneous actions.[11]

The Symptoms of the Time

What is the significance of the three leading motifs in Broch's novel? The term "Romanticism" does not refer to literary and ideological Romanticism—that movement with its predilection for history and landscapes and consciously direct experience, with its tremendous broadening of awareness and its already modern split in consciousness, with its program for giving poetic character to everything that could be comprehended, imagined, or experienced, and its absolutizing of the creative ego. It does, however, aptly describe the Pasenows if it is used with the derogatory meaning it has long had in popular speech; that is, of something dreamlike, vague, unclear, unreal, of an undue projection of feeling and an inappropriate clinging to an obsolete past.[12] Broch's romanticist avoids a critical encounter with reality. He is a commonplace man, who lets himself be driven by the dull impulses of his blood, and who glides through time with the superficial value norms of a society that has long since lost the true knowledge of its own standpoint and the ability to orientate itself, of a conventional, inbred society that is its own center. The romanticist avoids personal self-decision and responsibility. He gives absolute value to his own small "order," composed of uniform, social esteem, and family possessions. The romanticist has lost access to his own ego, to true community, and to genuine religious values. His relationship to the genuinely rational as well as to the genuinely spontaneous has been disturbed. Thus the invasion of the irrational, so long idealistically repressed, is all the more powerful, for it cannot be confronted by a genuine and valid system of order, nor sublimated by *ratio* and subsumed into the totality of the person. The order of "romanticism" is, for the most part, a deceptive order; its values are deceptive values. Broch's romanticist is, in the idiom of the present, a "fellow-traveler," not of the Nazi but of the Wilhelmine era. He is one who "fears knowledge," as the essays on the "Disintegration of Values" say in their direct analysis.[13]

Whereas the romanticist clings to a false order, the industrialist has lost order. The key word for this loss is "anarchy." Anarchy reveals itself in the second part of the novel on many levels, and ranges from a more or less extrinsic and social characteristic to a most intrinsically human one. Thus the trade-unionist Martin Geyring and the unemployed and dissatisfied members of the socialist Left are designated as anarchists, a label given them more by the "romantically" deceptive order of the world in which they live than by the narrator. These "anarchists" have a just cause, but their attitude, as the narrator suggests later, incorporates destructive forces. The need for a strike is but one sign of the social disorder. That Esch is unjustly dismissed from his firm is also an infraction of order. In pondering the bookkeeping mistake of which he has been accused, Esch comes more and more to the realization "that the world has a flaw, a terrible bookkeeping mistake, which only a wonderful new entry can redeem." [14] At the beginning of the novel, Esch's sexual life is anarchical. He is able, later, to overcome this form of anarchy by his attachment to Mother Hentjen. He considers the homosexuality of the distinguished president of the company, von Bertrand, to be punishably anarchical. And he is compelled to recognize as anarchical even the business undertaking in which he himself is engaged—Oppenheimer's vaudeville agency—which he considers "another sign of the anarchical condition of the world" (p. 248). The symbolic heightening of experiences is clear. It is obvious from what has been said that Esch is not an anarchist in the way in which Pasenow is a romanticist. In contrast to Pasenow, Esch recognizes the seriousness of the situation. He develops the ability to detect even the symptoms of anarchy and becomes a fanatical, grotesquely comical champion of order in the world. But precisely this vehement demand for order, like his longing for a "new life" and a "redeemer," arises from his irrational primitive instincts. These have, for their part, chaotic symptoms. As an ordinary man, dependent solely upon himself, Esch cannot distinguish the increasing demands of the irrational. He has no criteria for doing so. He allows himself to be guided and led by the irrational experiences of his subconscious. And in this sense he himself remains fundamentally bound to his original anarchy.[15]

Huguenau is not bound by Pasenow's romantic Wilhelmine system of order, nor does he experience in the depths of his person any longing for a new order and a new life. He has long since smothered this deep level of his personality. He is the typically modern man, who has reduced his thinking, willing, and doing to pure "objectivity." All his actions are acts of business. Distractions and the gratification of impulses are expendable. He is incapable of entertainment. He does not even know the sexual eroticism of Esch. Everything has become frighteningly simple for Huguenau. His business interests are completely coextensive with his existence. His human nature has become atrophied. Nothing can be more single-minded than such objectivity. His desertion from the front was objective; his entrance into Esch's business was objective; his derision of Esch's religious behavior was objective; his resort to murder, his return home, his survival, and his new success were all objective. The narrator characterizes him symbolically through his quasi-erotic relationship to the "machine." Completely cold, his reactions are always calm. He is so utterly lacking in human relationships that he is not even aware that their absence *is* a lack. It seems that nothing more can befall him. The symptoms of dissolution at the end of the war and his murder of Esch turn to his advantage. In 1918, Huguenau no longer asks questions about the meaning and totality of life. His radical objectivity has its source, if one looks deeply enough, in irrational compulsion. Thoughts and meanings outside his business concerns have no more interest for him; he is not even aware of their existence. There is no value for him except private and pragmatic objectivity.[16] Huguenau functions for his own benefit.

The Interpretation of the Age

"Each of the books attempts to capture in presentation as well as language the spirit of the age that is characterized, though certainly not adequately, in the headings Romanticism—Anarchy—Objectivity." [17] The epithet "lost generation!" which occurs in the epilogue, should be woven into the novel retroactively as a leitmotif.[18] It is missing in the edition used here. Instead, Broch, in pursuit of his intent to write an "epistemological" novel, has added to the Huguenau part of the trilogy those essays which, under the title "The Disintegration of Values," have been isolated as separate chapters and numbered consecutively throughout the novel. "It is self-evident," Broch wrote to Willa Muir, who translated the novel into English, "that the 'Disintegration' offers the (rational and intellectual, H.B.) key to the whole structure, but it is also something more: namely, the outline . . . of a new philosophy of history." [19] Whereas the action of the novel stresses the plastic phenomenon, the historical and philosophic reflection provides the conceptual analysis. In their efforts to reach a diagnostic understanding of the age, the essays extend backward in time and forward in space beyond the actual events recorded. The actual appearance of the characters and the concepts of "romanticism," "anarchy," and "objectivity" as symptomatic of the age are referred to the larger historical scene and to a metaphysical background. Thomas Mann and James Joyce embodied their intellectual reflections in the edifying conversations of their characters. Broch could not and would not do so. The historical background and the deeper insight into the superficial happening remain, in fact, closed to his characters, who possess no higher awareness and are, therefore, not capable of "edifying conversations." They cannot rise above their age, cannot separate themselves from it by reflection. Broch was aware that he had to introduce his thoughts "into an action and into characters . . . that had no relationship to 'culture' and who could not, therefore, carry on those dreadful edifying conversations." He spoke his thought "nakedly and directly." Through these analytical chapters, he hoped that the depth and "breadth of cognition in the whole work would receive an increase." [20] Nevertheless, it is not the narrator of the whole work who appears as its author, but rather "Bertrand Müller, Dr. phil.," the narrator of the "Story of the Salvation Army Girl." The introduction of this narrator belongs, in the history of the text, to the last stage of the novel. Despite the presence of this fictive narrator—a piece of self-portraiture—Broch emphasizes in his letters that he himself "has assumed, one might say, full scientific responsibility for the chapters on the 'Disintegration of Values,' showing that it is the author who speaks here without concealing himself behind one of his characters, that is, without burdening a character—which always involves some lack of sincerity—with a part of the responsibility for what has been said." "The author considers as indispensable a statement of meaning that lays claim to objectivity." [21]

The basic point of departure in Broch's theory of values was his discernment of the disappearance and loss of the "absolute" in modern times. In the novel, after the characters have demonstrated the phenomenon of the unreal and the pseudoreal, the essays take up the question: "Is there still reality in this distorted life? Is there still life in this hypertrophic reality?" (p. 400). Whereupon the narrator, "Bertrand Müller, Dr. phil.," reflects on the "style" of the age, its "logic," its "style of thinking," its "spirit." [22] The universally apparent "split in the totality of life and experience" (p. 403) has its roots in the "dissolution of former attitudes toward value." [23] As the cause, the essayist names the dissolution of the hierarchical and cosmic view of the world, that is, of the Christian and Platonic unity of values and absolute center of values in God. He discovers the reason for this dissolution in the impact of modern autonomous, individualistic, and scientific thought, which no longer finds its "point of plausibility," raison d'être in God, but seeks its explanations in its own thinking and in things themselves. With the Renaissance began "a sweeping revolution in the style of thinking and a revolutionizing of all the phenomena of life" (p. 510), the "disintegration of the world into separate spheres of value" (p. 514).[24] "Romanticism," "anarchy," and "objectivity" are, in content and form, products of this collapse of values; they represent romanticism and anarchy in the sphere of values and an objectivity that is private and individual. Pasenow's "romanticism" reflects a disintegration of values to the extent that it raises the finite, for instance, "uniform" and "honor," to the status of an absolute; that it has lost that claim to being absolute which is inherent in genuine religion; and that it is content to substitute a romantic, philistine order for critical watchfulness. "Anarchy" leads us to the realization that the collapse of values is a common situation. There no longer exists a scale of values constructed for life as a whole and generally regarded as binding. There no longer exists a standard of values by which one can criticize, purge, and bring order into the onslaught of irrational and pseudohuman strivings. Irrational experience of the world and the rationalization of even its smallest parts stand side by side, yet unconnected. The "latent anarchy within every social community" and the "anarchical animal" within every single individual are no longer restrained and checked by the strength inherent in every hierarchy of values.[25] In other words, man is no longer regarded as "the image of God." "Being in the image of God" and "anarchy" are for Broch the "positive and negative poles of the world mechanism." [26] For a "romantic" and "anarchical" world, revolution may be a necessity, yet it is the tragedy of all revolutionary forces that they bear in themselves the marks of anarchy and utopian romanticism. Complete disintegration of values is to be seen in an "objectivity" such as Huguenau's, an "unadorned," "commercial" objectivity that has become completely "devoid of values" [wertfrei]. In it, human reason and vigilance are concerned only with the partial values of the individual or the group, and in all areas of partial value, a "partial logic" is substituted for the "faith" that embraces the world. This basically inferior logic engenders and is converted into a "private theology" (p. 667). Such slogans as "war is war," "business is business," and "l'art pour l'art" (p. 457) acquire validity. "Man, ejected into the horror of the infinite . . . [and] helpless in a mechanism of values that have become autonomous, has no recourse but to subject himself to the single value that has become his profession, has no recourse but to become the function of this (partial) value—a professional man, consumed by the radical logic of the value into whose jaws he has fallen" (p. 477). The possibility of determining one's own position and attitude with regard to the "center of values" has been lost. This is Broch's clinical and considered diagnosis of the age. At the beginning of the year 1932, Broch added to the epilogue of his novel a diagnosis of the rising specter, both romantic and objective, of National Socialism. "Considered in its logical genesis . . . , every partial system is revolutionary; if, for example, the nationalistic partial system, following the course of its own logical development into an absolute, establishes an organon in which the National State assumes the central place of God, then this referral of all values to the idea of the State, this subordination of the individual and his spiritual freedom to the power of the State, not only puts the State in a revolutionary and anticapitalist position, but even more stringently compels it into an antireligious and antiecclesial position; and this, in turn, points unequivocally and clearly to an absolute revolutionary disintegration of values and, therefore, to the suppression of the partial system itself. If, then, the partial system wants to secure its own continuance despite the process of disintegration, if it wants to guard itself against its own *ratio*, which advances steadily toward the goal of disintegration, then it must have recourse to irrational means, and this engenders the peculiar ambivalence . . . that is inherent in every partial system" (p. 672f.).[27]

The "Sleepwalkers" and the Irrational

In *Die Schlafwandler*, the two poles of the novel and its characters are referred to as "the dissolution of former attitudes toward value" and "the eruption of the irrational."[28] Sleepwalking is in opposition to the state of wakefulness and rational awareness. As a state of trance, it possesses a characteristic certainty that is largely dissociated from reality and the ordered relationships of the world. Yet a dream-deflected knowledge of a visionary kind can be released from the dreamlike foundation of the psychosomatic states of man. Both the title and the characters of the novel have their place in the tension created by this ambivalence. It is possible to distinguish various levels of sleepwalking. On the lowest level, lack of watchfulness and awareness reveals itself in a kind of "animal and vegetative trance"; on the middle level, as the upsurge of an abysmal human longing for union, redemption, light; on the highest level, as a "perceptive," visionary, even "prophetic trance," as "sleepwalking which leads into the light," and which is aware of "the higher Platonic reality of the world."[29] Young Joachim von Pasenow and Ruzena are sleepwalkers on the lowest level. Esch inhabits the middle level. The narrator, "Bertrand Müller, Dr. phil.," has his place on the upper level. None of the characters in *Die Schlafwandler*, with the exception of the two Bertrands, is awake to reality. Pasenow is not awake to the romantic era of William I nor Huguenau to the totality of life and its meaning. As sleepwalker *par excellence*, Esch dreams his way through life. His transformation into a sleepwalker and his sleepwalking states are stylistically represented. His experience of the bitterness and loneliness of life, his momentary glimpse of the crucificial life of a vaudeville actress, and his exaggerated longing for an ordered and redeemed world of his own open to him the road "into the darker pits" (p. 314). For him there "dawns the knowledge of ignorance" (p. 316), an insight that enables him to participate in primeval human knowledge and experience. This level of sleepwalking, which was smothered in the businessman Huguenau, but is accessible to the half-primitive Esch, is at once irrational and religious. It is the "panic religion of experience . . . , a dark, dreamlike happening, in which man, led only by primitive emotions, childlike attitudes, memories, and erotic wishes, presses onward like an animal and without sense of time. The longing for awakening, for a discerning and rational awakening is not lost; it remains active in this dreamlike happening, though it retains its somnambulistic character." [30]

Sleepwalking and irrationality are not per se coextensive. There is an irrationality that has nothing to do with the sleepwalker's state as such, for example, Huguenau's sudden murder of Esch (p. 661). Apart from these exceptions, however, the concepts of irrationality and sleepwalking are, for the most part, inseparable in the novel. Like sleepwalking, "irrationality" is ambivalent and has many levels of meaning. On a level of neutral value, the "irrational" refers primarily to "the mute and very irrational life," which, as such, is still in that "primeval condition of formlessness" that provides the material for "the rational formation of the world" (p. 670).[31] These instinctive strivings and pillars of cognition lie before the threshold of rational consciousness and freedom and may be designated as prerational. It is true that they belong, as such, to man. But they are not specifically human, that is, they are not freely willed and accomplished human acts. What Broch regards as specifically human is any thought or action by which the process of a "rational formation of the world [*Welt*formung]" is accomplished in freedom. This process of forming the world ["*Welt*formung"] manifests itself in the artistic style, in the style of thinking, in the prevailing fashion of an epoch, and in the creation of "values" ("im Schaffen von '*Werten*'"). Style and the creation of values ["*Wert*schaffung"] of every kind are acts intrinsic to the forming of the world ["*Welt*formung"]. "The course of the creation of values ["*Wert*schaffung"] always proceeds from the unformed to the formed—or, at least, to the better formed; the unformed or incompletely formed is always the irrational." [32] If, through apathy, sloth, "romanticism," or "anarchy," man fails to bestow form upon the irrational, then the irrational acquires a negative significance and falls into the sphere of guilt and the "category of evil." In this sense, "romanticism," "anarchy," and an "objectivity" that gives form only to partial areas belong to the category of evil. In the present context, we can do no more than indicate the fact that the "primeval symbolism of an irrational and unmediated view of the world," the "irrational . . . in the form of primeval associations and symbols," belongs, in a more positive sense, like sleepwalking, which takes cognizance of a higher reality, to the "territory reserved for the poetic." Broch, and in this he clearly reveals his indebtedness to psychology and to the philosophy of life of the twenties, consistently attributes positive possibilities to the primitive shrewdness of the irrational. "Every approach to the absolute contains qualities of infinity, and all infinity contains the irrational, is the point at which the mysterious depths are revealed—the abyss of the human soul, of human existence, the abyss of the world. And, for that very reason, every shift into the irrational threatens to become, at the same time, a shift into the anarchical; the anarchical is always lurking in the depths." Only a genuine "power of sublimation" can overcome the threat of anarchy that is in the irrational. [33]

Therein lies, for the characters of *Die Schlafwandler*, the basic difficulty that besets the path to purification. Where can they acquire the power of sublimation? From the value system of the Christian church, which is certain of its absolute central value? For the "sleepwalkers" it no longer exists. From the irrational itself? "What is most essential to the three books lies, indeed, in the irruption of the irrational, in the ethical problems, in the disintegration of former value systems." Sleepwalking and irrationality release genuine life impulses: "longing for awakening, . . . 'redemption,' 'rescue,' 'the meaning of life,' 'grace.'" In depicting Esch's character and circumstances, the author sought "to demonstrate, as it were, the epistemological principles that grow from the soil of the irrational and lead to the primeval concepts of all religious thought, that is, sacrifice and self-sacrifice for regaining the state of innocence in the world." "From this there arises of necessity the new problem: what value can there be in longing for awakening and salvation when, in an age of decadence and disintegration of accustomed values, there is no goal toward which they can be directed? Can a new ethos arise from the sleep and dreams of everyday life at its worst?" Objective criteria from the "Christian and Platonic" view of life no longer exist for Broch's characters because their age as a whole has lost them. But the "sin of the compulsive and unawakened falls short of any value systems." The "sin of the rational (like Huguenau) and the diabolical rejects value systems." [34] "The man who belongs to no value group has become the exclusive representative of an individual value; the man who is metaphysically an outcast—an outcast because the group has dissolved and disintegrated into individuals—is freed from all values and styles and definable only in terms of the irrational" (p. 665). Can a genuine, objectively valid new system of values arise from the experience of the irrational? Can the road to redemption be found in the irruption of the irrational? Before considering the answer given in the epilogue of the novel, it will be well to regard the sleepwalkers' various attempts to achieve redemption.

The Search for Redemption

The longing for redemption is, in varying degrees of awareness, common to all the characters in the novel. The question as to the possibility of redemption in this age is the most intimate concern of both narrator and author. "All are waiting for redemption to come," says Esch (p. 507). In the essay "Leben ohne platonische Idee" [Life without the Platonic Idea], which he wrote shortly after he had completed *Die Schlafwandler*, Broch confesses: "All spiritual production, from its smallest beginnings even to the heights of philosophy, is guided by the thought of redemption: what is spiritual regards itself, and must so regard itself, as the creation of the Holy Spirit, and its work in the world is always intended as a work of redemption. Whoever is dominated by the spiritual element in the world views every event in the light of redemption." [35]

The search for redemption appears at its lowest level in *Die Schlafwandler* as sexual erotic longing. Young Joachim von Pasenow and Esch both seek it, at first in their mistresses, then in the "romantically" Madonna-like spouses, whom they so irrationally exalt. Each in his own way has to learn "that you are far from reaching the absolute when you opt for a woman" (p. 349). Even Esch's plans to emigrate to America, his search in dreams for the "new life" in a new paradisiac beginning, cannot be realized.

His drive toward the "new life" and toward "order" in life has its origin in an irrational, "sleepwalking" experience, through which he penetrates "to the primitive ideas of all religion." The narrator introduces Esch's exemplary longing for the discovery of religious meaning and for release from the chaotic aspects of his life by an epigraphic commentary in the nobly exalted language of a hymn: "That one may come who will take upon himself the sacrificial death and will redeem the world to a state of new innocence: such is the eternal wish rising up in mankind even to murder; such is the eternal dream rising up even to clairvoyance. Between dreamed wish and foreshadowed dream hovers all knowledge—the knowledge of sacrifice and the knowledge of the kingdom of redemption" (p. 319). Esch learns to regard his marriage to Mother Hentjen, who in her obtuseness possesses neither eroticism nor a knowledge "of the kingdom of redemption" and whose sterility he suspects, as "expiation" and self-sacrifice. "He realized that there can be no fulfillment in the sphere of reality, realized more and more clearly that even the farthest distance is still within the sphere of reality, that every flight undertaken in search of fulfillment and freedom or to find rescue from death is meaningless. . . . For the earthly is unchangeable, however much it may seem to change, and even if the whole world were born anew, it would, despite the death of the redeemer, never attain to a state of innocence on earth until the end of time had been reached" (p. 363f.).

Salvation Army and Biblical sects appear in the novel as a third aspect of the redemption motif. Esch had already become acquainted with the Salvation Army in part 2. In part 3, the "Story of the Salvation Army Girl in Berlin" is told "contrapuntally" to the essays on the disintegration of values, the depiction of Huguenau's "objectivity," and the episodes in the military hospital. In the Moselle region, it is true, Esch becomes a Protestant—it is "at the same time an act of homage to the Major" (p. 510)—but he establishes a private sectarian Bible group, whose structural similarity to the Salvation Army becomes clear in the "Symposium, or Conversation about Redemption." In both Esch and Major von Pasenow, a fanatical desire to overcome the fear of life and death and to conquer loneliness rises to the heights of hymnic and enthusiastic eulogies of "grace" and pleas for "salvation": "Lord God of Sabaoth/receive us into your grace . . ./Lead us into the Promised Land . . ." (p. 534f.).

In contradistinction to Joachim's and Esch's sexual and erotic search for redemption, Eduard von Bertrand's attempt at self-redemption is purely rational and aesthetic. Bertrand, a "type of the 'rational man,' often in the avant-garde of the real, is not freed by value; he denies it . . . [and] is destroyed by the sin of rationality." [36] Although highly aware of and disillusioned by the deceptive solutions of inert convention, he cannot escape from his exaggerated awareness and cold loneliness to become a human being. He is the first to founder. "If Pasenow seeks a solution in traditional religious forms," Broch comments in his letters, "and Esch 'saves' himself by resorting to an erotic mysticism, these are, nonetheless, only half solutions and bring no release from their dreamlike state, but rather draw the ethical into the sphere of darkness and compulsion—and this is the original type of tragic guilt." [37] It is clear that the novel regards as insufficient all previous attempts at a solution.

The last character to be shown in relation to redemption is

"Bertrand Müller, Dr. phil." He tells the story of the Salvation Army girl and her love for the Jew, Nuchem Sussin. This Bertrand II, as we shall call him for the sake of brevity, is the purified and spiritual brother of Bertrand I.[38] His intellectual awareness is greater than that of Bertrand I, but it is without the latter's Mephistophelean characteristics. He affirms the necessity of actively helping one's fellow man. "I am completely aware," he reflects, "that the meaning and ethos of my life are not to be sought in activity alone, but I have a presentiment that this time has no time left for the only true activity, for the contemplative activity of philosophizing" (p. 590). The Judaeo-Christian background of his, as well as of Broch's, search for redemption is clearly recognizable: "I have traversed many roads to find the One into Whom all others flow, but they have drawn farther and farther apart, and even God was not established by me, but by my forefathers." Bertrand's innate inclination to search for God and religion in a unity that comprehends the whole world and all of life creates difficulties for him when he is confronted with the great variety of religious denominations. Because of his desire for "Platonic freedom, which is all that matters," [39] it is inevitable that he will be at odds with every historically identifiable ecclesiastical or religious claim. He criticizes the Jewish nation because it "continually exercised new controls over God in His own book" and the "naïve and worthy people" of the Salvation Army because "you believe that all you need do to attract God to yourself is to do good and beat out music." And Bertrand II's own attempt? "I said to myself: 'you're a fool, you're a Platonist. You believe that you can form the world for yourself by comprehending it, and that you can redeem yourself unto God. Don't you see that you are bleeding to death in the attempt?' I answered myself: 'Yes, I am bleeding to death'" (p. 592). It is obvious that, from the Christian point of view, a good bit of Platonic self-redemption is still present in Bertrand II.

The question arises here as to why Bertrand did not embrace the "Platonic Christian church" of the Middle Ages, which he praised again and again in the essays and which he recognized as being still present in the form of the Catholic Church? We have already discerned a basic inner tension in this narrator with regard to every historical actuality. To this must be added his knowledge that the only "point of plausibility" in the medieval church, the comprehensive basis of its explanation of all phenomena, was "the faith, where every chain of inquiry reached its end." This basis of explanation in God and the logic of faith determined the "style of the epoch." The "unchaining of logic" since the Renaissance, that is, modern scientific thought, has transferred the "point of plausibility" into things themselves as well as "to a new plane of infinity." "Thought dared to take the step from monotheism into the abstract, and God, the visible and personal God in the finite infinity of the Trinity, became the one whose name is no longer to be uttered and of whom no image may be fashioned; who ascended to the infinite neutrality of the absolute and was engulfed by it; who disappeared into the dread entity that is no longer accessible because it is no longer in repose" (p. 476). "In one stroke, the binding of individual spheres of value to a central value was rendered impossible" (p. 477). "Apparently there are only two possibilities for the Christian: either the security that at present is still available in the Catholic system of universal values, in the truly maternal bosom of the church"—an alternative that modern scientific thought made inaccessible to Bertrand II—"or the courage to take upon oneself, in absolute Protestantism, the dread of standing before an abstract God" (p. 558). He is well acquainted with the "longing for reunion," but indicates, too, his belief that only a scientific man who is also a "mystic" would be able to achieve the needed synthesis in his own person (p. 558). This is already an intimation of the solution indicated in the epilogue. Bertrand II is unable to accept as singly and exclusively valid any of the historical and ecclesiastical materializations of redemption; not the Catholic Christian one, because it has no place for modern scientific thought; not the Protestant, because its image of God is extremely "abstract" and because its loss of unity is documented by "the many sects that have been formed"; not the Jewish, because it controls God by its unyielding "law." In the end, he recognizes, too, the lack of any real solution in the "Platonic" way that he has chosen for himself. It remains to inquire whether the narrator of the whole novel suggests in the epilogue a solution that leads beyond that of Bertrand II, the narrator of one part of the novel.

The Hope Expressed in the Epilogue

The epilogue of *Die Schlafwandler* does more than pursue the fate of Huguenau beyond the actual plot of the novel. It brings the "redemption motif," which contains the highest meaning of the novel, "to its climax." Broch calls the epilogue, which he has "crammed" with motifs and thoughts, his personal "*credo*." [40] The narrator of the whole work inquires here into the possibility of redemption, first for an average man of the modern era like Huguenau, and second for an epistemologically uncertain man like Bertrand II. Huguenau, the "Philistine" average man, product of the disintegration of values, can find the road to salvation if he questions his overrationalized system of partial values and is revolutionary enough to reach the "absolute nadir," "that nadir of the atomic dissolution of values" which makes possible the dialectic transfer into a "new system of values" (p. 683ff.). The total demolition of the existing system of values and the founding of a completely new one is reminiscent of Nietzsche, with whose efforts to overcome the rising tide of European nihilism by the establishment of a new system of values Broch was familiar. For an epistemologically uncertain man like Bertrand, the possibilty of a new unity of values and of redemption from abysmal "loneliness" is conceivable only "when the scientific point of plausibility of the 'this we hold for true' coincides with the point of plausibility of 'faith,' when the double truth again becomes one truth" (p. 676). But who can point out for men like Huguenau or Bertrand the way to a new attitude toward values and the right use of freedom? Answer: "the Leader who will take him gently and lightly by the hand, who will set all things in order and will show him the way; the Leader who follows no man, but who will go before him on the untrodden road of the closed circle, in the ascent to ever higher levels, in the ascent to ever brighter proximity to the goal; one who will build the house anew that the dead man may live again; one who himself has risen from the multitude of the dead; the bringer of salvation, who can make the incomprehensible events of this time meaningful in his own actions so that time may be retold. This is longing" (p. 685). Will it find fulfillment? No, at least not in the sensational manner that is expected: "Even if the Leader were to come, the hoped-for miracle would not occur; his life would be an ordinary one in earthly surroundings" (p. 685). The advent of the Messianic leader is the object of longing just as it was for centuries in the pre-Messianic Jewish era. The "bringer of salvation" whom the narrator envisages is not the Christian Messias, and the hour of salvation is not the Christian era. The Christian Messias has already come in the "fullness of time." From an eschatological point of view, he has irrevocably established the time of this world as the time of salvation. For the narrator of *Die Schlafwandler*, on the other hand, time exists "as an orbit to ever higher levels" (p. 682). This cyclic concept of time contains within itself the Neo-Platonic concept of spiral ascent. Even if the "Leader" never appears, this quasi-mystical experience of life promises hope. It is the higher "irrationality," "the small spark in the depths of the soul," that at the same time assures participation in the transcendent "Logos." [41] Each one bears a Platonic mystic seal, "each one bears the small spark in the depths of his soul." It reminds him of "sacrifice and propitiation for what has happened," "of the painful freedom of duty," and it bestows upon him "the prospect of grace" (p. 685f.). The "intellect" is by no means excluded. Its function is to make certain "that the irrational forces that have been unleashed (and that means, in this context, even those that are unleashed in a revolutionary manner) shall once more be incorporated into a system of values" (p. 681). But knowledge of the deeper foundations of life, hope of redemption—these are reserved to that small spark in the soul that bears the impress of the Logos. If "romanticism," "anarchy," and "objectivity" reach the nadir, if their disintegration becomes apparent in contact with nothingness, then hope will arise by virtue of the grace that is inseparable from the Logos, so that "the absolute may be fulfilled on earth . . . in an ever more accessible way" (p. 686), so that "the freedom of the age will flow again into the Platonic freedom of God" and "everything that has been separated will be reunited in one" (p. 683). This, then, is "that metaphysical age of the new faith," [42] which, as we have said, is not to be understood in a dogmatic or ecclesiastical way as the time of salvation after the birth of Christ, but as the "way of Zion, the way we all must tread . . . , the hope of a Messias to lead us is indestructible" (p. 686).

Jewish, Platonic, and Christian elements have been amalgamated in the crucible of the author's sensitive discernment of the spirit of his time and of his deep experience of humanity. The sleepwalker, dependent upon the hope of redemption, has not become a member of the visible church. Nonetheless, he has been deeply affected by the reality of redemption in the incarnate Logos. The combination of epochal contemporary criticism with the basic inquiry of Western man into the possibility of redemption in his age, and the excellence of the novel form itself, which is no longer linear and on one level, make *Die Schlafwandler* a unique novel, whose appositeness as a novel of contemporary criticism has not yet been really discovered.

6

Hundejahre

Some Remarks about
a Novel of Contemporary Criticism

Hochhuth's *Der Stellvertreter* [The Deputy], Böll's *Ansichten eines Clowns* [A Clown's Views], and *Hundejahre* [Dog Years], by Günter Grass,[1] author of *Die Blechtrommel* [The Tin Drum], were the most significant literary events of the year 1963. This triple "Teutonic nightmare,"[2] announced with great fanfare, given a rousing reception by the public, and persistently reviewed by critics, struts across the public stage with continuing success and holds the interest of literary markets throughout the world. All three works discuss Germany's recent political past. The generation of sons are the accusers. Smarting, restless, and belligerent, they lay charges against their fathers for the years of their responsibility. Among the accused are the guardians of truth, the preachers of law, the advocates of common sense, the institutions of public morality, those surviving fellow travelers of a terrible twelve years who are now established in honorable well being. All were accessories: spectators, witnesses, citizens who read the newspapers. When put to the proof, the partially clairvoyant consciences of these young accusers seem to emerge triumphant. That the historical forum was erected with so much more difficulty, on so many more levels, under so many more conditions; that it was more finely meshed and more widely spread;

that it was more secretive, more Philistine, more closely inter-
connected, and, despite all its blatancy, more dimly lighted than
its somewhat theatrical sequel, the literary forum with its prefer-
ence for chiaroscuro stage lighting—all this constitutes no *a priori*
argument against the authors of the literary forum. For to give
form means to abstract, "to remember means to select," [3] modern
presentation means montage.

The Construction of the Plot

Like *Die Blechtrommel*, the *Hundejahre* is also presented in
three parts: (1) "Early Shifts"; (2) "Love Letters"; (3) "Materniads." The action begins in 1917, the year in which both main
characters, Eduard Amsel and Walter Matern ("accent on the
last syllable"), were born. Amsel, the son of a fallen dealer of
Dutch Jewish origin, was baptized in April in "good Protestant"
fashion. The baptism of the miller's son, Matern, "was done the
Catholic way" (p. 32). With the birth of the two "heroes," the geographical locale of the novel is established as the mouth of the
Vistula, its nearby villages, and the City of Danzig. The broad
river of the homeland flows plastically, "becoming ever broader
in memory" (p. 9). The locale and its people are presented with
unusual force and with a profusion of individual characteristics
and detail. Aspects of time are developed along with those of
place: the relatively private years of the twenties; the public history of the development of the Free City of Danzig into the
Danzig of the Nazis; the wider scene of Germany at war; the
return of the soldiers to the Western Rhineland; the years spent
in restoring the public welfare. The private world broadens into
a public world. The public world takes concrete form in the characters. Nearly every problem of form or content in the novel arises
from the author's purpose of combining a nostalgic glorification
of the private world of childhood with a revelation of the totally
abhorrent and demonized world of public life. As a powerfully
artistic portrayal of the interaction of person and world, the novel
presents "the period of time in which the whole span of life is no

longer perceptible to the senses and in which the immanence of meaning in life has become problematical." [4]

The basic action that runs through the whole work is the Amsel-Matern narrative: the deeds, destiny, and encounters of two friends who were like blood brothers. Walter, a strong and sinewy lad, protects chubby, artistic "little Amsel," when his seven-year-old school companions call him "Kike," beat him, and push him into the nettles (p. 42). At ten, both of them are sent to the Gymnasium in Danzig-Langfuhr (p. 105).[5] "After Amsel had spent a gentle childhood on the right and left banks of the Vistula, Amsel's sufferings began far from the Vistula. They will not end soon" (p. 115). Both boys "pass their final examination, Amsel with distinction, Matern with some luck" (p. 200). Instead of "studying something proper," Amsel, who has artistic talent, spends his time in a studio, training to become a designer and painter and in the construction of "life-size scarecrows" (p. 217). Matern, on the other hand, "declaims into the wind with even more zest than Franz and Karl Moor" (p. 201). He began to live a sham into which he put only half effort; he distributed "Communist leaflets" (p. 225), "got into fights with the squadron leader [of the Hilter Youth]" (p. 224), accustomed himself to inertia and alcohol, became a rowdyish storm trooper. Because of his deeper and more artistic relationship to reality, Amsel was preserved from every Nazi enticement. He ridiculed the storm troopers with his scarecrows, "put Schmeling and Pacelli, the pugilist and the ascetic, under the visors of brown caps," and amused himself by "working like God" (p. 235f.). But those "whose mechanisms had been built in not by Amsel, but by the good God" (p. 252) climb over the garden fence in disguise, attack Amsel, and knock out all thirty-two teeth from his mouth. It is Matern's "crunching fist," the fist that had once defended young Amsel, that now knocks him down. Amsel's mouth, from which blood is running, asks his Judas-friend:[6] "Is it you? Si ti uoy?" (p. 255). The reversal of the letters, a game they had played together at school and the secret language of blood brothers, signalizes, in a way that is both grotesque and artistically forceful, the reversal of friendship, the rupture and loss of a world. The blood brothers have become "Cain and Abel" (p. 285). "Dies irae, dies illa," begins the sequence of mourning; "liber scriptus proferetur" begins the theme of judgment (p. 285f.). Matern, expelled from the SA [*Sturmabteilung:* "storm troops"] for theft, did not become, as SS [*Schutzstaffel:* "Black Shirts"] Company Commander Sawatzki advised, "a member of the SS; he became what he had forgotten, but what he had been since his baptism, a Catholic" (p. 284). Later, indefinitely discharged from the theater, he realized that "Catholicism is a lot of crap" (p. 292). He reports "voluntarily to the armed services" (p. 294) and gets to be sergeant, but is "then convicted for insulting the Führer and demoralizing the armed forces. Demoted . . . , transferred to the Fourth Punitive Battalion . . . , he deserted on January 23, 1945, to the Twenty-Eighth Division of American Infantry in the Vosges" (p. 433). Amsel, after the strange debacle, had traveled to Berlin with a passport made out in the name of Haseloff, become a ballet master, and, with his ballet, been assigned to entertain the troops. In Berlin after the war, Matern meets Haseloff, who, because of his thirty-two gold teeth, is known as "Goldmouth." Officially, "Goldmouth" is known as Brauxel, head of the "Firm of Brauxel and Co." (p. 648).

In the second part of the novel, the action involving Liebenau, Tulla, and Jenny is woven into this basic situation. Harry Liebenau is ten years younger than Amsel and Matern, and of the same age as his cousin Tulla Pokriefke and Jenny, a gypsy orphan adopted by the lovable, though eccentric, assistant master Brunies, who later died in the gas chamber. Growing up in his father's carpentry shop, Harry spends his childhood with Tulla and the neighbor's child, Jenny. He clings to Tulla and is fond of Jenny, but loses both of them: Jenny, who has a talent for dancing, to Haseloff and his ballet in Berlin; Tulla to the antiaircraft battery at Kaiserhafen as a prostitute (it is the battery to which Sergeant Matern belongs, as well as the philosophizing Air Force Auxiliary Störtebeker and Harry himself). Harry, who at twelve and thirteen had tested his sexual drives on Tulla with the allegedly innocent conscience of a child, finds his sixteen-year-old cousin pregnant; she does not know by whom (pp. 373, 382). Air Force Auxiliary Harry Liebenau is, at this point, presented to the reader

as a "know-it-all," [7] who "read books of historical and philosophical content without discrimination . . . He was an inquisitive man,
whose gray, but not cold gray, eyes reflected everything, and
who experienced his . . . body as something sickly and porous.
A constantly careful Harry who believed not in God, but in
Nothingness. . . . A melancholy man. . . . A man of inaction, who
attempted to murder his father . . . by means of long poems in
school notebooks. . . . A sensitive youth. . . . A visionary, who
lied a great deal . . . and regarded the interminable war as an
enlargement of his education" (p. 375). He learns with horror of
the heaps of bones and the smoke of burning bones in the concentration camps. Toward the end of the war, he is sent with a self-
propelled gun to defend Silesia and the capital of the Reich (p.
413). With the Amsel-Matern and the Liebenau-Tulla narratives
there is linked the history and fable of the dogs. Senta is the dam
at the Matern's mill. Her paternal grandmother was a wolf (p. 22).
"Senta whelped Harras; Harras sired Prince; and Prince made
history" (p. 22, 45). Harras is the watchdog of the Liebenau
family and therefore Harry's and Tulla's dog. The Danzig municipal police commandeered him for mating purposes. With Thek-
la he sired the sheep dog "Prince," whom the Danzig District
Leader Forster bought in order to "have him presented to the
Führer and Chancellor . . . on the occasion of his forty-second
birthday" (p. 181). From a technical point of view, Prince
makes possible the narrator's access to such historical places as
the Führer's headquarters in the "Wolfsschanze" and the Führer's
air raid shelter in Berlin, as well as his titillating participation in
the newsreels in which the Führer appeared. As "the last stations
are playing the 'Götterdämmerung' " (p. 423), Prince said "I dis-
engage myself" (p. 425). "At 4.45 A.M., early on the morning of
May 8, 1945, he swam across the Elbe above Magdeburg . . . and
looked around west of the river for a new master" (p. 427). This
turns out to be Matern, who has just been released from P.O.W.
Camp Munster (p. 431). As "Pluto," Prince accompanies the anti-
Fascist "cruncher" Matern on his private tour of revenge through
Nazi-infested and capitalistically macabre West Germany. In the
"hundred-third and lowest Materniad" (p. 648f.), the black-haired
Pluto advances to the rank of "hound of hell."

The author of the *Hundejahre* can tell a story. Events, stories, depictions of the historical period, myth, and fable flow from his notes.[8] If the developmental line of the modern novel is moving recognizably toward the disappearance of narrator, narration, and hero[9] and toward an increase in interiorization and reflection, symptoms from which many literary historians are diagnosing the death of the novel, it is nonetheless true that all three—narrator, narration, and hero—live on indestructibly and happily in Grass' work. Grass can tell a story, not because he does not know the difficulties of modern narration, but because, although he knows them, his epic strength is greater than the nonepic world or any nonepic awareness of the world.

The three parts of the *Hundejahre* are entrusted to three different narrators. Who tells the novel? Grass works, with complicated methodology and modern organization, with an "author collective" (p. 108). The novel begins: "You tell it! No, you! Or you can tell it. Maybe the actor should begin?" A discussion among the narrators. Who begins? Brauxel, Liebenau, Amsel, Matern? The narrator of the first part is introduced with the words: "He who wields the pen here is now known as Brauxel, he runs a mine that produces neither potash, ore, nor coal and yet employs . . . a hundred and thirty-four laborers and employees" (p. 7). But who introduces Brauxel as narrator? Apparently the author, who appoints and directs the narrators whom he has projected. Brauxel writes as "Chronicler" (cf. pp. 9. 32). As "an aid to memory" he uses Amsel's "diary, . . . the moving little volume wrapped in fragments of oilcloth" (p. 56). Later the reader suspects that Brauxel and Amsel are the same person. However, not only Brauxel, but also someone else is doing the writing, someone who stands above and behind Brauxel, someone who keeps Brauxel under observation. It is the epic, not the biographical, person of the author. He watches over Brauxel's shoulder, unfolds and comments upon the "Frühschichten" [early shifts]. He unfolds the whole novel. In the second "Frühschicht," he remarks: "Here, on top of Brauxel's desk, and there, over the Schiewenhorst dike, it [i.e., the Vistula] rolls day after day" (p. 11). In the fourth: "In the meantime—for while Brauxel reveals the past of a pocket knife . . ." (p. 16; cf. also the beginnings of the other "Frühschichten"). Probably with some kinship to the "spirit of the novel" in Thomas Mann's manner, the author whispers: "All children between Hildesheim and Sarstedt know what . . . was produced in Brauksel's (!) mine" (p. 14).[10] Brauxel works as "Chronicler." But who is the source of the mythologizing parts, Brauxel or the author himself without intermediary? The transitions and fluctuations from one narrative level to another, accomplished through nuances and often scarcely noticeable, will have to be subjected to an exacting stylistic investigation before it will be possible to speak more definitely about the relationship of narrative and narrator. In one sense, the chapters of the first part are "Frühschichten" because Brauxel writes them during the "early shifts" of his activity (cf. pp. 17, 121). In a figurative sense, however, they deal with the "early shifts" of the narrative itself, that is, with the childhood "shifts" in the lives of the main characters.[11]

Harry Liebenau writes the second part of the novel as "Love Letters" to and about his cousin Tulla. It is not long before one realizes that these are quite remarkable and questionable, very ironical, love letters. Grass intends the ironic alienation and lets this part of the novel, too, begin with the description of an explicitly held attitude toward the narrative: "Dear Cousin Tulla, I have been advised to put you and your given name at the beginning, to address you as if it were the beginning of a letter, since you were, are, and will be the material throughout. At the same time, I am telling myself, only and unalterably myself; or am I somehow telling you that I am telling myself?" (p. 139). Grass is telling the reader that the narrator is not using the form of love letters in a completely candid manner, which would hardly be possible in the context, but that these love letters are parodies and travesties in a complicated mixture of address and monologue, of subjective reminiscence and objective chronicle: "I am telling you. You are not listening. And the form of address—as if I were writing you one or a hundred letters—will remain a formal walking stick that I might as well throw away now . . . , but the dog, black on four legs and well-trained, will bring it back to me" (p. 139). Nevertheless, Harry Liebenau does throw away the "formal walking stick" in the last seventy pages of part 2. Grass has perceived the difficulty. How can letters to a completely private, politically uninterested girl convey a superpersonal, political account of the times? The transition is ready at hand. It conforms to the inner alienation of Tulla and the painful recollection: "There was once a girl called Tulla" (p. 357). Then, "there was once a sergeant" (= Matern; p. 359). "There was once an Air Corps Auxiliary" (p. 360). "There was once an order of the day" (p. 361). "There was once a heap of bones" (p. 370). "There was once a city" (p. 374). "There was once a self-propelled gun" (p. 413). "There was once a Führer and Chancellor" (p. 414). And, as a leitmotif, "there was once a dog" (pp. 389, 423, 427). The fairy tale tone thus conjured up releases a grotesque tension into this chronicle of war and immerses the daily happenings in the channels of the subconscious.

In part 3, Matern, the returned soldier, tells his "Materniads." [12] Tells? "Matern is supposed to sound off about those days" (p. 431). So it was with Liebenau, too (pp. 140, 227), when he was under commission to Brauxel (p. 431). The first part could be told; the second part could be subsumed under the heading "you." In the third part, there is much vituperation. "Everywhere scraps, dog food: the twenty-nine potato years," [13] the author says by way of introduction (p. 431). And we find this common denominator surprising, for the years of childhood were, as the author recalls them, more than just potato years, and the years that followed were considerably less than that. Matern, released into the narrative by the author and Brauxel, is not sounding off about those years. He is sounding off about the present, about the postwar era in which, to be sure, the earlier years are somehow present. Matern describes a grotesque tour of revenge through nearly all the cities of West Germany. There is a confusion of first and third person narration (cf., for example, p. 527ff.). Why, to what purpose, has the radio discussion been inserted between the Materniads (pp. 571–612)? The tour of revenge consists of Matern's private tour of de-Nazification and his condemnation of the economic wonderworld. He reads off the address of former acquaintances from the enameled fixtures in the "strong sweet stench of the warm, holy Catholic men's room in the main railroad station in Cologne" (pp. 447, 457, 461, 467, 479, 481). He alienates the wife of former Company Commander Sawatzki; he burns the valuable stamp collection of a second ex-Nazi; he deflowers the daughter of a third. In Saarbrücken, he contracts gonorrhea. As "demolition worker" (p. 477), "as bankruptcy accountant [for the Nazi regime], there appears the returning soldier dripping Johnny" (p. 479). [*Tropfhans* (= "dripping Johnny") is soldier's slang for one who has contracted gonorrhea.] "Matern wants to wander around, not to work" (p. 485). "The cruncher is going around" (p. 559), even after the "currency reform" (p. 483). Next, Matern publicizes the height of the economic miracle in press, industry, political reviews. Grass prefaced *Die Blechtrommel* with the remark: "Any similarity to persons living or dead is purely coincidental." Here he names dozens of persons who are still living: Springer, Augstein, Bucerius, Neckermann, Thyssen, Krupp, Flick, Stinnes, Grundig, Schlieker, Pferdmenges, Würmeling, Globke, Adenauer, Erhard, and others. "The clergy come, but not in vestments and not with Frings and Faulhaber at the head of a field procession" (p. 502). "The prelate Kaas, the nuncio Pacelli, the former SA-man, the repentant New Catholic, the crafty Old Catholic, and the representative of the Catholic wing of the SA. All, with the benevolent Virgin Mary, make their little dance" (p. 489). "Without being asked, heretics like Gerstenmaier and Dibelius eat out of the Virgin Mary's hand: 'Mary with your Child so dear, / Give us all your blessing here'" (p. 503). In between, there is Matern's copulation "in the church that alone makes holy, the unheated, i.e., the Catholic church . . . in a confessional. That at least is something new" (p. 486).

Matern has given no reason for his unbridled sexuality, only for his tour of revenge: "Revenge, hate, and fury" (pp. 476, 662f.). "Oh, leitmotifs and murdermotifs! Oh, syrup-sweet revenge! Oh, justice, riding hither and yon on the railroad" (p. 487). "The avenger savors to the full the aftertaste of revenge achieved" (p. 478). "I come to judge with a black dog" (p. 446), "a halfway rewarding business" (p. 546), and "the good God looks on" (p. 444). Matern judges the world, not the whole world—for that he would have to be God—but the part that is accessible to him, the part that is even partially known to him. The reader asks himself why the author has involved such a characterless, superficial, ranting creature in his condemnation of the political, economic, philosophical (Heidegger), and religious world? The unprincipled Matern is accredited by his facile use of words, his leveling off of differences, his talent for disillusioning, and his power of suggestion. Why was he commissioned by the artist Amsel, by the reserved Brauxel? Why does Grass lend him his magic word? Matern's revenge spectacles, his inability to distinguish value from lack of value, distort the world. It is this same Matern who must bring the whole novel to a close in a double finale, a personal one and one related to the historical events of the period. The personal finale takes place in the "artists' tavern" in Berlin, the "Chez Jenny" (p. 636), where, during a drunken reunion between "Goldmouth" and Matern, the tavern burns down. For the historical finale, "Director Brauxel" leads Matern into his mine: a representation of the world as an Inferno (p. 649ff.).[14] "Here all uniform discipline and civilian dignity are derided because hatred, anger, and stalking revenge, which had so recently seemed under control because they had been checked, blossom forth again . . . all uncontrolled, inhibited, and self-complacent scarecrows . . ." (p. 667).

And the unity, the inner necessity of the work and its narrators? All three "narrators" write from "memory." The levels of memory vary. The first narrator writes calmly and in a way that convinces the reader. Matern is least convincing. His poisoned memory spreads poison. All three write simultaneously (pp. 32, 55, 131f.), are called "chroniclers" (pp. 19, 32), and, in a variety of ways, show a tendency to mythologize. All three assimilate factual knowledge and strive to make their narrative seem like something witnessed in the real world. Any detailed structural analysis of the novel will have to inquire into the complicated relationship among the three narrators, into the character of Brauxel as he is represented and as he represents himself, into the inner harmony of the novel, into its unity, into the function and necessity of the extensive material, and into the method of narration. Often, ideas run riot; the author's verbal power and creative zest bolt like unbridled steeds, and Grass yields blissfully to his subjective impulse toward a universal deformation of his object. The formal development of a world viewed from within—and Grass has such a vision—is rudely destroyed by his exaggerated determination to reveal a world that is totally futile. His demiurgic method of composition, which blends organic elements with a montage of elements organized from without, produces a structure that is full of flaws. The unity is not convincing; the truth is not compelling; the final Inferno does not expand into vision. Inspired passages mingle with dross. How does Grass present his world formally? We shall investigate three great principles of revelation and deformation.

Revelation and Formal Destruction of a Vanished Reality

This oddly universal novel reveals a variety of thematic aspects. In parts 1 and 2, the themes of lost childhood and lost homeland are given a melancholy but transfiguring formulation. With the characters Amsel and Jenny, the theme of art and the artist is introduced. Matern's vital talent for adaptation and survival might well have been intended for a modern adventure or picaresque novel. The degree to which the characters are swept up and carried along by the historical happenings is a measure of the extent to which the novel itself undergoes a change from developmental [*Entwicklungsroman*] to historical novel [*Zeitroman*]. The latter reveals the world of Nazi totalitarianism with its destructive effect on the individual and, in part 3, the world of totalitarian economics and lack of principles. This destructive world itself falls victim to Matern's angry condemnation and the author's annihilating use of form.

With the title *Hundejahre*, Grass links the many parts of his novel to a common denominator. The dogs belong on many levels and serve the author for many purposes. As family dogs in part 1, they are physically real dogs. Through Perkun, they trace their ancestry to the magic, mythical realm of nature. In part 2, the trusted house dog comes into Hitler's possession, and the word "dog" acquires, from its association with the Führer's dog Prince, the force of an overwhelmingly pejorative metaphor. Through the medium of this metaphor, the novelist has rendered visible Hitler's attempted degradation of man into something subhuman. Man's years are revealed as "dog years"; man himself is revealed as expendable and debased, the maltreated dog of a brutal and despotic master. In part 3, the dog has lost the natural strength of his reality. Prince, who joins Matern as Pluto, is no longer a real dog, but a montage conjured up by the author and used as a novelistic device. The metamorphosis that changes the novel from the presentation of a living world into the presentation of a contrived one is apparent, to give but one example, in the changed character of the dog. Pluto is no longer present in the novel as Senta, Harras, or even Prince were present; he has become no more than a function of the narrator, an attribute of Matern's, who "has come to judge with a black dog" (pp. 446, 464). The intrinsic relevance of the dog is no longer indicated as before. When Matern, after concluding his picaresque and daemonic revenge, "makes his way without dog into the Eastern peace camp" (p. 614), he entrusts the dog—the meaning is tendentious—to the Station Mission for safekeeping. Yet, while Matern sits in the interzonal train, "a black shepherd dog grows younger by dog years between Genthin and Brandenburg" (p. 621), for he is still needed: first of all in the reunion celebration with "Goldmouth"-Amsel, who, as an "honest finder," leads Pluto, *canis ex machina*, back to Matern at the Zoological Gardens Station of the interzonal train. At the end, Prince-Pluto is needed as the hound of hell in the lowest Materniad. Brauxel and Matern make the real "start" to their descent [into Brauxel's mine], "with British European Airways to Hannover Langenfeld" (p. 648). And Pluto? As soon as he is needed, he is there. Harras was a living creature. The pejorative metaphor was already linked to Prince. Pluto is primarily an attribute, a principle of revelation and composition, a fact which, in a historical novel that strives to create a real background, cannot fail to result in a loss of reality. The logical thread, the "parable" (p. 608), is easily recognized. The dog, originally a family dog, is increasingly disparaged, wrapped in darkness, made increasingly daemonic. "The dog stands in a central position," begins the third part of the novel. What the author is trying to show is a "close-up of ghosts!" "a close-up of final victory!"

"a close-up of a dog!" (p. 621), a close-up of hell. It may be questioned, however, whether the author has not, by his arbitrary use of structure, defeated his own purpose.

Matern and Liebenau furnish the dogs as a principle of revelation. Amsel furnishes the scarecrows as a principle of deformation. "When he was about five and a half years old, he made the first scarecrow worthy of the name" (p. 39). A definite purpose is bound up with Amsel's childhood game: "The scarecrow is made in the likeness of man" (p. 38). The words are intentionally reminiscent of the Bible. What is play for Amsel the child becomes a profession for Amsel the artist. As human need and artistic pleasure are intensified, the forms of the scarecrows become ever more grandiose. The artistic deformation of man into a scarecrow demonstrates the distorted image of man that has been and is yet to be found in physical reality. The deformity of man becomes visible in the grotesque figures created by the artist. Amsel constructs the SA men as mechanized scarecrows. For this revelation of truth, the artist is beaten by the SA men. The author's presentation is particularly compelling at this point. Dehumanized man can no longer endure the mirror of art because he is at variance with the truth. The artistic and historical aspects of the novel are mutually intermingled in the ballet-creation of Haseloff-Amsel in the central part of the novel: "The Scarecrows," or "The Revolt of the Scarecrows," or "The Gardener's Daughter and the Scarecrows" (p. 400). There follows a sketch for a ballet that one would like to see realized on the stage. An integral part of the scarecrow ballet is "that shaggy black dog" (p. 402).

Like the dog motif, the motif of Being and Time is linked to the scarecrow motif: a parody and travesty of Heidegger. Matern, traveling for vengeance, called to Heidegger: "Open the door, Stockingcap! Matern is here to proclaim revenge! . . . Skiing Nothingness, open up!" (p. 475). On the verbal level, one reads: "The question about the scarecrow-as-such puts us—the questioners—in question." "He, the pre-Socratic . . . has a thousand words for being, for time, for essence, for world and basis, for the with and the now, for Nothingness, and for the scarecrow-as-such as [verbal] prop; thus: scarecrowness, scarecrow-hood, scarecrow-structure, scarecrow-view, not-scarecrow-as-such; scarecrowing away, antiscaresrow-as-such, scarecrow-prone, scarecrow-essence, scare-crow-state-of-mind, descarecrowed, ultimate-scarecrow, scare-crow-yielding, scarecrow-wholeness, basic-scarecrow-as-such, and: the proposition about the scarecrow-as-such" (p. 669). The Heidegger parody constitutes, in my opinion, one of the author's great flashes of wit. Obstructing the world by an abstruse system of mythology that has no foundation in history is a preliminary to every form of nihilism, including that of Hitler. The destruction of such a system by parody is one of the stylistic devices permissible to an author who is also the critic of his age. But it is vexing to the reader to find the author losing control of the narrative out of sheer delight in his own artistry, committing gross generalizations, and admitting unrestrained and excessive repetitions. It seems grotesque that the same uninhibited, pubescently angry, deluded Matern who tears open Heidegger's garden gate on his tour of revenge and spits out in homely idiom: "C'mon out, ya profligate! Monstrous louse! Misshapen oaf!" (p. 477), that this same Matern, who puts himself so subjectively in the wrong, should be entrusted with the objectively intended judgment contained in the verbal parody. If Matern is able to see through Heidegger's philosophy, though his intellect is so limited that he passed his final examination only with difficulty, and if even Harry Liebenau, in his role as narrator, is able to parody Heidegger, it is surely pertinent to inquire into the identity of the narrator whom the author has thus projected and the necessity of such a projection. It cannot be denied that the deformity of the language itself conveys a sense of destruction and of the loss of a life worth living. Therein lies its artistic justification. Dogs, scarecrows, and Heidegger-imitation reveal the deformation of man and his world.[15]

The Inquiry into Effect and Objective

The Socialist writer Tibor Déry said recently at the Writers' Congress in Leningrad at which representatives from the Federal Republic of Germany were also present: "My first general question is as follows: Are we ourselves sufficiently clear about the effect of the work of art? . . . A work of art that affirms nothing and denies nothing is, of course, inconceivable, but I believe that the questions which the work of art poses by its mere existence are like the Shakespearean mirror in which the world views itself." Déry names as the first effect of the work of art the "purely moral" one; "the supplementary effect . . . is divided into various levels of a political, historical, or economic nature." Déry demands "propaganda—intentional or unintentional—for human virtue or for a nation's will to life." It is clearly a question of "catharsis, which is the artist's ultimate goal." [16]

What is Grass trying to achieve with his novel? To destroy the Shakespearean mirror? To spice the salad of the Federal Republic's household with his satire? To create the wholesome view that makes catharsis possible? Is he trying to reveal our vanished history, our vanished living space, our vanished human image? The reply can be only partially affirmative, and it is doubtful if the purifying effect has been achieved at all. Grass draws into the light of his historical magic mirror and unmasks there much that the normal peace-loving person does not admit or would prefer to conceal. The role of public nuisance inspires his fancy and increases his courage. Nevertheless, he oversteps to a marked degree the limits of permissible distortion. In the second part of the novel, that is, not merely in the "Materniads" with their lust for revenge, the action of Count Stauffenberg is commented upon as follows: "His attempt at assassination failed because he was not an assassin by profession and, in his inexperience, did not go at it wholeheartedly enough, but slunk away before the bomb had clearly said 'yes,' and wanted to spare himself for great tasks after the successful assassination" (p. 395). The later totally negative presentation of the economic world of the Federal Republic, reaching its height in the presentation of the world of production as "Hell and Co." (p. 673), permits of no evaluation, no exception, no differentiation, no problem. The descent in the last Materniad could have become a great vision if the atmosphere of the narrative had not already become expansive and unproblematical.[17] Certainly, the author is not to be identified with the ranting Matern. But Matern is the author's creation. And one must ask whether Grass has separated himself sufficiently from his revenge-riding

Matern, the "demolition worker" and "bankruptcy accountant."
Traces of his failure to do so are recognizable when the "dog"
is expressly designated as a principle of "parable" (p. 608); when,
in the "lowest Materniad," the scarecrow-as-such is described in
the words: "Projecting itself into the Nothingness, the scarecrow-
as-such is already beyond the scarecrow essence as a whole . . ."
(p. 669; the ellipsis points occur in the novel). But the author
samples Matern's revenge too eagerly. His sympathy for his
creation Matern is so great that it is impossible to recognize any
objective framework or alienating barb of satire in the extremely
subjective "Materniads." We seem to be hearing the author himself when "Goldmouth," the artist and producer, increases his
vitality to the point of grotesquerie in the burning nightclub:
"Don't lose the thread, folks. As long as we're still telling stories,
we're alive. As long as we can think of anything at all—with a
point or without it—dog stories, eel stories, scarecrow stories, rat
stories . . ." (p. 641). At night, the story-telling narrator rises
superior to existence as "hell" (p. 641). Fine and good. With
proper epic preparation this might have seemed great tragedy.
But can the mere teller of stories judge the story even though he
does not let the true remain true? When he tells stories instead of
history? Uses grotesquerie as a substitute soporific? Art instead
of life? Thomas Mann was wiser in this regard; his attitude was
more critical. The man who is nothing-but-artist is a questionable
judge of life. Only the artist who accepts life itself, who is alive
to the tensions and tragic moments of history, can judge history.
One who recognizes no values makes a poor judge. One whose
credo is nihilism cannot have the proper attitude toward a nihilistic
history unless his theme is to read "Variations on Nothingness."
We recognize too few values in the author of *Hundejahre*.[18]
Matern is characterized by his destructive rage. Liebenau makes
open confession of his *credo* of "nothingness." [19] Nowhere does
Grass indicate that he is at variance with Harry Liebenau's views
and judgments. Matern is a doer of Nothingness, Liebenau a believer in Nothingness. Liebenau's words annihilate values through
the principle of linguistic leveling: "Swine, Jesus Christ, Marx
and Engels . . . , swinish, salty, devilish, Christian and Marxist,
laughing, roaring, chewing the cud . . ." (p. 357). Everything is

reduced to the same level, everything is equally trivial. Matern blusters: "Throne and altar, being and time, master and dog" (p. 445); "Inge-mouse and Inge-hole and tidings of joy" (p. 457); "the Main Railroad Station in Cologne . . . Jesus Christ, who can multiply loaves and turn off drafts, had it glassed in" (p. 514). Liebenau mourns over his anonymously pregnant cousin: "There was once a girl called Tulla and she had the pure forehead of a child" (question of the reader: when was this shrewish, egotistic creature, this half sister of the tin-drummer Oscar ever pure?). Yet Liebenau continues with generalizations, equatings, and every appearance of proof: "But nothing is pure. . . . No virgin is pure. Even the swine is not pure. The devil never completely pure. . . . Jesus Christ not pure. Marx-Engels not pure. Ashes not pure. And the host not pure. No thought keeps one pure. Even art does not flourish purely" (p. 357). An experience that begins by being truly human is here linked to a nihilistic destructive tendency, becomes suggestive through the magic of words, and is made convincing where, humanly speaking, one might have demanded differentiation and where, historically speaking, one might have demanded truth. Such a message is too paltry, even when it is artistically clothed. Brauxel, too, the first narrator, reveals a tendency to reduce everything to the same level and to devaluate it, as, for instance, when he explains: "like the devil and God" (p. 73, twice), and when he relates with an expression of guilelessness: "When God was still going to school, it occurred to Him . . . to create the world with his schoolfriend, the gifted little devil" (p. 107). Grass writes tendentiously. And his tendentiousness is anything but harmless. Not only Hitler but economy, philosophy, even religion are to be annihilated or at least gnawed away by a pejorative lack of differentiation. "Is there a God, or is God the primeval scarecrow?" (p. 670) is the cynical query in Brauxel's Production and Mine Works.

Metaphors, sequences, word plays and combinations of words, sudden flashes of wit, and stories are all at the disposal of the author. Human, social, and historical realities, however, are not equally at his disposal. In the last analysis, structures of a deeper order resist the ranting demiurge. Precisely where he most wants to reveal and judge, Grass alienates reality and turns it into unreality before it is sufficiently under his control. The play of phantasy begins too soon. The claim of artistic freedom is not sufficient justification for unbridled phantasy nor the rod of justice for evil emotions. Grass might have had the talent to write the epic of his generation and of our age. But the binding power of truth and epic form demands more than stories, brilliant wit, and spasmodic display of talent. Contemporary criticism of the kind attempted here presupposes fairness, discipline, and a more comprehensive and differentiated sense of the real. To the degree that these are lacking, the epic that essays contemporary criticism remains only a ranting, disfiguring, albeit perhaps great, artistic game.

7

Doomed Existence
Franz Kafka's Story:
"A Country Doctor"

Though it requires only eight pages in the *Collected Works*, Kafka's short story "Ein Landarzt" is distinguished both by the unusual attraction it has for critics and by their unusual embarrassment in interpreting it. Kafka himself submitted it for publication to the Kurt Wolff Publishing Company, where it appeared in 1919. It is one of the most compact texts in all epic literature; there are no paragraph divisions in the printed text. It is strange to the listening ear, cluttered to the eye of the imagination, nonsensical to the censorious intellect. Written in the winter of 1916–1917, the story originated in Kafka's middle creative period, which began in 1912 with "Das Urteil" [The Judgment] and ended in January–February 1920 with the notes for "Er" [He]. In writing "Das Urteil," Kafka, purified by his inexorable artistic intellect, experienced a new intensity. The *Diary* notes: "I wrote 'Das Urteil' in a train between ten in the evening and six in the morning on the night between September 22 and 23 . . . . Several times during this night I bore my own weight upon my back. How everything can be said, how for everything, even for the strangest fancies, there is prepared a great fire in which they perish and rise again . . . . The slight heartaches. Weariness that disappears in the middle of the night . . . . Only thus can one write, only in such a context, with such a complete opening up of body and soul." A decade later he wrote to his trusted friend who had translated his works into Czechoslovakian: "In that story each sentence and each word, each—if it is permissible to say it—music is linked with 'Angst'; at that time the wound broke open for the first time in a long night." [1] It was with just such a complete opening up of body and soul that Kafka composed "Ein Landarzt." A wound is its central symbol. The *Diary* gives evidence that Kafka ranked the story high among his works. The entry for September 25, 1917 reads: "From works like 'Ein Landarzt' I can still derive a temporary satisfaction, provided always that I am lucky enough to produce something of the kind (very unlikely). Happiness only then, when I can raise the world into the pure, the true, the unchangeable" (T 534).

The Story

One does well to insist that "Ein Landarzt" is "first of all a real story, and only then a symbol and a puzzle." [2] How does the story go? At night, during a blizzard, a doctor is summoned to a distant village to treat a patient who is seriously ill. His horse has died of overexertion. No one will lend him another. What is he to do? Perplexed and distressed, he kicks open the door of his unused pigsty. A strange man is crouching inside. He drives out two horses and holds them in readiness. The doctor can go. But the "beast" of a groom demands as "price" the doctor's "servant girl," Rosa. Under such a condition, the doctor wants to renounce the trip. But his "carriage is whisked away like a log in the current." Within seconds, the country doctor is standing before his patient, a boy, whom he does not find really ill. And for this he has had "to sacrifice Rosa, this pretty girl." He wants to drive back, but, faced with the tearfully disappointed behavior of the family, he is "somehow ready to admit with reservations that the boy is perhaps sick after all." "In his right side, near the hip, a wound as big as the palm of my hand has made its appearance." It proves beyond healing. People from the village join the group. "They have lost the old faith." They no longer need the pastor.

They expect "everything" from the doctor, whom they unclothe and put into bed beside the boy in order that his healing power may be more effectively transmitted. Despite the fact that it cannot be healed, the wound "is not so bad"; it is a "beautiful wound," a proper wound, a wound unto death. After the boy's death, the doctor hurries home. Without waiting to dress, he leaps onto one of the mysterious waiting horses. The horses carry him off, wander through the wastes of snow, and never reach home. The country doctor has lost everything. The ringing of his night bell has betrayed him.

Alienating Elements

If the metaphorical elements are, in a generally empirical way, ordinary, their arrangement into scenes is nonetheless extraordinary, and the story itself is above the ordinary. Totally absorbed in the uncanny affair, the country doctor tells a story that is at once elemental and alienating as it moves from highlight to highlight with the compactness of a ballad and in a tightly structured series of metaphors that have their own logic. The separate parts of the imagery seem familiar: a village, an icy winter, a country doctor, a night bell, an instrument case, a horse and carriage, a village family with a boy sick in bed and with magic confidence in the doctor, village elders, a school choir with their teachers. But the metaphorical sequence and the arrangement of scenes bear no relationship to the ordinary events that we might expect on the basis of our conscious day-to-day experience. As though in a fairy tale, horses emerge from the pigsty at exactly the right moment. The boy's wound, though the size of one's palm, is at first invisible, then suddenly visible like a picture in a peep show. The doctor's horses are at his disposal and not at his disposal, present, yet at the same time "unearthly." Their whinnying has been "ordained in a higher place." The village assembles in the middle of the night. The doctor is overcome by some magic means. Only because he does not want to delay long enough to dress, he rides back without clothes through the winter. Neither the nonarrival of the horses nor the loss of the doctor's practice is motivated.

The story violates our concept of causal relationships and the logic of everyday understanding. The peculiar logic of the imagery itself, which only Kafka uses in this fashion, reveals deeper truths and opens up new existential meanings.

The Narrative Technique

It will be profitable to postpone our inquiry into the meaning of what has been narrated until we have considered the unusual narrative technique and the unique structure of events and metaphors. The disconnected and only partially motivated action as well as the metaphorical relationships, which are unfamiliar to everyday consciousness because they contradict its firm and over-emphasized sense of order, indicate that this is a dream structure. Kafka cultivated his "dreamlike inner life" not merely as a protection against the importunities of the outside world, but even more as a means of perception, of inner vision, as a source of images, a descent into the dark wells of consciousness, as the condition and the possibility of writing. "The dream reveals a reality behind which presentation lags," he said to Gustav Janouch. "That is the frightening thing about life, the terrifying thing about art." [3]

To this dreamlike consciousness belong the unusual and sudden links between person and problem which appear in images beyond the reach of controlled reflection and which both interpret and unmask by means of metaphorical associations. Outside and inside, ego and world, man and animal are not fully distinguished from one another. Ordinary details of time and space appear, if not suspended, at least displaceable; distances seem not so much quantitative as qualitative, that is, in relation to their narrative function and meaning. Places that lie far apart and events that are separated from one another in time can be momentarily linked if they have anything in common, however hidden it may be. What has been buried, immured, or suppressed comes to light. Man's suppressed desires are expressed in images. In the dusky openings of the dream horizon, intensive images meet with a logic all their own. To the excessive clarity of the individual images and relationships there is often linked ambiguity in the interpretation of meaning.

The structure of both plot and imagery in "Ein Landarzt" arises, to a large extent, from some such dream order. This is obvious in, for instance, the doctor's almost immediate arrival at the sick man's home and the practically endless procrastination of the movement which issues in his nonarrival at the end of the story. Corresponding to the ability to remember dreams, to the possibility of channels of knowledge that communicate on a deeper level, is the fact that the country doctor-bachelor suddenly sees, for the first time, the girl whom he has been overlooking for years, and that seeing her, he loves her. The moonlight atmosphere, the mysteriousness and rich implications of the wound, the forms of nakedness, the various ways of not-being-able-to-help, the guilt feelings and the verdict of guilt, the subliminally present question as to meaning, the aphoristic "key" to the explanation of the evil fate that encompasses the whole person at the end of the story belong to the mood and consciousness of a dream. But there is no question, in the story, of what one might call the photographic or naturalistic reproduction of an autobiographical dream. Not only has the material of the dream been chosen by a critical and supervising consciousness and shaped in advance by observation of real detail,[4] but the structural principle of the dream has also been given a completely new and more intensive form by the artistic consciousness and by the process of critical creativity. All metaphorical and dream elements have been absorbed into the higher organization of the literary construct and into the consciously intended integration of the work of art as such, that is, of the structure uniquely and properly presented by the artist.

Mythical elements and a concentration of fairy tale themes are linked to the dream elements and dream character of "Ein Landarzt." "Struggle, the assigning and carrying out of tasks, intrigue and assistance, harm and healing, . . . overpowering and redeeming, liberation, rescue, as well as contact with a world that surpasses the everyday one, with magic, 'supernatural' powers" [5] are fairy tale motives in this compact and direct narrative. But the harmonious solution of the fairy tale, the rescue of the "hero," the winning or rewinning of order on a higher earthly level, the good fortune which is finally achieved through trial and which confirms the "hero"—all these are lacking. This nonappearance—or rather this active prevention—of success, this lack of goal caused Clemens Heselhaus to apply the concept of the anti-fairy tale to Kafka's tales. Kafka himself noted in 1913: "I would gladly have written fairy tales (why do I hate the word so?) which W would have liked" (T 323f.). Later he explained to Gustav Janouch, "There are no unbloody fairy tales. Every fairy tale issues from the depths of blood and anxiety." [6]

The country doctor reports his experience as a first-person narrator. There is no place for an explicit address to the reader. But an implicit awareness of and consideration for the public is often recognizable, as, for instance, when the doctor explains at the beginning: "Of course; who would lend his horse in this weather for such a trip?" Or when he justifies himself to an imaginary public: "I am no world reformer and I let him [i.e., the patient] lie. I am employed by the district, and I do my duty to the limit, even to the point where it becomes almost too much" (E 149). The ending is similarly aphoristic. In general, however, the predominant impression is of a monologue, although, from a formal point of view, only the beginnings of the interior monologue are discernible. The narrator is so stricken by his fate that he loses sight of the reader in the course of the story. Only before, between, and after the individual episodes does the doctor as first-person narrator overtake the suffering "hero" and present the narrative situation. He does not narrate simply from hindsight, which overlooks what is past and presents the danger as overcome. He cannot achieve such detachment from the facts he is narrating. The event is presented directly, as though it were happening here and now and had significance for the present. All unnoticed, the time level of the past pushes its way into the present; the report acquires scenic immediacy. Only at the end of the uncanny sick call does the narrative past tense make its hesitant appearance, even then slipping back often into the present. At the end, the narrator summarizes the action in an aphorism that is at once an interpretation and a complaint—an unbelievably compact epic form.

Thematic Structure

The narrator is telling more than just the story of a country doctor, more than just an interesting and perhaps unique event, more than just this professional story, or that family story. As doctor-narrator, he is diagnosing the peculiar basic frame of mind of an inevitable and doomed existence. The country doctor is charged with a threefold "rescue": the rescue of Rosa (E 149), the rescue of the boy (E 151), and finally his own rescue (E 153). In the last analysis, the first and second rescues are also rescues of the doctor himself. They are partial aspects of the doctor's single comprehensive existence, shown from three points of view and knotted together in one; and, beyond that, they are a typically Kafkaesque model of human existence in general. In a this-worldly —one is tempted to say in a bourgeois—sense, all three rescues fail to achieve their objective. The bourgeois existence, the adaptation of the Kafkaesque "hero" to ordinary human situations, is a failure. His surroundings and his own inner life challenge the isolated country doctor to an integration of his human personality. The forces that condition his existence call him to the struggle ("struggle" is one of the most important words in Kafka's vocabulary). He responds to the summons—and fails, because the exigency of his bondage cannot be here and now dissolved, because a harmonious solution and a happy existence are not accessible to him. According to the law by which he is governed ("law" is another key word for Kafka, though it has an entirely different meaning for him than for Goethe), and which he learns here and now, but with which he is not sufficiently conversant, he is doomed to failure in this world.

The Critical Moment

In "Ein Landarzt," as in the other stories and in the two great novels, Kafka plunges into the situation with which the story opens. There is no initial exposition, no friendly hand extended to the reader, no introduction to the strange happening. Like the imprisonment of Josef K in *Der Prozess* [The Trial], like Gregor Samsa's awakening from restless dreams in "Die Verwandlung" [Metamorphosis], the ringing of the night bell is revealed as a critical moment, pregnant with existential meaning.[7] The doctor's whole concept of life is shaken, his whole previous existence is placed in question, thrown into confusion, into crisis. His confrontation with an antiworld is sudden and unexpected. It is true that it already existed as a world. But until now the unreflecting "hero," who had not yet come to himself, had been immersed in it as in a coexistent world. Now, for the first time, from one moment to the next, the coexistent world appears as an antiworld and does so with a merciless intensity that the country doctor (and the Kafka hero in general) cannot withstand. As an antiworld, it draws the country doctor into the process of confusion and, by exploiting his weaknesses and proving his failure, draws him also into the indictment, into the expulsion from human society, into its own earthly court of justice. At first, the "great dilemma" evoked by the ringing of the night bell does not seem to exceed the bounds of the usual and the imaginable. It is only through the later sequence of events that the first sentence, "I was in a great dilemma," acquires an ironic meaning, a deeper significance, which the doctor, who is experiencing the dilemma, has not perceived and which it is, in fact, not yet possible for him to perceive. Almost as we watch, the "great dilemma" acquires the characteristics of a fate that makes too great demands upon his freedom, that jeopardizes his existence, apparently without admitting a catharsis, and throws it into utmost confusion.

The country doctor lives in isolation from society. That is why he has to send the servant girl to find a horse: none of the villagers would have trusted him with one of theirs. Corresponding to his isolation from the village is his lack of contact in his own home. The "pretty girl" has lived "for years" in the doctor's house, but he has "hardly noticed" her. He is a bachelor not only in actuality, but by his own decision, or better, by his own evasion of any binding decision.[8] Professionally, he describes himself as being "employed by the district," as one who does his "duty to the limit . . . to the point where it becomes almost too much," as one who is "poorly paid," yet "generous and ready to help the poor"

(E 149f.); according to his own moral concepts, he is professionally above reproach. Yet even here his difficulty in establishing contact with other people is apparent. "It is easy to write prescriptions, but it is usually hard to get to understand people" (E 150). The difficulty lies with the people, too.

The Failure to Rescue Rosa

A strange "man" thrusts his way into the country doctor's bachelor (= unsociable) behavioral pattern and professional "dilemma." He "crawls" out of the "pigsty that has not been used for years," holds "two horses, enormous creatures with powerful flanks" (E 147), in readiness, removes the dilemma—and creates a new one. His designs on the girl are immediately evident. "The groom puts his arms around her and presses his face to hers. She screams and takes refuge with me . . . 'You beast,' I cry in fury, . . . but recollect at once . . . that he is helping me of his own free will where everyone else had failed" (E 147). Less aware of the girl than of the "fine team of horses" that can take him to his patient, the country doctor climbs in "happily." For an instant he had been aware of the danger that threatened the girl, but he reacts only to the "fine team of horses." He has not really come to terms with the dilemma-like danger; in the critical moment of decision, he sacrifices the initiative. His getting into the groom's carriage was an uncritical act. Afterwards it was too late and could no longer be "retrieved" (E 153). The girl realized at once the extent of the danger. She had the proper "presentiment." The country doctor became conscious of it only at her second scream. If the loan of the horses is linked to the loss of the girl, he "will renounce the trip." Easy to say, but impossible to execute. The horses whisk the carriage irresistibly away "like a log in the current" (E 148). Once he is in the carriage, the counterforce is too strong.

Even in the very first moment of surprise at the discovery of the groom and his horses, the girl had shown her keen presence of mind. More quickly than the doctor, she had found the *mot juste;* with her humorous, yet ambiguous, comment and its reference to her own person: "You never know what kind of thing you'll find ready at hand in your own house," she had encompassed the present situation so well that both the doctor and she had had to laugh. Despite the momentary rapport and her helpful interest (which is also characteristic of Fräulein Bürster in *The Trial*), and although the doctor-narrator includes her for the first time in a "we," he falls back at once into the impersonal "she" when he again speaks of the "girl." It is worthy of note that it is the groom, who has just made his appearance and whose attitude toward her is unequivocal, who first calls Rosa by name. Only when it is too late, only in his growing sense of irreparable loss, does the doctor-bachelor become aware of this "thou" of the opposite sex as potentially worthy of love, and of duty, omission, doom, and guilt in relation to her. At the very moment in which she might have been redeemed from a useful "thing" to an erotic "thou"—humanly speaking, not yet a total redemption, but here and now at least a first rescue[9]—he knows that she is the groom's "victim" (E 150, 153) and relegates her even more completely to the dominion of the subhuman. "The representative of life with whom you must come to terms," Kafka noted at the beginning of 1918, "is woman, or more exactly, perhaps, marriage" (H 118).

At the decisive moment, the doctor failed to cut through the fatal knot that bound the possibility of rendering medical assistance to his patient to the impossibility of rescuing Rosa. In his belated realization and hesitant decision is hidden—and with this we move into the realm of interpretation—a deeper cause: the split personality of the country doctor. The groom from the pigsty, the "unearthly horses," and the "earthly carriage" (E 153) symbolize the forces and total structure of the country doctor's existence. The groom signifies the lower drives, an "animal" sensuality; the unearthly horses signify the higher forces, or, more specifically, the call which the doctor has thus far not recognized and which is so opposed to his own will to live, namely, the call to contemplation of the wound and to an existence that leads out of the world. Both of these, the lower drives and the higher inclinations, dwell, meet, and struggle together in the one "earthly carriage"—the human vehicle of body and soul.

The Failure to Rescue the Boy

The doctor, arriving instantaneously at the patient's house, finds the boy at first "wasted, without fever, not cold, not warm, with vacant eyes." The patient, "without a shirt on," raises himself up under the feather coverlid and whispers in his ear, "Doctor, let me die" (E 148). The parents do not hear him. The doctor, intending to leave the boy to his own devices, wants to return to Rosa: "How can I rescue her?" (E 149). The family takes measures to prevent his departure. The sister, who has been taking care of the boy, removes the doctor's fur coat. "The old man claps me on the shoulder." "The mother stands at the bed and coaxes me to it." Unlike Gregor Samsa's parents (this is the positive side of Kafka's portrayal of his parents), they are concerned about the cure of their only son. The mother's coaxing is almost siren-like. The family lures the doctor against his will deeper and deeper into the fate of the sick boy, not suspecting that they are hindering another rescue. A second time the doctor attempts to take his leave. Then he sees the mother standing there "biting her lips and with her eyes full of tears, and the sister waving a blood-soaked towel"—the one disappointed, the other displaying the evidence of the wound that he has failed to notice. Once again, as when he was sitting in the carriage behind the groom's horses, he cannot escape. Was he unwilling or unable to see the wound because he was not supposed to see it? When it is expressly pointed out to him, he is "somehow ready to admit with reservations that the boy is perhaps sick after all." And now he discovers: "In his right side, near the hip, a wound the size of my palm has made its appearance." It is described as being "rose-red, in many shades, dark in the center, becoming lighter at the edges, somewhat granulated, with unevenly distributed blood clots, open to the daylight like a mine. So it appeared from a distance. When I drew nearer, a complication presented itself. Who could see such a thing without a soft whistle of amazement? Worms as long and strong as my little finger, rose-red themselves and spattered with blood besides, were held fast inside the wound and were wriggling with their white heads and many little legs toward the light" (E 151). The "rose-red" color of the wound is more than just a subliminal reference to the girl Rosa. For the wound and for Rosa, existence is both a state between the color of blood and the white that signifies innocence and a preordination of death. The narrator sheds light on every detail of the rose-red color, from the blood-dark center to the lighter edges of the wound, and to the white heads of the worms, which are themselves an indication of death. Despite the naturalistic details, this is not a naturalistic description. How can there be "worms as long and strong as my little finger" in a "wound the size of my palm"?

The wound is shown to the reader in a kind of enlargement. Not only is it observed psychologically; it is regarded symbolically as well. The narrator annotates its significance and importance in the course of the narrative itself. "Poor lad, no one can help you. I have discovered your great wound; you will die from this blossom in your side" (E 151). The boy's "great wound" is not to be classified either wholly or partially among the various kinds of bodily illnesses. Even its location is of a central and symbolical character. It is located "in his right side, near the hip." Similarly, in "Ein Bericht für eine Akademie" [A Report for an Academy], the shot by which the ape dressed as a man was captured wounded him "below the hip" (E 186). Whether this is a direct reference to the wound in the hip received by Jacob in his wrestling with God (Genesis 32:23ff.) and to the wound in Christ's side cannot be determined with certainty. It is more important to realize that the same central location in the human body that is singled out in the Bible is also singled out by Kafka, though in a secular way and under another aspect. The boy's "great wound" is the wound of his existence, the wound of birth and the wound unto death, as is made clear in the course of the narrative. The country doctor realizes at once that the people with their magic confidence in the doctor "demand the impossible of him." Without verbally expressing any causal relationship—the structure is paratactic, a typical procedure for Kafka, especially in this story—the narrator inserts a reflection that contains the explanation of his incompetence to treat the wound. "That is the way the people in my district are. Always demanding the impossible of the doctor. They've lost the old faith; the pastor sits at home and unravels his Mass vestments one by one, but the doctor is supposed to accomplish everything with his sensitive surgeon's hand" (E 151). The wound, then, extends into the religious dimension, into the world of the believing community and the pastor with sacramental function. But the pastor can achieve nothing more in this community. These people, because they have lost that dimension of their existence in which the "great wound" has meaning, are deceived as to the nature of the wound. The experienced doctor recognizes it, but is aware of his own incompetence to treat it. In their recourse to the doctor, these people who have lost their faith resort to both rationalistic flight and archaic magic. The family and the "elders of the village," who have arrived in the meantime, unclothe the doctor and put him into bed, not beside Rosa, but "beside the wound." The "school choir with their teacher leading them" (in the middle of the night!) sings the "new but erroneous song" (E 153):

> "Let's undress him, then he'll cure him,
> If he doesn't, then let's kill him!
> He's just a doctor, just a doctor" (E 152).

Just a doctor, not a pastor. The "new song" is an "erroneous" one because the doctor cannot help here and the superstitious expectation of the village rests upon a loss and a misconception that are not without guilt. The doctor, aware of his profane role, cannot prevent himself from being "misused for sacred purposes." But he has changed his attitude toward the helpless and deeply isolated patient, just as the patient has changed his attitude toward the doctor. Though the boy had at first begged with romantic longing to be allowed to die, he sobs after the discovery of the wound, "Will you save me?" And it is possible to detect a ballad-like brevity, irony, and alienation when, without transition, we are told in the briefest of phrases that the boy was "completely blinded by the life in his wounds" (E 151). The worms live; the life of death is blinding. But just as the doctor realizes the significance of the boy's wound, so the boy realizes the situation of the doctor who has been laid beside him. Through the boy's mouth there speak precisely that singular maturity and knowledge that are lacking in the adult "people" around him. He realizes the twofold helplessness of the doctor: his personal helplessness and his professional helplessness. "You know, I have little enough confidence in you. You've just been dropped off here somehow or other, you didn't come on your own feet. Instead of helping, you're crowding me on my deathbed." Now, too, his aggressiveness bursts forth: "What I'd like best is to scratch your eyes out" (E 152). The doctor understands the outburst. He tries to ward it off by protesting his incompetence.[10] "Right, it's a shame. Nevertheless I am a doctor. What am I supposed to do? Believe me, it's not easy for me either." It is a shame that he is there and is unable to help. He is a doctor who is supposed to heal somatic wounds, not a pastor, who would be competent in the present situation. The boy undersands the doctor's answer correctly as an "excuse," but this would have been impossible if he had been able to regard the doctor as medically competent. Now he, for his part, expresses the first and only explanation of the wound; realization is opposed to realization. "I came into the world with a fine wound; that was my only endowment." The existence-wound reveals itself as a birth-wound, the birth-wound as a death-wound. The experienced doctor can offer the troubled boy no more than his "better perspective," can do no more than attempt to give mediocre comfort through mediocre classification and rationalization. "Your wound is not so bad. Done at an acute angle with two strokes of the ax. Many offer their sides and hardly hear the ax in the forest, let alone having it come nearer" (E 152). The "two strokes" and the "ax in the forest" refer in all probability to the human act of procreation (ax = penis). It is the parents who engender the wound and with it death. The "wound is not so bad," partly because the one who bears it is not guilty of it and partly because it makes the sensitive youth more perceptive in regard to death. He received the wound at his entrance into the world and experiences it as given before and with his own free decision. It prepares him for his exit from this world. Again with ballad-like brevity and understatement, the narrator announces the boy's death in the unlikely little sentence: "And he took it" (i.e., the doctor's "word of honor" as to the meaning of the wound) "and became still" (E 153).

Just as the groom from the pigsty represents, on closer observation, a part of the country doctor's ego, so the boy afflicted with the wound symbolizes another aspect of his existence, namely, the innocent "I," wounded from birth, basically in need of care, and foreordained to death. The innocent "I" and the suffering though innocent "I."

The Prevented Rescue of the Country Doctor

The country doctor neglected to rescue Rosa and was thereupon compelled to "sacrifice" her as a "victim." It is not his task to attempt the rescue of the faithless "people." With a single exception ("Josephine the Singer"), the need for positive activity on behalf of a larger social community never occurs to any of Kafka's heroes. They are and remain I-figures, exclusively concerned with the threatened and hopeless state of their own existence. When his attempt at rescue fails and becomes impossible, the country doctor turns his attention to his own person. "But now it was time to think of my own rescue," he says to himself after the boy's death. What can he mean? Answer: the recovery of his "house," his "bed," his "flourishing practice" (E 153).

Rescue means first of all the return home. His departure, as it were in full flight, is described as follows: "Clothes, fur coat, and bag were quickly collected; I didn't want to take time to dress." As means for the return journey, the (only apparently) "obedient" horses present themselves. "If the horses went as fast as they did on the way here, I would, in a sense, just spring from this bed [that of the boy who has died] into my own." But the magic formula which the country doctor remembers and uses correctly produces the opposite effect. "Gee up!" (E 148), the "disgusting groom" had said. And the horses had sprung forward with the carriage. " 'Gee up!' I said, but they didn't spring forward; we crept slowly, like old men, through the wastes of the snow . . . I'll never get home this way" (E 153). On the trip to the patient's house, time and place were almost completely as one; on the return trip, they expand and become endless, goalless. From the empirical point of view, they seem alienated; from the narrative point of view, they are expressionistic, that is, they are used purely as means of expression. They are present exactly as they are experienced by the subjective consciousness of the

163

"hero" and as the narrator needs them in order to render the hero's inner experience visible. As such, they are no longer presented materially and as ordering the event, no longer as greatness contained independently in itself (as in all epic works until the end of the nineteenth century), but only functionally. If the arrival happens suddenly, time and space coincide. If it is indefinitely delayed, the details of time and place seem not so much quantitatively prolonged as qualitatively changed. Movement in "Ein Landarzt" is retarded; it leads neither to the next nor to the wrong village, but into the wastes of snow. Time and place cease to exist as purposeful details. The mysteriously ready horses reveal themselves as instruments of doom. It avails the country doctor not at all that he has answered the ringing of the night bell. This world challenges him and, in doing so, proves to him the impossibility of standing the test, of succeeding, of making himself at home in it. The doctor not only gains nothing. He even loses what he had. "I'll never get home this way; my flourishing practice is lost; a successor is robbing me" (i.e., of his practice). At the end, he is robbed of his last share in an existence linked to community and possessed of earthly meaning. A last intensive metaphor reveals the objective state at which he has arrived. "An old man, naked, exposed to the frost of this most unhappy age, I wander about. My fur coat hangs behind in the carriage, but I can't reach it, and not one of my agile crowd of patients will lift a finger" (E 153). This is like a passive variation of the myths of Prometheus and Sisyphus, the Kafkaesque version of existence. The cunning and the physical strength of the "heroes" in the two myths are lacking here, it is true, as are the great rebelliousness of Prometheus and the will to achieve of Sisyphus. But the hopeless subjection, not to the rock, but to the "earthly carriage," and the uselessness proper to it seem to have been retained from the original metaphor. The purposeful onset of human activity ends in total frustration and in the grotesqueness depicted here, which is a revelation of Kafka's basic experience of life, the artistically organized "proof that it is impossible to live," as the second part of the early story "Description of a Struggle" is entitled. Even the level of existence that the country doctor had achieved before the beginning of his ordeal is taken from him by fatal powers. Not one of his "agile patients" lifts "a finger" for the harassed doctor. The friendly powers of earth are completely absent. Fatal forces expel him from his home and his profession. Not expulsion from Paradise (on which Kafka had so frequently meditated), but expulsion from a minimal earthly existence that was sufficiently tenuous to begin with.

Expressionistic and Symbolic Character of the Metaphors

Time, place, course of events, and imagery reveal their expressionistic character. "Winter" is not intended as a specific season of the year. The description hardly touches upon the natural scene but refers instead to unprotected, exposed space. In the course of the story, the "icy winter" (E 146) logically becomes "endless winter" (E 150), the "snowdrifts" become "wastes of snow" (E 153). "Night" is set into the imaginary atmosphere of "moonlight" (E 148). The country doctor, whose age is indeterminate at the beginning of the story, becomes an "old man" (E 153). Nearly all the metaphors are meaningful. Nakedness, emphasized by being made a leitmotif, has from the beginning, and throughout the process of unclothing, a meaning relevant to existence: incapacitation, exposure, creatureliness thrown back upon itself (the boy) and repulsed (the country doctor); lonely poverty; preparation for death. The "bed" in which the boy lies and into which they put the doctor is a significant place in Kafka's stories. Generally speaking, it is the place of dreaming and awakening, the place of union and rejection by a woman, the place of metamorphosis and the revelation of ultimate truth, even the place of judgment (cf. "Die Verwandlung," "In der Strafkolonie," and the diaries). It is not without irony that the country doctor must share the bed, not with Rosa but with a dying person. From the fact that he never returns to his "bed," he learns symbolically an ultimate truth: this earth has no further place for me.

Groom, horses, carriage,[11] boy, and wound, the figure of the country doctor himself—all these have a symbolic as well as an expressionistic character. The groom from the pigsty symbolizes the lower, basely sensual drives. The "unearthly horses" stand, in the structure of "Ein Landarzt," for the higher powers of man that are directed toward spirit and death. The boy who is doomed to die reflects the innocent "I." The wound in his side represents the wound of existence. In the letters and diaries of that same year (1917), Kafka refers explicitly to the "symbolic" character of the wound in "Ein Landarzt" (B 160f., T 529).

If one prescinds from their alienating effect, Kafka's images say both more and less than does the classical symbol. Less, because the level of imagery is not pure; it does not exist as a self-contained order that, in a broad sense, signifies primarily itself and establishes an a priori order in the narrative action. More, because the referential character of the imagery is stronger, and its expressionistic character, its symbolic nature, its system of metaphors were intended from the beginning, Kafka's images are more interior, more spiritual, but also more explicitly intended, closer to actual existence, and, even at their first appearance, subjective, metaphorical, fragmentary, dissonant, grotesque.

Doomed Existence

At first glance, the question of guilt seems not to have been so explicitly stated in this story as in "Das Urteil," "In der Strafkolonie," or the novel *Der Prozess*. The country doctor stands before no humanly visible, authoritative court of justice. The leading character is neither exposed by an express complaint nor condemned by a public statement of his guilt. The complaint seems rather to have been reversed: the country doctor makes explicit complaint; Rosa and the boy make implicit complaints. Rosa complains against the "inexorableness of her fate" (E 148); the boy, against his birth-wound (E 152). All the complaints of the main characters are directed toward the forces of life that prevent a meaningful earthly existence and ordain birth, fate, and death.

It cannot be denied that a latent feeling of guilt is recognizable in the person of the country doctor. Even his attempt to justify his professional existence by the statement that he does his "duty to the limit, even to the point where it becomes almost too much"

(E 149) is an indication of his latent guilt. He has no desire to be a "world reformer"; he simply wants to live himself. But this is basically impossible. To the extent that the country doctor reflects upon himself, he projects his guilt onto others. It falls upon that "agile crowd of patients," those people who have lost their faith and "demand the impossible of the doctor" (E 151). The "new but erroneous song" (E 153) shows the whole village as guilty. The *new* consists in the rationalistic view that the doctor can and must "accomplish everything"; the *error*, in precisely this view, which has emancipated itself from the "old faith" (E 151). The narrator refers the people to the larger background "of this most unhappy age." The people incur guilt toward both the doctor and the dying boy. For the boy, they fail to do what is right. For the doctor in his new helplessness, they do not "lift a finger." The boy's parents, it is true, are guilty in a different way and from the beginning, not in a moral sense, but in a sense that conditions his very existence. If our interpretation of the wound made by the "two blows" at birth is correct, then they account for the wound of existence. But are they also responsible for it? Or have they merely done what they were obliged to do? The question is not answered in the story.

Not only the unfortunate people and parents of this age but also the other forces that exert an influence on the country doctor are responsible for his fate. The groom from the pigsty and the "unearthly horses," these two irreconcilable and diametrically opposed forces, prevent the rescue of Rosa and wreak havoc in the doctor's own existence. He attributes the superiority of their powers to the "gods" (E 149; cf. T 546). The gods "help"; they "send the needed horse, add a second because of the urgency, and, to crown it all, donate the groom too" (E 149). But their help is an ironic help, an ambiguous help that exploits his need. Not only do they use their groom to prepare the "inexorableness of her fate" (E 149) for Rosa, but, with their "uncontrollable horses" (E 149), they prepare a fate for the country doctor as well. It is true that the doctor's verdict of guilt against the gods and his exoneration of himself are accomplished not with a pure conscience but "blasphemously." It is true that he accepted the "fine team of horses" from the groom and, despite his initially clear insight into the meaning of the situation, climbed thought-lessly and "happily" into the carriage and let himself be led astray by temptation. It is true that, in a moment of "thought" (E 149), of reflection, he disavowed his own causative role in Rosa's fate and his own. But actually there is, after his first nondecision and false decision, no further hope for him. Fate takes its course. Whatever "superior" awareness he possesses and whatever he en-dures or accomplishes thereafter in the exercise of his profession "is of no help to him" (E 152) once the horses and the people have had their way with him. It is, to be sure, of some help to the boy that the doctor can offer him his "better perspective," his diagnosis of the wound. But, except for that one instance, the doctor's immunity from the superior forces that surround him is partially hindered, partially rendered ineffectual, partially turned into its opposite. It is true that the disturbing summons of the night bell makes him aware of his inadequate contact with his fellow beings. But the forces that are at work upon him do not help him. They show themselves merciless and send him his fate. They make him aware of the deficiencies of his existence, but they hold him fast to his destiny even after insight has gripped him, and they do not permit that insight to issue in the deed that will make him free. Rather, they drive him from the position that he has already attained by depriving him of house and practice. The powers of the "gods" play their cat-and-mouse game with him.[12] It seems scarcely just that they punish him.

In the end, the country doctor emerges as plaintiff and judge of just such a foreordained fate: "Deceived! Deceived! Once you have answered the false alarm of the night bell—it can never be made good again." People, groom, horses, and gods have deceived him. The people have summoned him "falsely" with the night bell. He was not competent to treat this wound. The groom and horses have deceived him (and Rosa) because he could not overcome such extreme and powerful forces. The situation introduced by the "false alarm" has gone amiss and is hopelessly doomed; it is a fatal situation, never to be remedied: the hideous face of absurdity. It is a situation in which it is not humanly possible for a person to be self-determined and freely in control of himself, a situation in which nothing is possible but an earthly existence that is completely doomed from within, from without, and from above.[13]

The Landarzt-Pattern and Kafka's Own Existence

In September, 1917, in the very year in which he wrote "Ein Landarzt," Kafka's tuberculosis of the lungs made its appearance. He coughed blood. It is astonishing to what a degree Kafka has indicated his own sickness and existence by means of the *Landarzt*-pattern and the *Landarzt*-wound. The anxious dream and its construction seem to have had a prophetic character. The "wound," it is true, no longer appears in a figure of pure innocence, as in the case of the young patient. Rather it has been enlarged to include the whole personal existence of an adult who is an outcast from the bourgeois world. After the outbreak of his illness, Kafka wrote to his friend Max Brod: "But I am not complaining. I had predicted it myself. Do you remember the bloody wound in 'Ein Landarzt'?" (B 160). Some days later, he again spoke to Brod of the "wound, of which the lung-wound is only a symbol." From the perspective of the boy in "Ein Landarzt," he complains about the lack of "understanding for such things [that is, for "inner concerns"], because there is no better perspective. . . . I am always searching for an explanation of sickness, for I have not yet been able to track it down." He referred then to the possible resolution of the "misery" through "women" (B 161). Perhaps on the same day, September 15, he addressed himself in the diary: "If the lung-wound is only a symbol, as you claim, a symbol of the wound whose inflammation is called F(elice) and whose depth is justification, if this is so, then the doctor's suggestions (light, air, sun, rest) are also symbols. Grasp this symbol" (T 529). In the following month, he informed Brod: "I have come to the opinion that tuberculosis, as I have it, is not a particular illness, not an illness deserving of a particular name, but only an intensification of the general seed of death, whose significance cannot at present be estimated" (B 177). Kafka understood his own wound psychosomatically as encompassing his whole existence, inescapably and personally. In it lurked the "father's curse" [14] and the inadequacy of his own attitude toward his family (inadequate from birth) and toward Felice and his bourgeois calling; in it lurked the "general seed of death," the half-suppressed awareness of guilt and the awareness of innocence, the hopelessness, the impossibility of getting along in this world, the question as to the "justification" of his whole human existence. Like the country doctor, he cannot reconcile the claims of the woman ("Felice"), of the "people" who have lost their faith, and of his own profession among people. And in this failure to find a means of reconciliation he encounters—like the country doctor against his own will—the "great wound," for which there is no healing in the here and now; he encounters the tragic call to death.

On the basis of Kafka's notes, it must be mentioned that the wound as birth-wound contains a reference to the doom of original sin. "Original sin," he notes in 1920, "the old injustice that man has committed, consists in the reproach that man makes and does not cease to make that an injustice has been done him, that an original sin has been committed against him" (BK 295f.). It was committed even against the parents who "engendered" the wound (E 152). Therefore justification extends beyond the freedom and the potentiality of the individual. "The situation in which we find ourselves is sinful independently of any guilt" (H 48), that is, of personally incurred guilt.

The perception of the "great wound" drives the sensitive person out of the world of "people" with all their self-deception and loss of faith. This results necessarily in homelessness, nonarrival, displacement, and flight from such a world. From this point of view, there lurks in the "doom" pattern of "Ein Landarzt" an irony of irony and a sense of the absurd. We recognize objective irony in the "help" rendered by the horses. And yet, by compelling the country doctor to contemplate the "great wound" and by leading him out into the "wasteland," they do confer a boon on him. After the disillusioning struggle, there comes the true realization that, in the world of "people" and "of this most unhappy age," there is no place for him. The loss of all his earthly possessions shatters his existence; he becomes a modern secularized (psychologically, sociologically, pathologically, and existentially conditioned) Job-figure. And yet, he *has* gained something from all his loss; he has gained the disillusion and resignation of the "old man" in his attitude toward antinomy; he has gained the ability to be himself in truth and to be human in desolation. In the autobiographical notes for "Er" [He] in 1920 Kafka observes: "He wants no consolation, but not because he does not want it—who would not want it?—but because to seek for consolation means: . . . to live on the edge of his existence, almost outside it" (BK 296).

In the reflections in his diary, Kafka tried to understand his own existence under the double aspect of the boy foreordained to death and of the country doctor who both flees from and wants to flee from death. Eventually, the two coincide, for they lead to the border line of the earthly. Like the boy, Kafka is aware not only of protesting against the wound, but also of yielding to it, of becoming still. Toward the end of September, 1917, after the outbreak of his illness, he makes the entry: "I would, then, entrust myself to death. Remnant of faith" (T 534).

An autobiographical note that further interprets the fate of the country doctor who wanders around the world of men and never arrives at a destination reads as follows: "This search takes its direction from mankind. The loneliness that for a long time has, to a large extent, been forced upon me, though it was partly sought by me—but what was that either, if not compulsion?—is now becoming quite unambiguous and extreme. Whither does it lead? It can—and this seems most compulsive—lead to madness, about which nothing more can be said; the search pierces me and rends me. Or I can perhaps—I can?—if only in the smallest measure, hold myself up and let myself be borne along by the search. Where would I arrive then? 'Search' is really only a symbol: I could just as well say 'assault on the last earthly barriers,' and, in fact, an assault from below, from man; and I can, since even this is only a symbol, replace it by the symbol of an assault coming down upon me from above. This whole literature is an assault against barriers" (T 552, 1922).

For Kafka, the story of "Ein Landarzt" meant a growing awareness of his own antinomies; it meant presentiment, conjuration, determination, and defense in the face of a doomed existence; it meant an assault—not yet against the last barriers of the earthly, but against banishment to these barriers. For Kafka, what the boy and the country doctor had to face separately have been united. He faces "two opponents: the first (this is the opponent of the sick boy) oppresses him from behind, from his point of origin," from birth. "The second (the opponent of the doctor-ego) obstructs his road from in front. He struggles with both." But "it is not a question of just these two opponents, but also of himself" (BK 300). The antinomian experiences of hostile forces cannot be reconciled in the *Landarzt*-narrative. An existence of this nature is driven out of the circle of mankind. All three "rescues" have their goals within the confines of earth and, as such, are doomed to failure. And this failure that lies totally within the confines of earth has a tragic character. The possibility of a painfully lonely existence on the edge of the world seems to be indicated in the narrative, a call to death seems to have been uttered there. "Ein Landarzt" contains, as its literary pattern, the basic experience that is typically Kafka's. The diaries have reflected further upon this basic experience. Existence within the barriers of earth, revealed as beyond hope of redemption, realizes its abandonment, seeks rescue in an assault on the barriers of earth, fastens upon an "indestructible hope" (cf. H 47), and schemes to surmount its barriers.

8

Skeletons of the Sayable—
Demonstrations of a World
On the Verse-Texts of
Helmut Heissenbüttel

Beda Allemann, the Swiss literary historian, would find it "very distressing if there were no Heissenbüttel." He finds, "in the field of power" of Heissenbüttel's language, "elementary lines," a new "constructivity." Georg Böse singles out Heissenbüttel's "transgression of the bounds of the endurable." "Montage effects," ". . . increases considerably our power of perception," "poetological experiments," "uninhibited speech" with an "admixture of self-torment"—these are some comments by the critic Karl August Horst. "Neatly done," concedes Dieter Hasselblatt; then he proceeds to object, "interesting but without intrinsic worth," "ordinary stuff, not style." "The destruction of the word, the dissection into syllables, and the path to letterism were not first attempted by Franz Mon," grumbles the elderly Erich von Kahler, but "by Heissenbüttel." "In his *Textbooks*, Heissenbüttel exposes the language to tensile tests," the much younger Heinrich Vormweg counters with approval. Horst Bienek, another of the younger critics, declares flatly, "It is really nothing but intellectual Pop Art; instead of empty jam jars, he pastes on words." Karl Schwedholm—a writer-critic of the middle generation, who, as director of the literature department of the Stuttgart Radio Station, may well be on friendly terms with writer Heissenbüttel, who is director of the department of radio essays in the same station—sees in Heissenbüttel's verse-texts "the formation of structures with a strict formal logic"—and this despite a "certain tendency toward the technical manipulation of language. Operative here is an extreme seriousness of purpose that does not seek an easy course, does not resort to intuition as an explanation, and leaves nothing to whim or chance." We will not ask whether anyone who has written verses with any degree of understanding has ever taken the easy course or left anything to whim or chance. Jürgen Becker, in his early years a disciple of Heissenbüttel's, is of the opinion that today's literature is concerned with "satisfying the subjective longing for understanding and bringing light to the troubled consciousness. This is Heissenbüttel's message." "The changed experiences of contemporary reality form the basis of his literary style." Is Heissenbüttel, then, a secular Messiah? Kurt Leonhard, a connoisseur of contemporary lyric—Heissenbüttel honored him with the dedication of "Pamphlet IX"—believes it possible to observe, on the stylistic level at which Heissenbüttel has arrived, "no more metaphors, no images; or, at least, the images and metaphorical mode of expression disappear more completely from his work with every book he publishes." Peter Hamm, lyricist and editor of an anthology of lyrics by the younger generation, includes Heissenbüttel among those "builders of constellations, combinations, topographies, etc.," whose "texts are alienated from the real, including also the verbal, milieu." "The absolutizing of language, as can be gathered from the theoretical utterances of Heissenbüttel, Bremer, Mon, Gomringer, Kriwet, etc., originated in and corresponded exactly to the general ability to communicate within the late bourgeois community. The world, which has become abstract, appears simultaneously in these texts as a shadow-play that has subsumed even structurally the disconnected appearance of reality . . . But purposely distorted syntax and reduction produced no alternatives; rather they led ever deeper into the dead-end street." These catchwords and evaluations have been garnered from the critics.[1] They indicate a broad range of interest, from approval through reservation to a harsh "no." Anyone who approaches these texts will do well to keep his reactions in check until he has familiarized himself with the subject.

What speaks to us out of Heissenbüttel's verse-texts? Intensified awareness? Hermetic depth of meaning? Partial meaning? Lack of meaning? And if lack of meaning, is it to be blamed on the author or on the world that he describes? Or perhaps on both? Reduced reality and reduced awareness? Contracted meaning and contracted form in a complicated involution of necessity and non-necessity? Heissenbüttel does not call his verse-structures poems, but "texts." His *Textbooks* also contain compositions in compact prose, but we shall discuss only the verses. The word "text" has a completely neutral meaning. It prevents the application of already existing expectations and categories of lyric (as well as of epic), detaches itself from tradition, and extends the boundaries of the genre. Let us subject ourselves to the "exercises" required by the critics and by Heissenbüttel himself in order to sample some of the texts and perhaps, eventually, gain the necessary vantage ground for evaluating them.

Saying the Sayable

"The right method of philosophy would really be this: to say nothing but what can be said," stated Ludwig Wittgenstein at the end of his *Tractatus logico-philosophicus* (Proposition 6.53), which was completed in 1918, not printed until 1921, and rediscovered in the 1950s by some German writers on the search for new objectivity and logic. In the introduction, Wittgenstein wrote: "It would be possible to summarize the whole meaning of the book in somewhat the following words: What can be said at all, can be said clearly; and one should keep silent about what he can't talk about" (cf. Proposition 4.116 and Proposition 7). "Today's poets," wrote Kurt Leonhard in 1963, "make their appeal to Wittgenstein: 'The limits of my speech are the limits of my world.'" [2] Wittgenstein's propositions find a literary echo in Heissenbüttel's works, too. He has developed in a logical sequence Wittgenstein's basic proposition about the sayable:

> say the sayable
> experience the experienceable
> decide the decidable

attain the attainable
repeat the repeatable
end the endable

the not sayable
the not experienceable
the not decidable
the not attainable
the not repeatable
the not endable

not end the not endable[3]

That is logical. It is clear. It is rigidly constructed. Two parallel strophes are presented: the first is formulated positively, the second negatively. Except for the negation and the shortening, nothing in the first strophe—neither the choice and sequence of words nor the sequence of ideas—has been altered in the second. The negation, "One should keep silent about what he can't talk about," already stands as the final proposition in Wittgenstein's tract. Previously it had been said of philosophy: "It shall set limits to what can be thought and thereby to what cannot be thought. It shall set limits from within to what cannot be thought by means of what can be thought. It will interpret what cannot be said by presenting with clarity what can be said" (Proposition 4.114 and 4.115). Thus basic words of Heissenbüttel's text: "the sayable" and the "unsayable," are already found in Wittgenstein. From the linguistic point of view, it is noticeable that the subject and the finite verb are missing in the first strophe, and that even the infinitive predicate is missing in the second. At the end of each line, the reader expects this predicate, but the author withholds it beyond the end of the strophe. It appears at last in an isolated line at the end of the poem, thus opposing resistance, tension, and a surprising climax to the smooth flow of verse and expectation in the second strophe.

Each verse in the first strophe presents an object and, by means of a *figura etymologica*, a part of the predicate. Who is the subject of these sentences? And what mode or expression is being used here? Indicative? Subjunctive? Imperative? The reader who is perturbed by the apparent attempt to mystify will perhaps remember that he is surfeited in his daily life by just this kind of abbreviated sentence structure: "Right turn," "Yield," "No Smoking"—these are only some of the directives in our highly organized society.[4] Although they are abbreviated, the statements are unambiguous. No one inquires as to the grammatically omitted subject or the missing *verbum finitum*. Who is meant? Everyone. What is the auxiliary verb that belongs to the infinitive? "Must" or "may not." In the Decalogue, Everyman is called "thou"; "must" and "may not" become "thou shalt" and "thou shalt not." Whether or not we expand the lines of Heissenbüttel's text to read "Everyone must (shall) say the sayable" or "Thou shalt say the sayable," it makes no difference. Each line is both an apostrophe and an imperative of the author to himself and of the author to the reader. Whereas the first strophe requires only a slight productive increase, the second is more difficult. Should one expand it to read:

> not say the not sayable
> not experience the not experienceable
> not decide the not decidable(etc.)

or:

> not end the not sayable
> not end the not experienceable
> not end the not decidable (etc.)?[5]

The first possibility is suggested by the formal parallelism of the first and second strophes, the second by the isolated last verse (*"das nicht Beendbare nicht beenden"*) in conjunction with the preceding strophe (which is in need of an infinitive-imperative). The author must have seen and wanted this ambiguity. An analysis of the text leaves both possibilities open. Therefore, both must have been intended. What is thus created is an artistic involution, a play on words on two levels. Even on the first level, one must ask: ought, may, or can one not say the not sayable, not experience the not experienceable? Is one not supposed to say the not sayable because one cannot say it? But if one cannot say it, one may not act as if one could say it. Even on this level, it is a game with many balls. A further question presents itself: whether the not sayable is absolute, that is, not sayable under any circumstances or at any time, or if it is only relative, that is for now and under these circumstances for this person. Then there is the second possibility: *not end the not sayable*, for its present nonsayability could become a later sayability. In other words: the boundaries of the sayable might be extended. That one ought to say the sayable and not end the not endable—that is unambiguous. The ambiguity lies in what one must and can do with regard to the not sayable. From this ambiguity, the text derives tension, compactness, and a certain enigmatic quality. Either the sayable is not sayable at all—or it is sayable at a later time. In no event ought one to act as if it were here and now sayable. In the second instance, one ought not to be content with nonsayability, but should strive to realize the potentialities of the sayable.

A series of statements formulated in this way about the imperatives of human activity can be accepted by a Jew, a Marxist, a Christian, an atheist, a scientist, a man in the street, a poet. No attempt has been made to say what is experienceable, what is decidable, what is attainable either now or later. Each one is free to interpret the *what* in his own way. The text has reference, then, to no specific content. It is a purely formal program, a formal literary credo. As such, it gives access to all texts. We may inquire what these texts reveal as sayable, not sayable, not now sayable, as experienceable, repeatable, not endable, and so on.

Simple Sentences

A year earlier, in 1953, Heissenbüttel had written the text "Einfache Sätze" [Simple Sentences]. It was first published in *Kombinationen* [Combinations] and is now the first poem in *Textbook 1*:

> simple sentences
> as I stand my shadow falls before me
> morning sun sketches the first design
> blossoming is a deadly business
> I have given my consent
> I live[6]

This is not just a formally logical program, but a confession with content, the explanation of a fundamental consent,[7] and an insight that might be designated the modern author's parallel to Descartes' "cogito, ergo sum."

The first line of the text is its title. The following lines, each of which is a sentence, are simple sentences in both form and content. The text comprises three thought units that correspond to the strophes of a traditional poem; the first two lines contain an observation and a statement of fact; the middle one, an aphorism; the last two, a confession. The text begins with an action, a happening. The remaining statements summarize the comprehension that comes from individual observations and facts. The speaking "I" has its place from the beginning within the action. Where it stands, how long it has been standing, if it has just stood up, how it feels—all this is left unsaid and is clearly not important. The degree of abstraction and the reduction of the text have left such details behind. The shadow cast by the morning sun is that of the speaking "I." It makes the "I" aware of its own existence. The sun outlines for man his own body. The casting of the shadow is designated as sketching, the shadow itself as a design; thus the business of outlining is compared with the process of artistic creation and is clearly in a special relationship to the "I" of the text. The next line with its aphoristic statement, "blossoming is a deadly business," does not proceed directly from what has been said. The intermediate steps of individual observations and experiences that led to this sentence are not named, nor is the relationship of the sun to life mentioned in detail.

Despite the abstraction, reduction, and paratactic structure of the lines, the text incorporates a causal relationship: sun-life-blossoming. The description of the sun's activity as "business" may prove alienating. But the German word *Geschäft* [business] is etymologically related to both *schaffen* [to create] and *Schöpfung* [creation]. Schiller had used the word in his youthful ode "An die Sonne" [To the Sun]: "Sie aber bleibt in der Höhe . . . und erfüllet ihr grosses Geschäft, erleuchtet die Sphären" [But she (the sun) remains in the heavens . . . and does her great business, illuminates the spheres]. Unexpectedly, Heissenbüttel's word is one of the linguistic properties of classicism. Many a man has already rebelled against this monstrous business of death. But— and this is not without its element of surprise—the "I" of the text does not protest, but rather announces his consent, or, more exactly, his consent already given (in the past), to the way life is, that is, to death. This is done without rhetoric, without pathos, without revelation of feeling with regard to the repeated stock experiences of this deadly business. The final sentence, "I live," is formal, and of a simplicity that could hardly be surpassed. Even rhythmically, the line is clearly a conclusion. The cool, unemotional processes of perception and thought come to rest. Such a concluding verse would be unthinkable in a classical poem. But it reveals the changed content of the modern author's awareness, a new Cartesian caesura. Life is no longer a thing to be understood automatically. It must be expressly recognized—and accepted. For many readers, the predominating element in the literature that has appeared since 1945 seems to be the "no" of its authors. Yet closer observation of this literature discovers everywhere the signs and forms of consent. Thus, for example, the narrator in Max Frisch's novel *Mein Name sei Gantenbein* confesses unexpectedly at the end of his tragicomic marriage fictions, "I like life." Face to face with the "deadly business," both Frisch and Heissenbüttel react with wonder and assent.

Heissenbüttel's text elicits a variety of emotional reactions. One reader in the *Frankfurter Allgemeine Zeitung* reacted as follows: "In this niggardly curtailment the structure is incapable of enkindling sensual impressions that can awaken the emotions or of inducing complex insights . . . The linguistic construct lacks not only that playful lightness and grace that charm the senses, but also, despite its pretentious posturing, any substance worthy of note." And the reason? "Wherever this substance cannot be encompassed in a stimulating word, it is lacking." The older reader and critic, with his classical and romantic norms, will, perhaps, make little sense of this difficult intellectual text. The final sentence in the review just cited is a case in point: "I cannot call a poem like the one quoted either bad or good; it seems trivial and superfluous." [8] Undoubtedly, the text is neither trivial nor superfluous. This rejection had, in fact, been preceded by an enthusiastic eulogy of the poem by a member of the younger generation of writers, Gert Kalow. In his interpretation, the verses are made to bear the weight of the recent carnage during World War II: " 'As

I stand, my shadow falls before me': that is 1945; the darkness falls away like a black cloak, becomes a shadow, but in doing so it determines the *I*; the end of tyranny comes like the morning sun, but freedom is not hailed with jubilation; it is recognized as a burdensome challenge," for "blossoming is a deadly business." [9]

The text "say the sayable" was a formal program. The "Simple Sentences" were programmatic in content as well. Behind such sentences, there is no longer a consistent philosophy of the world, a traditional and preordained manner of contemplation, an obvious division into cosmos and world. In the text "Pamphlets VI," written in the following year (1945), the simple affirmation is made:

> I give my consent
> I do not give my consent
> I say the truth
> I do not say the truth [10]

The statements are placed in contradiction to one another without any attempt to show a higher synthesis. This is irritating. It is provoking. But we should not immediately be on our guard against it. It is true that the text does not say to whom or to what the "I" has given and has not given its consent. Judging from the context of the "Pamphlets," there is no reference to a basic consent to life, but only to a consent to the forms and facts of public life. At one time, the "I" agrees; at another time, it does not. Both reactions meet in the same person, and he may well wonder at it. Indeed, even a this-as-well-as-that is conceivable, an ambivalent attitude, a partly-this-partly-that. This is especially true of the following sentences: "I say the truth / I do not say the truth." One might think of Luther's *simul iustus et peccator* as comparable to this this-as-well-as-that, though Luther made the conditions clear under which the one or other side of human existence would be valid. Heissenbüttel does not do this. Not only does his text come closer, in this way, to pamphleteering provocation, but it becomes more broadly meshed, more inexact. In writing thus, he makes it easier for himself, but harder for the reader. Perhaps this kind of antithetical writing and ambivalent attitude was inspired by Wittgenstein's later philosophy. In the *Tractatus logico-philosophicus*, he was still saying: "The proposition must establish reality upon a firm 'yes' or 'no' " (Proposition 4.023), and he was still representing a "kind of absolute categoricity." Later he posited a "constant dialectic between thesis and antithesis." [11]

Without doubt there lurked behind Heissenbüttel's "Pamphlets" and pamphlet-like texts a typically modern form of criticism and scepticism. Robert Musil had given it its most exemplary expression in *Der Mann ohne Eigenschaften* [The Man without Qualities]. It is not by accident that Musil is allowed a word in Heissenbüttel's "Pamphlets III" (a seven-line text with seven quotations from seven authors): "Attitude: that of a man who is not in agreement with himself." In Musil's work, there emerge the hydra heads of an intellect that crosses the threshold of criticism in the direction of total criticism. But it is an intellect that, for all its mathematical logicity and sagacity, does not see that it is incapable of communication, of turning to a "thou," and of a small, modest, creative act of love; an intellect that itself produces a pathological character. No reconciliation is possible with comic and compromising man. The ability to forgive is lacking. Traits of a total criticism reveal themselves in the whole direction of Heissenbüttel's texts. They live on criticism and suffer from it.

Topographies

There are no "simple sentences" in this group of texts. The vocabulary is more difficult, the breaks in the thought sequence are greater, the involution of interior and exterior elements has become more complicated. The combination of image, metaphor, and concept, of name, quotation, and description creates a unique kind of text. Whoever comes to this textual structure from the traditional poem finds it strange. The combination of quotation, image, and thought, including the use of foreign words, was already to be found, it is true, in the works of Ezra Pound and T.S. Eliot. But in German-speaking countries, the text gave voice, at the time of its inauguration, to something quite new in form and content. "Topography, Greek: description of a place; locality; hence, pertaining to a country and its individual regions and places," the author quotes from Brockhaus; and he prefixes this information, not without irony, to his text, which appeared for the first time in 1956, in a volume of the same name. Later, because of its exemplary description of a locality and of an awareness of locality, it was included in *Textbook 1*. We are familiar with topographies from geography—today, for the most part, from Merian's prints. In the literary realm, there have been poems about landscapes and cities. The latter were popular during the Renaissance and among the Humanists, especially since praise bestowed upon a city was appropriately rewarded by the city fathers. There have been landscape poems of a descriptive nature in nearly every European language. They were either pure nature poems or poems of nature and mood. We might recall, for instance, Goethe's "Ilmenau," Eichendorff's "In Danzig," or "Wer hat dich, du schöner Wald." In his "Lament of a Devastated Germany," from the time of the Thirty Years War, Gryphius offered a topography that already extended far beyond any purely representational descriptions of cities or nature. At the beginning of the present century, the Expressionists supplanted nature with their poems about cities. These were no longer poems in praise of the city, like those of the Renaissance; they were poems of protest, curses, revelations of the hostile and daemonic forces in a modern metropolis (as, for example, in the poems of Georg Heym, Johannes R. Becher, Alfred Wolfenstein, Jakob van Hoddis). What wonder, then, that the genre has recently undergone a new change? Did not T.S. Eliot lead the way here, too, with *The Waste Land* (1922)?

Topographies

a

breathless the birds of world history traverse
   the defenseless terrain
the irreparable shocks skin without shame losses
Big Sid Catlett Art Tatum Fats Navarro
reminiscence about the subterranean space of my own landscape
for I a novel by Gustav Freytag
isolated white patches wandering quickly
   over the visible contour
a white gull frees itself from the profile of one in flight

estranged faces on the stairs of the subway tunnels
the faces of the dead
in mad haste multiply glowpoints of night
rusty frameworks swing slowly desperately
    incessantly into the steel blue protective layer

b

time
past ages increase future ones decrease
among the rust yellow October trees move the
    lemon yellow autos
the dusky beauty of a hydrangea mummy
the slow tread of those who expect nothing
loss of time
the cessation of identity upon the bridge
scents of anise in the air
doors of anise
death is so permanent
the brass rods of the awareness of time beat blindly against one
    another

c

the same faces meet endlessly in streams
    that flow in opposite directions
the loudspeakers talk on uninterruptably
the piano playing of little girls digs a tunnel
    through the years
the screech of the sea gull that shreds my early dreams is
    still my sister
from the tunnels emerge the lighted front surfaces
firewood sky of the remotely situated districts
open-standing doors of the shunted railway carriages
    in the November sun
shallow smoke area hung over shunting yards
latticed mirror-images in the corrugated iron of the canals
in this canal and bridge area
the glittering parallels of the terrain stretching before me

d

to deduct days to count annoyances to function exactly
without interest in the interests of the interested
that with what can be achieved less is achieved
    than when nothing is achieved
the temptation to always the same kind of sentences
hiding place Benjamin Péret and Francis Picabia
canceled notions
surviving thoughts
everything is different from its hypothesis
truth is my memory
I collect passers-by who talk to themselves
I signify the absence of thoughts
    in the estranged faces

e

sentences without content in the nightdrift
real nocturnal snatches of conversation in a streetcar
voices over the ice
the face empty of humanity that I recognize
a day before Christmas
nightland nightblue
winged peripeteia of night
the milk-brown circle
now
now now now[12]

In the struggle for a new objectivity (we might think, too, of the
efforts of the *nouveau roman* since the 1950s), description has become a typically modern stylistic device. The literary attitude behind this fact is in obvious contrast to the "Clang-and-Bang"
poetry of the expressionist era. The place described in the text
just quoted is the metropolis. That the prototype is Hamburg is
not important, though it may help the reader's imagination. It is
not important because the text is not concerned with the individuality of this or any other metropolis. What is described is the typical, which changes only in unessential ways from city to city.[13] It
is not so much a geographical place that is being described, as a

living space that determines and surrounds man, into which the textual "I" (an exemplarily modern consciousness, if one will) knows that it has been admitted. The five parts of the text describe the one locality from within and from without, from objective observation and from subjective consciousness, and under more or less varying partial aspects. The goal is a kind of polyperspective and simultaneity. Subjective elements of association, summarizing statements, and interpretation are mingled with the description. The two poles of the "Topographies" are outer locality and inner consciousness. The polarity between subject and object is obvious. The structure that comes into being is neither something linear nor a causally and logically constructed closed form; it is rather the assembling of elementary parts, large and small, for a (not regularly constructed) latticework, screen, field of consciousness. In other words: an exemplary locality is introduced into an exemplary consciousness. But the reverse is also true: an exemplary consciousness is introduced into an exemplary locality. The ego is seeking its outer and inner place and wants to become orientated in this area. The orientation is only partially successful.

Heissenbüttel himself distinguishes "in principle two categories of verse: aphorisms and illustrations. The change from one to the other determines the course of the rhythm. The thematic context, if one can use the term, can be determined from the sequence of aphorisms. In 'Topography,' *a* is the something in which reflection about something general ('world history') coincides with reflection about something antecedent to the individual ('subterranean space of my own landscape'). This is true of 'Topography' in general ... Divided line by line, line 1 is an aphorism, 2 is mixed, 3 is an illustration, 4 an aphorism, 5 an aphorism, 6–7 an illustration, 8–9 mixed, 10–11 illustration. In the illustrations there may be a question of pictorial elements, quotations, names, or (rarely) particles of sound. In line 3 it is a question of names. It is a question of three jazz musicians who died young: Big Sid Catlett (percussion instruments), Art Tatum (piano), Fats Navarro (trumpet). I have determined the sequence of these names on the basis of sound-values alone." [14]

The text begins with a comprehensive observation: "breathless the birds of world history traverse the defenseless terrain." This is a kind of superframework for the place that is to be described. What takes place, what is to be found in this world, in this city? "The irreparable, shocks, skin without shame, losses" (punctuation has been added as an aid to reading). Association takes place too—memory[15] and the almost free play of thought. Association: the three jazz musicians. Memory: "reminiscence about the subterranean space of my own landscape." This line, too, is abbreviated and without a verb. What does it mean? Heissenbüttel has given us the information in a letter. "Extended into a full sentence or, perhaps better, to a completed reflection, it could mean something like this: For when I ponder and consider what the backgrounds of that convention look like into which I have entered, then am I (or that which is down there where this I dwells, that which takes effect later, not perhaps somewhat like) a novel by Gustav Freytag. The abbreviation has two functions. It is supposed, first of all, to maintain an ambivalence between question and answer; and, secondly, to spur the reader to completion or, to put it more subtly, to the chain of association between the 'I' and Gustav Freytag." [16] Next, there occur in the verse-text impressions and images with elements of interpretation, of sententiousness, of reflection. In lines 8–9, the phrases "estranged faces" and "faces of the dead" belong to the level of interpretation; the phrase "on the stairs of the subway tunnels" belongs to the metaphorical level. The interpreter cannot point to a tangible conclusion that can be summarized in a single sentence, to a peak of meaning toward which the text hastens, to a principle or system of order that would be found by the textual "I," for there is none. Heissenbüttel had cited in a previous text, "Pamphlets III," the proposition of Wittgenstein's that was most important for him: "All sentences are of equal value." "Topography a" shows this. What is described is an irregular outer and inner area reflected in the consciousness. "Topography b" reflects "time," lost time ("past ages increase, future ones decrease," "loss of time"), the time "of those who expect nothing," the sad, black time of nearness of death ("death is so permanent"),[17] the disoriented awareness of time ("the brass rods of the awareness of time beat blindly against one another"). There are echoes of Marcel Proust's "lost time" and of Hofmannsthal's

Reitergeschichte [Rider's Tale] ("the cessation of identity upon the bridge"). But it is no refound time, even less is it a redeemed time, as is made even clearer in "Topography d." Time is here even less susceptible of a meaningful orientation than was place in "Topography a." The knowledge of nearness of death is, it is true, inescapable, but the "brass rods of the awareness of time beat blindly against one another."

What else happens in this place that is so poor in hope? "The same faces meet endlessly in streams that flow in opposite directions." "The loudspeakers talk on uninterruptably" (c). But it is not only the streams of traffic, the noise from the loudspeakers, the loudspeaker-civilization, the nonstop of the loudspeakers; the "piano playing of little girls" takes place here too. And it "digs a tunnel through the years." Such activity is meaningful activity, illustration, a part of the counterworld, like "the screech of the sea gull that shreds my early dream" and "is still my sister." The proximity to the natural, the uncontaminated, the living is affirmed; a wishful reference is made to something like animal or childlike innocence. Traffic images predominate among the impressions of the metropolis that are reported so succinctly here: "The lighted front surfaces emerge from the tunnels," "shunted railway carriages," "shunting yards," "canal and bridge area." In the last line (as in "b"), there is a kind of recapitulation: "the glittering parallels of the terrain stretching before me." Parallels of canals, of tracks, of vehicles, of the open doors of the shunted railway carriages. The separate and component parts of the picture, illustrations of the terrain, are introduced into the framework of the "defenseless terrain" of the first topography. Through the tunneled world of traffic and of lost time, "the piano playing of little girls digs" another tunnel of its own. Such a positive factor manifests itself in the life of adults, but not the signs of a meaningful and fulfilled existence.

Proof of this is offered in the new beginning of "Topography d." "To deduct days," "to count annoyances," "to function exactly." Our punctuation is itself an interpretation. It would also be possible to read: "to count; annoyances." Heissenbüttel has purposely left room for what is ambivalent, open on more than one side, equivocal. In this way, the field of association is compressed.

It is, for instance, not clear whether one who is under contract to this technical world deducts days (of his own accord) because they do not really count, or whether he has to deduct them on his time chart so that it will function. The highest principle, the imperative and slogan of this world, is "to function exactly." Man is a functional part within a functioning world. Gottfried Benn had already expressed this in his poem "Verlorenes Ich" [Lost Ego]. Heissenbüttel's textual "I" has no interest in this whole functional bustle, "without interest in the interests of the interested." Even more, this "I" refuses—when and insofar as it can—to join the bustle. The lack of meaning in this world with its "temptation to always the same kinds of sentences" is notorious. The protesting "I" introduces its flight, introduces a kind of counterworld into the arena: "hiding place Benjamin Péret and Francis Picabia." The two names evoke and illustrate the world of surrealism and dadaism. Péret (1899–1959), most consistent in his application of surrealist theories, was, among other things, editor of the journal "La Révolution surrealiste." Picabia (1879–1953), painter, illustrator, and poet, was editor of several avant-garde journals. Here, then, in the realm of surrealism are to be found, in the opinion of this textual "I" that has withdrawn from the functional world, freedom from the need "to function exactly" and freedom from the "temptation to always the same kinds of sentences." Here, in the "hiding place," are "canceled notions" and "surviving thoughts." "To cancel" [*Stornieren*], a word taken from the jargon of the business world, refers to the removal of a false bookkeeping entry by the substitution of a correct one. Are surrealist notions, then, the corrected entries to be substituted for the incorrect entries of the business world? The textual "I" marks its own position more negatively than positively with the sententious observations:

> everything is different from its hypothesis
> truth is my memory
> I collect passers-by who talk to themselves
> I signify the absence of thoughts
>   in the estranged faces

Here is a twofold dictum drawn from his own experience. "Everything is different from its hypothesis." No reason or proof is given for this statement; it is a summary assertion. The assertion is drawn into the topographical field and included in the "I's" own referential position. The second personal dictum is also summarily stated: "truth is my memory." What truth? Of the natural sciences, of history, of sociology, of theology? The context yields only a personal experiential truth. But, provocatively, the formulation is made general and undifferentiated. Or is the textual "I" treating his own statement with irony? That is inconceivable. He takes himself too importantly and seriously. The "estranged faces" are the "faces on the stairs of the subway tunnels" from "a" and they are always "the same faces" from "c." As observer, the textual "I"—a modern Lynkeus-watchman—has seen a superabundance of such faces on passers-by. His recognition indicates that "the absence of thoughts on the estranged faces" has been observed; his presentation in the text shows that the observation has been recorded. But what has the disappointed "I" really gained by such a recording? Does the observational memory build a bridge of communication? Or does it isolate itself further? It does the latter.

In "Topography e," the last attempt at the description and discovery of locality, we see a withdrawn, meditative textual "I" at nighttime. Except in the dependent clause ("which I recognize"), predicates and the mention of the "I" as an observing center of consciousness are lacking. They are abstracted, yet clearly present by implication. What does the nighttime "I" remember, associate, contemplate? "Sentences," "sentences without content," which hurry past, "snatches of conversation in a streetcar," "voices over the ice" (ice can be both description and metaphor). What does the "I" recognize in all this? "The face empty of humanity," not a particular, individual face, but the human countenance of the "sentences without content," of "those who expect nothing," of those who merely "function exactly," the faces of the species man in this observed and described world. Man alienated from himself, nonhuman man. This is observation, lament, judgment, and protest all in one, told without any excess of feeling, and presented under the aegis of the objective. Again there occurs the transition from the world of the others to the world of the "I." Chronology is introduced into the topography. Calendar chronology extends in the "Topographies" from October ("b"), through November ("c"), to December: "a day before Christmas" ("e"). But it is more than just calendar time. Was not "the slow tread of those who expect nothing" already observed topographically in "b"? Now suddenly there is expectation after all (for man cannot live without expectation). Now suddenly the night is to change. From the world of futility and of recognition of "the emptiness of human life," there is magically to be born "the winged peripeteia of night," a something, the sign of a coming. The expectation rises, is repeated for a fourth time, and reaches a climax in the "now" that is distributed over two lines. But nothing happens on "a day before Christmas." Advent fails to arrive—must fail to arrive in the "hiding place Benjamin Péret and Francis Picabia," must fail to arrive in the extreme isolation of an isolated observer. Is the textual "I" demonstrating here against its own will its own helplessness? It has furnished proof not only of the hopelessness of the place of the others, which it has described, but also of the hopelessness of its own "hiding place" and observation post. "The milk-brown circle" of night does not open up. Cyclic time is not a rising, eschatological, Christian time. In form, the text of the "Topographies" is, in contrast to the most classically closed poems, an extremely "open" [18] structure. In content and meaning, on the other hand, the field of consciousness of the "I" is completely closed, incapable of contact, incapable of an encounter that might bestow inner peace and happiness. The text demonstrates the lonely "I" in a world of "estranged faces."

No positive orientation is achieved. The "I" which, from the beginning, has been concerned about its own image has discovered no relationship to the place or time it has described, not even the relationship of radical alienation. It might be asked if important aspects of reality have not been omitted in this topography? Are the "estranged faces" the only men whom the observer-"I" has met, and do all men bear the lineaments of "estranged faces"? If the author, who comes forward with his scientific, logicianist, concretist[19] demands, does not ask himself this question, the critic must do so. Heinrich Vormweg, a critic well disposed to Heissenbüttel, comments on "Topography e": "It contains a series of statements, of things heard and seen, and ends in a kind of expectation with the structure left open. This is not syntactic arrangement, but something that has been jumbled together almost in a moment's time—order would be something that would have to be added to it, but the language does not permit it. The multiplicity forces itself into the foreground." [20] Order would, indeed, be something that would have to be added. But is the language responsible for its absence? That is a fashionable excuse with quasi-scientific pretentions. As if language, in the first place, had no principles of order in itself and, in the second place, has and does not have other principles of order than those which man has imposed and is now imposing upon it. What did the aged Goethe say in his "Noten und Abhandlungen zum West-Östlichen Divan" [Notes and Discussions on the West-East Divan]? "The discretion of the poet is properly referred to the form; the world will give him the material only too generously; the meaning arises freely from the fullness of his inner self." Order would have to proceed from the writer's consciousness. Granted, it is several degrees harder to achieve in a text like the "Topographies" than in Goethe's *Römische Elegien* [Roman Elegies] or *Venetianische Epigramme* [Venetian Epigrams], which also contain some topography. But that the positive should end with the "piano playing of little girls," with the "screech of the sea gull," and in the "hiding-place Benjamin Péret and Francis Picabia," with elements of a retracted reality and an emaciated new romanticism, is, despite all protestations of a new sincerity, something that cannot be accepted. In the lyric texts of a Nelly Sachs, whose testimony is indeed significant in our time, something more is to be found. "For the elements set in motion like brother and sister the blessing of Scripture . . . And Israel, warrior on the horizons / sleeps with the seed of stars / and heavy dreams unto God." "If the prophets broke in / through the doors of night / and sought an ear like a homeland— / Ear of man, / intertwined among the nettles, / would you hear?" In her works, there is a quite different intensity of night and loneliness than in Heissenbüttel's. But "after midnight only brothers and sisters speak." In Nelly Sachs' poetry, the lyrical "I" is always ready to learn living and dying anew. And: "the inner language redeems / what a victory." [21]

Such a confrontation seems meaningful and necessary if only to

point out the limitations in the completely one-sided and pretentious talk of some modern authors of texts and some theories of
authors. Wherein do the topographies of an author like Heissenbüttel differ from those of a Nelly Sachs? Even more than in language, they differ in intrinsic worth, in insight into a direction of
order, of meaningfulness, of salvation. The world presented by
Heissenbüttel—and this applies to all his texts—is without grace.
In the world of Nelly Sachs, grace has its role. And it shows its
strength by changing and transforming reality. In Heissenbüttel's
most recent "13 Hypothesen über Literatur und Wissenschaft
als vergleichbare Tätigkeiten" [Hypotheses about Literature and
Science as Comparable Activities], it is true, it is stated program-
matically: "Literature and science are comparable in two of their
fundamental attitudes: (1) they no longer admit that proof or
reason can exist in revelation, myth, empathy, higher insight, and
so on, but only in experience, on the principle that experience is
accessible to everyone; (2) they attempt to shed light without
prejudice, insofar as that is possible, on the living space and living
conditions of man as well as on the laws of nature and of the world
in which man lives . . ." [22] This is not the place to inquire as
to what, if there can be such a thing as freedom from prejudice,
is or is not supposed to be signified by it. It is and is not surprising
that Heissenbüttel considers himself and his experience free from
prejudice.

9

Journey into Dustlessness
The Lyrics of Nelly Sachs

Klaus Nonnenmann does not even mention Nelly Sachs in his *Schriftsteller der Gegenwart* [Present-Day Writers] (Walter, 1963). The *Kleines Lexikon der Weltliteratur* [Small Lexicon of World Literature] (Herder, 1964) allots her only a third as much space as has been allotted the biography of Ingeborg Bachmann. Michael Landmann, a Berlin professor of philosophy closely connected with the ivory tower of Stefan George's former circle of disciples [the *Georgekreis*], complained in 1963: "Even today, fashionable abuse allows poems to be written—not certainly for the sake of musicality, but rather from extreme aversion to what can be rationally comprehended—which, like those of Nelly Sachs or Perse, either say disturbingly little—are little more than emoted printer's ink—or else remain so inaccessible to even the most genuine attempt to understand them, that one longs for a return to banal clarity." Hans Magnus Enzensberger, who trumpeted his *Landessprache* [Vernacular] angrily across the land, knew her as early as 1961, when he wrote: "In the center of Stockholm . . . between the neat Paalsundpark and the little grocery stores opposite, the visitor could, if he were so minded, meet at certain hours of the afternoon a dainty, friendly, shy, elderly woman: the greatest poetess who is writing in German today." And he continues,

"Don't utter it, that superlative! Go past, stranger! For the little dwelling . . . is a refuge, the sanctuary of a woman who has been persecuted." There, in this little dwelling, Rolf Italiaander visited her in the first of his postwar visits. He reports: "Nelly Sachs' kitchen was her bedroom, living room, and workroom, as well as her reception room for visitors. In the other room, her old mother lay in great pain. When I arrived, Nelly Sachs took off her kitchen apron. I was surprised to see how small and frail she was. I found her manner typically Berlinish. I . . . was enchanted by her cordial simplicity. Even as she was pushing the peeled potatoes to one side, we began to talk about literature." [1]

Nelly Sachs has been called "Kafka's sister." But her experience and linguistic expression are structurally different from Kafka's. For her, darkness does, indeed, hold a painful meaning, but it is one that illumines existence. Grief can be transformed. The way of flight stands open, not from here to there, but from here upwards, from immanence to transcendence. For her, God has not disintegrated, as He had for the merchant's son Kafka; for her He is ever present as He was for the elect of the Old Covenant. With more justice, she has been called "a sister of Job." [2] She is, indeed, a sister of Job, separated from him by two and a half millenia, but not by any difference in the intensity of her experience of suffering, in her enduring of earthly losses, in gnawing doubt, in attachment to Yahweh-God, in searching for God in grief and finding Him in hope. Not by accident is the exemplary figure of the suffering and believing people of Israel the main theme of Nelly Sachs' poetry.

> *Job*
> O thou weathervane of suffering!
> Lashed by primeval tempests
> into this storm's course and that;
> even thy South is called loneliness.
> Where thou standest is the navel of pain.
>
> Thine eyes are sunk deep into thy head
> like cave doves in a night
> that the hunter brings out blindly.
> Thy voice has become silent
> for it has too often queried *why*.

Thy voice has gone to rest among the worms and fish.
Job, thou hast wept through all the watches of the night.
But there will come a time when constellations of thy blood
will cause all rising suns to pale.[3]

Suffering comes from every direction of the wind to surround the sufferer. There is no possibility of avoiding it in time or space. Wherever he stands, there "is the navel of pain." Escape is impossible—but not transformation. In *Glühende Rätsel* [Glowing Riddles] the last cycle of her poems thus far published, the poetess dared to write: "Thine anxiety has issued into the light."

Life and Work

Nelly Sachs was born in Berlin on December 10, 1891, the only child of a Jewish manufacturer, William Sachs. She grew up in a villa in the Zoo Section, in a cosmopolitan atmosphere. She was taught by private tutors. As a girl, she enjoyed her father's musical efforts. In his library, she found books on German Romanticism, which fascinated her. She herself soon began to play an instrument, to dance, and to write. At the age of fifteen, she read Selma Lagerlöf. Later, she dedicated her own first work, *Legenden und Erzählungen* [Legends and Tales] (Berlin 1921), to the Swedish authoress. In the 1920s, Stefan Zweig became her first literary mentor. Her first poems appeared in 1929 in the *Vossische Zeitung*. In 1932, Leo Hirsch printed the verses of the still unknown poetess in the *Berliner Tageblatt*. Her works were printed even in the formerly well-known Munich journal, *Jugend*. Soon, however, only *Der Morgen*, journal of the Jewish cultural group, was open to her. She could no longer publish in Aryan Germany. After 1938–1939, when the extermination of the Jews was rigorously pursued, her life was in danger. In the summer of 1939, in response to the pleading of a friend, Selma Lagerlöf in conjunction with the Swedish royal house, intervened on behalf of Nelly Sachs and her mother. In June 1940, they fled by plane from Berlin to Stockholm. In the meantime, Selma Lagerlöf had died. It seemed a miracle to Nelly Sachs that her rescue had been so successful. Her relatives were being put to death in the concentration camps of the

Third Reich. With all the ardor of her thinking and loving soul, she suffered the murder of those dear to her and the systematic extermination of her people in the gas chambers.

From this suffering there arose, after 1940, her verses *In den Wohnungen des Todes* [In the Dwellings of Death]. They appeared first in 1947 in the Aufbau-Verlag in East Berlin. The cycles in the volume *Sternverdunkelung* [Eclipse of the Stars] were written from 1944 on. She meditated on the figures of the Old Testament and inquired unceasingly into the meaning of life and death in this world. In 1949, the poetess was able to have her verses published by the Bermann-Fischer Publishing Company, which was then located in Amsterdam. The greater part of this printing had to be destroyed. No one knew her or wanted to buy her poems. No literary journal presented her to the public. Her next volume, *Und niemand weiss weiter* [And No One Knows Anything More] (1950–1956), contains elegies on the death of her mother and further Biblical reflections. The Hamburg publisher Heinrich Ellermann printed this collection in 1957. Two years later, the Deutsche Verlags-Anstalt in Stuttgart published her new cycle, *Flucht und Verwandlung* [Flight and Metamorphosis]. The later cycles, *Fahrt ins Staublose* [Journey into Dustlessness] and *Noch feiert der Tod das Leben* [Death Is Still Celebrating Life], as well as the earlier poems, appeared in the Suhrkamp Verlag in Frankfurt in 1961. The collected edition of her poems bears the title *Fahrt ins Staublose*. A selection, to which has been added the first part of the cycle *Glühende Rätsel* from the year 1962, was brought out in a Suhrkamp edition in 1963. It offers a kind of lyrical summary of her work. Parts 2 and 3 of *Glühende Rätsel*—her last publication to date—appeared in *Späte Gedichte* [Late Poems] (Suhrkamp, 1964).

Nelly Sachs also wrote dramatic scenes. *Eli*, a mystery play about the sufferings of Israel, became well known. Eli is an eight-year-old shepherd boy in a small Jewish city in Poland that was destroyed during the last war. German soldiers drag his parents from their beds. In his nightshirt, Eli runs after them, raises his shepherd's flute, and with it calls God to their assistance. One of the soldiers fears that it is a signal and strikes the boy dead with the butt of his rifle. Samuel, the old grandfather, who had also

197

run after them, is struck dumb with fear. Later, the soldier suffers and dies from pangs of conscience.

As a sign of gratitude to her host-land, Sweden, Nelly Sachs translated modern Swedish lyrics into German.[4] For this work, she received her first public honor, the Literature Prize of the Association of Swedish Lyricists. There followed in 1959 a presentation from the Cultural Committee of the Federal Association of German Industry. A year later, she accepted the Droste-Prize in Meersburg. In her speech of acceptance, she pleaded: "My brothers and sisters, bestow on me more of this courage with which you help me today to overcome my weakness. I have nothing to forgive: I am a human being, like all the rest." Had they read her poetry? Or did they want to make "restitution"? In 1961, she was honored again, this time with the Literature Prize of the city of Dortsmund. The last token of esteem from Germany came to her in the Paulskirche in Frankfurt on October 17, 1965 when the Peace Prize of the German Book Trade was bestowed upon her. A disinterested observer noticed that, as the cameras flashed, the prizewinner assumed no pose. Where speakers were eloquent, she was silent. Heroes and stars, even writer-stars, are corruptible. But hymns of praise could not corrupt Nelly Sachs. The show, the bustle, the fawning publicity had no effect on her. What unadorned sincerity, what a sign, what a consolation in this world! She had chosen suffering as her lot. Her work is "inconceivable without the additional notion of substitution. . . . Out of her mouth speaks more than just herself." [5] On October 20, 1966, Nelly Sachs, together with the Jewish novelist Samuel J. Agnon, was awarded the Nobel Prize for literature.

The Jewish Fate

After the war, Theodor W. Adorno, a man who had himself experienced exile, expressed a thought that has subsequently often been quoted: Since Auschwitz, it is impossible to write a poem. Nelly Sachs has written poems not only since Auschwitz but even about it. She proves Adorno right in that she has been unable to produce specimens of the post-Romantic or of the Expressionist "Clang-and-Bang" tradition. But she disproves the philosopher's contention by her own concentrated, prophetically astringent, religious tone, which has been purified by her encounter with death and is radically suited to an age of horror.

In the Dwellings of Death is the title she gave the four verse-cycles in which she meditated on, prayed over, and conjured up the incomprehensible occurrences in the concentration camps. They are dedicated "To my Dead Brothers and Sisters." The first part pertains to the Jewish people as a whole; the second contains the "Gebete für den toten Bräutigam" [Prayers for a Dead Bridegroom]; the third, a series of "Grabschriften in die Luft geschrieben" [Epitaphs Written into the Air]; the fourth, "Chöre nach Mitternacht" [Choruses After Midnight]. Several of the poems have epigraphs from the Bible, Hasidism, and the Cabala. The speaker belongs to the tradition of the believer, of the devout Jew.

The epigraph of the first poem—it supplied the title of the first volume—is taken from the Book of Job, where the context implies an "invocation of the Muse," but not the Muse of antiquity, nor a new mythic Muse,[6] nor even a Muse of Job's own making. In his fifth reply, Job pleads with his accusers and friends for pity, wishes that his words might be written down, inscribed on rock, because they confess his experience, document his belief in the counsel of Yahweh, and reveal his endurance of the incomprehensible, his reaching out to the Savior-God. The poetess—Gottfried Benn would have said "the lyrical I"—chose the central verse as a pertinent motto, an epigraph. It reads: "Even after my skin is flayed, without my flesh I shall see God" (Job 19:26).[7] The title poem reads as follows:

> *O the chimneys*
> On the ingeniously conceived dwellings of death,
> When Israel's body released in smoke went forth
> Through the air—
> A star, like a chimney sweep, received him
> And became black
> Or was it a sunbeam?
>
> O the chimneys!
> Paths to freedom for Jeremiah and the dust of Job—
> Who conceived and built you stone on stone
> The path for fugitives from smoke?

O the dwellings of death,
Invitingly constructed
For the master of the house who formerly was guest—
O you fingers,
Laying the threshold at the entrance
Like a knife between life and death—

O you chimneys,
O you fingers,
And Israel's body in smoke through the air!

The situation presented here is the murder of the Jews and their cremation in the extermination camps of the Third Reich. The verses are a lament for the dead. The anonymous killing and dying seek a memorial—a direction with meaning. The murder is done to "Israel's body." It is the Jewish people in its visible, earthly form, regarded from the standpoint of religion, not of race. The occurrence is not so much described as invoked, evoked, and expounded. Its brutal and monstrous shape is subsumed by invocation, evocation, and suggestive query into the person who commemorates it.

In the "dwellings of death," the descendants of Israel were put to death. Through the chimneys of the cremation ovens, they were pursued into the air. What irony in the word "dwellings." These are dwellings, not to dwell and live in, but to be killed in. And what perversion of thought, what reversal of meaning, that these dwellings, these murder-factories, are "ingeniously conceived." The cosmos grieves. The "star" that shone "like a chimney sweep" down the chimneys of the cremation factories was "black"—black from soot, black from smoke, black from grief. "Or was it a sunbeam?" queries the last line of the strophe—participation has been added from the direction of the supernatural. Star and sunbeam are lament, lamenter, and consoler in one. The murderers wanted literally to pursue "Israel's body" into the air and destroy it. But "Israel's body released in smoke went forth / *Through* the air," through the beyond. Whither? Into what dwellings? Into cosmic, supernatural realms. "Star" and "sunbeam" did more than turn black, did more than endure the situation passively. They, too, inaugurated an action: against banishment, reception; against annihilation, rescue. They "received" Israel's body. A higher, lighter irony answers the wicked irony of the "ingeniously conceived dwellings." It surpasses the wickedness but is unable—and therein lies, for man, the incomprehensible darkness—to hinder the earthly course of annihilation. The supernatural realms receive only what is left, what is immortal.

One who ponders in faith recognizes (strophe 2) the chimneys of death as "paths to freedom for Jeremiah and the dust of Job." "Dust" belongs to the basic vocabulary of the poetess. It defines one pole of human existence. The definition is rooted in the Biblical formula of experience: Dust thou art and unto dust thou shalt return (Genesis 3:19). But the lyrical work of Nelly Sachs continues the Biblical sentence in a manner that is Biblical: and thou shalt return *through* dust. The dust is at the same time the "ashes of resurrection" (p. 384)—and as such the point of departure for the last metamorphosis. From this perspective, the experience of dust ("Disinherited, we bemoan the dust," *Späte Gedichte*, p. 170) and the becoming dust, in whatever forms, become stations on what the later lyrics have called the *Journey into Dustlessness*. All this has not been said expressly in the poem, but it has been intimated. The poem inquires expressly into the identity of the one who conceived and built the chimneys that became, though their innovator had not intended it, "paths to freedom." "Who conceived and built you stone on stone / The path for fugitives from smoke?" As opposed to him who conceived and built the "chimneys," the poem recognizes him who conceived and built the "paths to freedom"; as opposed to the dispositions below, it recognizes in wonder the dispositions from above. The paths to annihilation built by murderers are at the same time "paths to freedom"; the paths to freedom are "paths for fugitives"; the paths of flight—so says the later work—are paths of "metamorphosis." There is no express answer here to the query as to who conceived and built the paths of freedom. It has already been given in the context. It is the God "of Israel," the God of Jeremiah and of Job. It had also been expressly stated in the epigraph: "Even after my skin is flayed, without my flesh I shall see God."

In sharp contrast to the interpretation of death as victorious escape for the slain, the third strophe speaks insistently of the remembrance of what has happened and of lamentation. What language, what pathos would be adequate to portray this death?

The primeval movement of lament cries out: "O the dwellings of death." In a combination of euphemistic understatement and irony, the simple lament is commented upon in a verse heavy with antithetical tension: "Invitingly constructed / For the master of the house who formerly was guest." This master is death. The use of the present participle *einladend* [here translated in its adverbial form, *invitingly*] makes the event more graphic. And just as the first strophe apostrophizes the ingenious thought of the manufacturers of death, so now the perpetrators are represented in shuddering memory by their "fingers" (*pars pro toto*). "O you fingers/ Laying the threshold at the entrance / Like a knife between life and death." That such a thing existed can be proclaimed only with lamentation, only in a form that is at once as simple and as intensive as possible.

The last strophe is a summary. It conjures up the whole poem with the utmost brevity and condensation: one verse each for the place, the perpetrators, the dead; report and reflection, lamentation and consolation combined:

> O you chimneys,
> O you fingers,
> And Israel's body in smoke through the air!

Here is utmost economy of words, a great poem, a unique statement.

In quite a different way, Paul Celan, in his famous "Todesfuge" [Fugue of Death], has made the same occurrence the object of a poem. As a "Fugue," his poem is not only more artistically constructed; it is also linguistically richer. Instead of the primitively simple, faltering tone of lament in Nelly Sachs' poem, Celan has employed a swifter, lighter, almost dancing rhythm and a magically whirling tone. He makes no attempt to interpret the occurrence. In long, artistically constructed lines, he offers a visionary presentation unsurpassed for power of imagery and suggestion. But there is no search for meaning, no ascent to religious transcendence. Celan's poem is tremendously beautiful; Nelly Sachs' verses are reflective, prophetical, and simple.

The cycle "Dein Leib im Rauch durch die Luft" [Thy Body in Smoke Through the Air], whose title poem has just been interpreted, was followed by the "Gebete für den toten Bräutigam" [Prayers for a Dead Bridegroom]. These are at once love poems and prayers. The all-pervasive pain of separation at the threshold of death, the address to the absent one, the speaking to God and to creatures about the beloved dead, this directness of address and compact consciousness,[8] this unity between the experience of suffering and the contemplation that penetrates its meaning—all this is unique as well as completely personal, religious, and cosmic in tone. One might say that no one else since Dante has achieved such intensity, purity, or transcendent power of longing. Like "dust," "longing" is one of the words most frequently used by the poetess. If "dust" defines man in the existence that has been predetermined for him, "longing" defines him in his character as wayfarer and in his freedom to transcend it.

> *But perhaps* God needs longing,
>   or where else would she be found,
> She who with kisses and tears and sighs
>   fills the mysterious spaces of the air—
> Perhaps it is the invisible kingdom of earth
>   from which the glowing roots of stars emerge—
> And the radiant voice over the fields of separation
>   that summons to reunion?
> O my beloved, perhaps our love
>   has already borne worlds in the heaven of longing—
> As our breathing in—and out
>   builds a cradle for life and death?
> Grains of sand, we two, dark from parting
>   and lost in the golden secret of births,
> And perhaps already lighted round about
>   by future stars and moons and suns.[9]

The words seem conventional; any one of them might have been written two generations earlier. Whence comes, then, their undeniable power to convince? From the purity, the interiority, the spiritualization of love and pain, from the mystic consciousness of the omnipresence of the beloved and of cosmic and personal union.

The "Prayers for a Dead Bridegroom" were followed by "Grabschriften in die Luft geschrieben" [Epitaphs Written in the Air].

They are epitaphs for the individual acquaintances designated in the headings by professional title or initials. The memorial words are written in the air because these people have no grave and no gravestone. They all belong to "Israel's body released in smoke ... through the air."

The last cycle in the volume *In den Wohnungen des Todes* is formed by the "Chöre nach Mitternacht" [Choruses After Midnight]: a "Chorus of Things Left Behind"; a "Chorus of the Saved"; a "Chorus of Wanderers"; a "Chorus of Orphans"; a "Chorus of the Dead" and a "Chorus of Shades"; a "Chorus of Stones" and a "Chorus of Stars"; a "Chorus of Clouds" and a "Chorus of Trees"; a "Chorus of Invisible Things"; and a "Chorus of the Unborn." All the choruses reflect a real world and time: the cosmic, historical, interpreted, present time of the world. It is the "time after midnight," after the great murder, after the war; the time when a new day is dawning. It is not improbable that the midnight of Jeremiah is concealed in the midnight-cipher of the poetess. In Jeremiah, the "energy of chaos and creation [bears] its own name. This is midnight. Midnight is primarily a place: the region of the North where darkness and night reign. All harmful powers are concentrated around midnight. When the portals of midnight are opened, evil wins free course. It is impossible to predict the physiognomy of evil—neither its degree nor the duration of its harmfulness can be known in advance. But midnight is also the exciting hour into which—with Jeremiah—all men are plunged. Jeremiah saw the portals of midnight open." [10] In Nelly Sachs' works, midnight is also the time of inner confidence, as witness the later verses: "und nach Mitternach / reden nur Geschwister" [After midnight, only brothers and sisters speak] (p. 149). The "Chorus of the Saved" pleads: "Lasst uns das Leben leise wieder lernen" [Let us learn life gently once again] (p. 50). The "dead of Israel" speak: "Wir reichen schon einen Stern weiter / In unseren verborgenen Gott hinein" [We have progressed one star farther / Into our hidden God] (p. 56). The "unseen things" console the "separated loved ones" and rise up, conscious of their strength, against the "Klagemauer Nacht" [Wailing Wall, Night]:

Wailing wall, night,
Thou canst be shattered by the lightning of a prayer
And all who have missed God in sleep
Awaken unto Him behind
Thy falling walls.[11]

Lastly, there speaks the "voice of the holy land" (does not this name spring from the Christian domain?). She speaks: "O meine Kinder / Der Tod ist durch eure Herzen gefahren / Wie durch einen Weinberg—" [O my children, / Death rode through your hearts / As through a vineyard—]. She queries further: "Wo soll die kleine Heiligkeit hin / Die noch in meinem Sande wohnt?" [Whither the little holiness / That still dwells in my sand?] And she answers admonishingly: In forgiveness.

Lay upon the plowed fields your weapons of revenge
That they may become gentle—
For even iron and grain are brother and sister
In the bosom of the earth—[12]

Who could utter these words today and be believed? A Christian? What Christian? But the Jewess Nelly Sachs can and does. In the poem "Auf dass die Verfolgten nicht die Verfolger werden" [That the Persecuted May Not Become the Persecutors] (p. 77), she admonishes her brothers and sisters to renounce the spirit of revenge.

According to all current theories about the lyric, from Benn to Brecht and from Höllerer to Heissenbüttel, this kind of speech is old-fashioned; themes of Biblical import are not admissible. At least, they never occur to the programmatic mind of the programmatic poet. They have all defined knowledge and wisdom after their own fashion. They omit the greater reality. They seem to know nothing of mystic community.

Flight and Metamorphosis

The very first poem in the *Wohnungen des Todes* mentioned the key word "flight." The fact that those exiled to the gas chambers are received supernaturally, that the most radical restraint upon them is recognized as a possibility of utmost freedom, points to a metamorphosis. The cycle *Glühende Rätsel* is still concerned with the puzzle of her own existence as flight and metamorphosis. Flight and metamorphosis are themes in all of Nelly Sachs' poems. The cycle published in 1959 bears this title. It is concerned with the same radical, inescapable, and indestructible existence which, in a later formulation, was called "Fahrt ins Staublose." Man's life begins in the birth of dust. It ends in dustlessness. Between lies the journey, with its many stations of farewells, of death, of metamorphoses, of gradual, often violent, birth. Man, "dark from parting," but "lost in the golden secret of births" (p. 25); man "exploding," charged with the "stuff of longing" (p. 331), is always "the ashes of resurrection" (p. 384):

> Upward from daily destructions
> his prayers have winged their way
> seeking the eyes' inner thoroughfares.
>
> Craters and dry seas
> filled with tears
> traveling through the starry stations
> on the journey into dustlessness.[18]

The "journey into dustlessness" is a flight from and a flight toward something: a flight from the "dwellings of death" in this world, with their "breath of Sodom" and their "burden of Nineveh" (p. 254); a flight from the world that has slain the "bridegroom" (pp. 23ff.) and affords no "homeland" ("Heimat," p. 262); a flight from this world that is nourished on the "shrub of despair" (p. 378). But whither? In the very concretely recognizable, personal "refugee" situation on the "pavement of a strange city," where the show windows present their "picture-book heaven," the "survivors" [*Überlebende*, title of one cycle] protest: "World, do not ask those who have been snatched from death / whither they are going, / they are always going to their grave" (p. 114). In the cycle *Von Flüchtlingen und Flucht* [On Fugitives and Flight], this experience is portrayed: "That is the flight that draws fugitives with it / into epilepsy, into death!" (p. 160). The lyrical "I" of these verses knows that it is "fleeing the land / with the heavy baggage of love" (p. 259). Fleeing the land to go where? Into the other world, into the world of the bridegroom and of God, for it is one world. "Always on your luminous trail" (p. 383), i.e., the trail of the dead bridegroom. In accordance with strict Israelite reverence before the absolute spirituality and infinity of the totally Other, God is not addressed as "Thou" in these verses. He is the God of "creation,", of "births," of the "source" (p. 386), of "what is hidden," of "resurrection," of "salvation" (p. 141). Despite the teleological role of His world, the "trails" to it and to Him are again and again "darkened in epilepsy" (p. 383). In June 1961, the poetess confessed in a letter: "The poems that I write from time to time—in the beginning it was done to be able to breathe—are now tumbling as though epileptic to their end." [14] The intensity of the ecstatic flight compels the fugitive at times almost into madness.

> Flight from the black-bloodied constellation
> of farewell,
> Flight into the lightning-tapestried
> inns of insanity.
>
> Flight, flight, flight
> into the coup-de-grâce of flight
> from the ruptured arteries
> of a brief stopping place.[15]

Since the days of "Abraham" (p. 162), Israel's fate has been flight. Nelly Sachs' personal flight has its place within the larger exodus of her people. But even this larger exodus of her people must be understood as encompassing more than just the one most obvious and visible exodus in a movement of flight that is actually cosmic. For Nelly Sachs, the whole world is proceeding endlessly toward the start of flight and its goal. The whole universe is putting on a new condition, a new birth.

> *Whither* o whither
> thou universe of longing
> who, even in the caterpillar bewitched yet dimly surmised,
> unfurl thy wings,
> and with the fishes' fins
> incessantly describe thy origin
> in depths of water that

a single heart
can measure with the plummet
of grief.
Whither o whither
thou universe of longing
with the lost kingdoms of dreams
and the ruptured arteries of the body;
as the curled soul awaits
its new birth
under the ice of the death mask.[16]

The poem seems to be a parallel to the eighth chapter of the Epistle to the Romans: "For the eager longing of creation awaits the revelation of the sons of God," St. Paul says. "For creation was made subject to vanity . . . in hope, because creation itself also will be delivered from its slavery to corruption into the freedom of the glory of the sons of God . . . And not only it, but we ourselves . . . groan within ourselves, waiting for the adoption as sons, the redemption of our bodies" (Rom. 8: 19–21; 23 passim).

In the poem "Wohin," the poetess develops for the first time her great image of the transformation of the caterpillar into the butterfly.[17] It is one of the central images in the mysticism of both Orient and Occident and is even found in a secular form in Goethe's poem "Selige Sehnsucht" [Blessed Longing] in the *West-Östlicher Divan*. For the "flight and metamorphosis" that she had both experienced and understood in faith, Nelly Sachs found an objective correlative[18] in the image of the butterfly. The caterpillar has many metamorphoses before it; the butterfly has already experienced them: from caterpillar to chrysalis to flying lepidopteron—each one a process of dying and of being reborn. Nelly Sachs sees—and this is the fruit of her reflections on Hasidism and the Cabala—the "origin" of the butterfly's wings as implicit in the "fishes' fins" (p. 140). For her, fish are creatures that lie farther back in creation, farther below in longing, nearer the beginning. They, too, are objective correlatives, namely of the soul's "consciousness of water" (cf. pp. 354, 162, 262).

Repeated reflection reveals in the aspect of the butterfly yet another level of comparison. An otherworldly splendor has been painted onto the dust of its wings. The image of metamorphosis becomes an image of promise and transcendence. Unlike Mörike in his poem "Im Weinberg," Nelly Sachs portrays, even at the outset, a butterfly that is diaphanous, and so allows a glimpse of transcendence. In Mörike's poem, the lyric "I," sitting in the vineyard, recognizes the butterfly first as a shimmering natural being, as a charming sylph, as an aesthetic encounter. Only as a second step and from without does the lyric observer, who holds the New Testament in his hands, draw any connection between the butterfly and the Word of God—and even then only in the narrowest sense. For Nelly Sachs, the butterfly is, itself, an image of promise.

> *Butterfly*
> *What* beautiful otherworldness
> has been painted on thy dust.
> Through the fiery core of earth,
> through its stony crust
> thou wert passed,
> farewell web in the measure of mortality.
>
> Butterfly
> the good night of all creatures!
> The weights of life and death
> sink down with thy wings
> upon the rose
> that wilts as the light ripens homeward.
>
> What beautiful otherworldness
> has been painted on thy dust.
> What a symbol of royalty
> in the secret of the air.[19]

The butterfly is neither described naturalistically nor regarded in the manner of Goethe or Mörike. From the beginning, its image is viewed from the horizon of that transcendental knowledge that comes from faith, its symbolical character is recognized, and it is depicted in precisely this referential character. This kind of writing existed in the Middle Ages and in the Age of Baroque. Transcendental faith seeks its symbolical analogue; existence that is but dimly directed to the world beyond seeks its objective correlative. Everything visible must serve faith; the whole representational world must serve the nonrepresentational world. To the degree that a rationalistic and scientific point of view was declared the only legitimate one, such a contemplative attitude was rejected as unscientific. It found its natural sphere among the mystics. In the poem here quoted, the butterfly is understood a priori as the sign of an existence that is subject to change, but whose goal is not of this world, and whose return home is through the portals of death. This attitude does not turn the butterfly into a thin allegory or a formal emblem. On the contrary, presentation from the standpoint of faith intensifies it until it becomes most truly what it is in the plan of creation, a being that points beyond itself.

The poem begins with an exclamation of astonishment: "What beautiful otherworldness has been painted on thy dust." In the dust that the wings have accumulated in flight is concealed all the transitoriness of all dust, the birth of the dust of created beings. But it bears also the traces of immortality, the beauty of the world beyond—in the polar tension between the world beyond and dust. The beautiful flaming structure of the wings passed, as the poem says, "through the fiery core of earth." It springs from the fire that is innermost, strongest; from the creative fire. But then it passes "through [earth's] stony crust," through the limiting and limited confines of earth. The regions from which the butterfly emerges, to which it is bound by its origin, are named. The last line of the first strophe identifies the butterfly itself. What is it then? A "farewell web in the measure of mortality." What a definition! What a metaphor! What a combination of image and concept! Whose "farewell web" is meant? In the first place, of course, that of the butterfly itself. In its own development from caterpillar to chrysalis and from chrysalis to butterfly, the web of wings is the last web to be formed, the farewell garment. As such, the web is, at the same time, a cosmic sign of farewell for the one who beholds it, a *memento mori* in the fullness of its beauty and in the fragility of its design. Therefore, it is "the *good* night of all creatures" (strophe 2); it is not only the sign of night and the night of death, but a promise that both of these will be turned to good. This promise is based on the butterfly's own being, whose process of becoming and dying rises in a single direction, from lower to higher, from the heaviness of the cocoon to the lightness of air. It is, by definition, a being between "life and death." In this role, the weightless "weights" of its wings "sink down . . . upon the rose." The rose is the second correlative, the second sign of the human soul. Even in bloom, it is on its way home; it attains the high point of its existence in the face of encroaching death. Between butterfly and rose there exists, then, an inner relationship. They attract one another mutually, show themselves to one another, and, as the butterfly sinks to rest upon the rose, speak to one another the word of love and of farewell. This is also an image of man and wife, together an intensified sign of "light ripening homeward."

The poem begins with a statement. It ends with a proof. It is astonishment at a higher level, the fruit of meditative reflection, when the poetess repeats at the end: "What beautiful otherworldness has been painted on thy dust." In conclusion, explicit reference is made to the symbolic character of image and event. "What a symbol of royalty in the secret of the air." *Symbol of royalty*— the highest among signs. The poetess uses the metaphor of royalty frequently. She speaks, for instance, of "the fish with the purple gills torn out / a king of sorrows" (p. 97); of "this chain of riddles / laid around the neck of night / a royal word written far away" (p. 385); and she knows about the "royal road of secrets" (p. 354). The metaphor of royalty points beyond what is highest and most worthy on earth and into the regions of the divine kingdom of Yahweh, i.e., once more into transcendence. This word, too, is a cipher in the Jewish Cabala.[20] In the poem we have been discussing, the sign of royalty is the butterfly, the rose, the meeting of the two: a "secret" in a double sense. Not everyone heeds the image in its character as a sign. They see and do not see. But the process remains a "secret" even for those who do see. There is no definitive interpretation for the process of living and dying. The referential function of the image empties into infinity.

The penetrating experience of the "I" that speaks out of all these verses is flight—flight as destiny and freedom, as necessity and grace; flight as both the potentiality and the predestination of life; as "epilepsy" and "pursuit" (cf. pp. 77, 95, 160ff., 258). / Compelled to flee, the "I" prays "for the blinking of an eye: /

Rest upon the flight" (p. 258). The prayer is heard. The "hearing" is depicted in the following lines:

> *During the flight*
> what a great reception
> on the way—
>
> Wrapped
> in the winding cloth of wind
> feet in the prayer of the sand
> that can never say Amen
> for it must be transformed
> from fin to wing
> and further—
>
> The sick butterfly
> will soon have knowledge of the sea again—
> This stone
> with the inscription of the fly
> has come into my hand—
>
> In place of a homeland
> I hold the metamorphoses of the world—[21]

The man forced into flight is accorded not only a "brief stopping
place" (p. 164), as in an earlier poem, but "a great reception."
In what does the reception consist? Who grants it? The reception
"during the flight" (an echo of "upon the flight") consists in
becoming aware of an image, more specifically, of the poetess's
great image of metamorphosis. She recognizes at once its character as a sign, as an objective correlative, as the reflection of her own
condition. In the encounter with the image of the butterfly, the
"I" experiences rest during the flight, confirmation, direction,
hope, and consolation. The butterfly is a "sick butterfly" at rest.
It, too, is on its way—on its way to the sea. What is its sickness?
We are not told explicitly, only implicitly. It is sick from weariness, from longing, from flight, from the long journey.

"Wrapped / in the winding cloth of wind / feet in the prayer
of the sand," it stands, sits, and lies there. "Wrapped in the winding cloth of wind" is an ironic euphemism, for it means not
wrapped in the winds, but exposed to them. "But the wind is no

home / it only licks, like the animals, / the wounds of the body," we read in the poem "Jäger, mein Sternbild" [Huntsman, my Constellation] (p. 258). The wind is no house, no covering, no vis-à-vis. And yet it is a kind of place, of covering, of vis-à-vis: a place *sui generis*, i.e., the place in which "flight and metamorphosis" occur, where the barriers of space are removed—a kind of unpredictable "being-spoken-to" from all sides. It indicates her symbolic and cosmic view of the butterfly, her extraordinary awareness of this removal of barriers, as well as of space, person, and transcendence, when the poetess says that the butterfly's "feet [are] in the prayer of the sand." That is, of course, a mystic interpretation. The butterfly is understood as the reflection of the speaking "I." But that does not exclude the possibility that the butterfly achieves, precisely through this recognition by another, its own cosmic individuality (cf. Rom. 8:19ff.). It stands in the sand "that can never say Amen." If we tried to count the grains of sand, we would never come to an end. In this not-coming-to-an-end, the sand is like the endless sea toward which the butterfly is moving. To the objective endlessness of the goal there corresponds the subjective endlessness of the "I's" own condition, of prayer. It is not only the sand "that can never say Amen," it is also [stylistically, this is the figure of enallage, of extension of the basic reference of a word] the butterfly; it is also man "during the flight": "it [the butterfly] must be transformed / from fin to wing / and further." "Fin" and "wing" are formally shortened expressions. We have already seen that, in the imaginative world of the poetess, longing—the necessity of flight and the task of metamorphosis—has its origin in the "fishes' fins" (p. 140). In man, flight and metamorphosis begin "back among the stars in memory / borne on the waters of sleep" (p. 162). The way, "the vein of gold in mortals / sinks under the awareness of water / and works for God" (cf. p. 354). From this state in which it has fins and is aware of water, the creature that is subject to flight and metamorphosis must be transformed into "the cocoon of the silkworm" (p. 258), into "wing / and further." But even the winged state is not a final state. As a winged creature of dust, man must—the "sick butterfly" must—be further transformed until the last metamorphosis of "death" has been completed by the "resurrection" (p. 317) from "the ashes of the resurrection" (p. 384).

At present, the sick butterfly has lost its awareness of the sea and therewith its inner compulsion toward the goal. The loss is part of its sickness. But it "will soon have knowledge of the sea again," of the nearness of what it seeks and the goal of its predestination. Surprisingly, the poem offers a second image of encounter: "This stone / with the inscription of the fly / has come into my hand," says the lyric "I." This is no egotistical grasping for the object seen, but a reverent contemplation, which comprehends the stone as a gift, the gift as a sign. What kind of stone is it? Probably a piece of amber found in the sands on the beach, in which an insect has been embedded. Far from being valued for the sake of adornment, the amber is a sign for faith. Was not the slain Christ entombed in the rock as the insect is in this stone? The stone thus found is an image of death. "Job's four-winds-cry / and the cry hidden in the Garden of Olives / like an insect in crystal overcome by weakness," so reads the poem "Landschaft aus Schreien" [A Landscape of Cries] (p. 221ff., cf. p. 225). As the Christ of Easter, the Christ entombed is the sign of a "resurrection in stone" (cf. p. 190). The stone with the "inscription of the fly" is, for the believing "I" who contemplates it, a sign of its own death and its own resurrection.

Butterfly and stone-enclosed fly are, symbolically, forms of the "metamorphoses of the world." The rest during the flight, the reception, the contemplation, the gift—all consist in this: that they reveal to the lyric "I" both its own inner condition and its own state. The point of departure for the poem was a situation of flight. The two middle strophes showed two images of metamorphosis. On the basis of these strophes, the final one points, on a higher level, to the flight of the "lyric I," a flight transformed by the sign of death and resurrection. The final verses read: "Instead of a homeland / I hold the metamorphoses of the world." Critics have recognized in them the lyrical interpretation of the poetess herself, the sum of her existence incorporated in a poetic formula. It is no accident that not only the word "flight" but also the word "reception" appeared in Nelly Sachs' first poem, "In the dwellings of death." Star and sunbeam received there the "fugitives from smoke." In this poem, the "sick butterfly" and the "fly" in stone receive the fugitive. Unlikely hosts give a "great reception," behind which stands the God of Israel. The "sea" is a sign of Him; the "metamorphoses" are paths to Him. The man who is in flight throughout his existence possesses no home. He cannot cling to anything, cannot rest; he is not rooted in what we generally call a "homeland." What is a "homeland" for other men is for him the "metamorphoses of the world." What poverty! What a presentation of life—an exceedingly challenged and symbolical existence—the most exposed path to the God of creation and of resurrection.

In the twentieth century, destiny has replaced the medieval pilgrim with the refugee. Yet we refuse to recognize his existence. Regarded from its brighter side, flight means "journey." Whatever is found on the journey: fish, butterfly, rose, or loved ones; whoever "comes from the earth" (p. 331) is, in the language of the Bible, "dust"; born in dust, perishable dust, dust of metamorphosis, "dust, that stands open to a blessed encounter" (p. 149). The man who is completely and finally transformed, the resurrected man, will be the "dustless" man—goal of all flight and of all metamorphosis. Surpassing all the definitions of man that have been hurled at us in recent times, Nelly Sachs defines man out of her Biblical faith as one "on the journey into dustlessness." What definition could be more necessary for us? Technical man wants to change; mystical man lets himself be changed.

Notes

Chapter 1

[1] Cf. R. Guardini, *Das Ende der Neuzeit* (Basel, 1950; Würzburg, n.d.); H. Freyer, *Theorie des gegenwärtigen Zeitalters* (Stuttgart, 1955); A. Hauser, *Sozialgeschichte der Kunst und Literatur*, 2 vols. (Munich, 1958); A. Gehlen, *Die Seele im technischen Zeitalter. Sozialpsychologische Probleme in der industriellen Gesellschaft* (Hamburg, 1957); D. Riesman, *Die einsame Masse* (Hamburg, 1958); G. Lukács, *Literatursoziologie*, ed. P. Ludz (Neuwied, 1901).

[2] Even the word "nature" itself has received new connotations. It is no longer regarded as "saving" nature, nor as romantic or youthful nature; it is not even regarded primarily as the opposite of the great city. Nature is, for the average consciousness of a technical world, above all the object of scientific research; the description of nature is no longer something analogous to Stifter's description of a lake or a threatening thunderstorm; it is rather a most precise, brief, but comprehensive collection of information about nature as governed by laws. Cf. W. Heisenberg, *Das Naturbild der heutigen Physik* (Hamburg, 1955), p. 11f.

[3] More than fifty years ago, Malte Laurids Brigge, in Rilke's novel of the same name, delivered his monologue about standardized life and impersonal death.

[4] The attempt at a new mythologizing of the hero in parodistic form and language, as, for instance, the inferior superiority of the shrewd Tin Drum cretin in Günter Grass' novel, does not contradict what has been said. This totally unidealistic figure has been consciously conceived as an anti-hero. The anti-hero remains a possibility, as does, in a certain sense, the negative hero.

[5] E. M. Forster, *Aspects of the Novel* (London, 1927); trans. *Ansichten des Romans* (Frankfurt, 1962), pp. 53, 95. The tradition of "characters" in a

country where the "character novel" was more widespread than the *Bildungs-roman* in Germany is hardly to be wondered at.

6 N. Sarraute, "Das Zeitalter des Misstrauens," *Akzente*, vol. 5 (1958), p. 34ff. Eugènie Grandet is the chief character in Balzac's novel of the same name, published in 1833. The novel tells the story of a disappointed woman, who, at the end, is "not of this world though living in the midst of it; who has been created to be a wonderful wife and mother, but who has neither husband, nor children, nor family." Cf. S. O'Faolain, *The Vanishing Hero. Studies in Novelists of the Twenties* (London, 1956); W. Weidlé, *Die Sterblichkeit der Musen* (Stuttgart, 1958), p. 47ff.

7 Alain Robbe-Grillet, "Bemerkungen über einige Wesenszüge des herkömmlichen Romans," *Akzente*, vol. 5 (1958), p. 28. Forster, *Ansichten des Romans*, p. 34. In *Theorie des Romans* (Helsinki, 1935), p. 167f., R. Koskimies says "In all literary creativity, the literary plot is doubtless the central core whose clarification (!) either by momentary illumination of the intuition or as a result of lengthy meditation gives every, even the least, literary work of art with a narrative content its own right to exist and its own reason for being."

8 Weidlé, *Die Sterblichkeit*, p. 11.

9 Cf. Forster, *Ansichten des Romans*, pp. 38 and 92f.

10 Ibid., p. 59.

11 Cf. E. Lämmert, *Bauformen des Erzählens* (Stuttgart, 1955), p. 24f., and Koskimies, *Theorie des Romans*, p. 166ff.

12 W. Kayser, "Wer erzählt den Roman?" in *Die Neue Rundschau*, vol. 68 (1957), p. 451.

13 Cf. F. K. Stanzel, *Typische Erzählformen des Romans* (Göttingen, 1964).

14 W. Kayser, *Entstehung und Krise des modernen Romans* (Stuttgart, 1963), p. 34. Separate printing of article in *Deutsche Vierteljahrsschrift*, 1953. Cf. E. Kahler, "Untergang und Übergang der epischen Kunstform," *Die Neue Rundschau*, vol. 64 (1953), pp. 1–44.

15 For comments on "narrative time" (*Erzählzeit*) and "narrated time" (*erzählte Zeit*), see G. Müller, *Die Bedeutung der Zeit in der Erzählkunst* (Bonn, 1947).

Chapter 2

1 Hermann Broch, *Gesammelte Werke*, vol. 8 (Zürich, 1957), p. 282. To say that Kafka wrote "without any artistic intention" is a misunderstanding on the part of Broch that has since been sufficiently disproved. The highly sophisticated Broch had a predilection for the seemingly naïve creative genius.

2 Klaus Mann, *The Turning Point* (1942). Enlarged German version: *Der Wendepunkt* (Frankfurt, 1952; posthumously), pp. 232, 347.

3 Cf. *Dichtung im Unterricht*, vol. 9: "Franz Kafka. Sieben Prosastücke, ausgewählt und interpretiert von Franz Baumer" (Munich, 1965); *Wilhelm Königs Erläuterungen zu den Klassikern*, vol. 279: "Erläuterungen zu Franz Kafkas Erzählungen" (Hollfeld).

4 H. Tauber, *Franz Kafka. Eine Deutung seiner Werke* (doctoral dissertation, Zürich, 1941).

⁵ Heinrich Politzer, *Franz Kafka, der Künstler* (Frankfurt, 1965), pp. 512–525.

⁶ *Nachwort zu Kafkas "Prozess,"* 3rd ed. (Frankfurt, 1946), p. 316; cf. p. 317f. On the subject of Kafka's penultimate will, see Politzer, *Franz Kafka*, p. 418f.

⁷ Max Brod, *Franz Kafka. Eine Biographie,* 3rd ed. (Berlin, Frankfurt, 1954), p. 207; Brod, *Franz Kafkas Glauben und Lehre. Kafka und Tolstoi* (Munich, 1948). See also Brod's concluding remarks on the novels *The Trial* and *The Castle.* Brod's distinction between the Kafka of the aphorisms and the Kafka of the novels and novelle was attacked by D. Hasselblatt, *Zauber und Logik. Eine Kafka-Studie* (Cologne, 1964), p. 190. Where Brod simplifies and overemphasizes, Hasselblatt rejects completely—hardly a less extreme position.

⁸ Brod, *Franz Kafkas Glauben und Lehre,* pp. 85, 90. Brod denies that Kafka "felt the need of finding God outside the Jewish community. Kafka never experienced a need to leave the Jewish community. On the contrary, . . . in his later life, he continued to tighten the bonds that linked him to the Jewish community" (p. 54). Brod continued his interpretations along these lines in *Verzweiflung und Erlösung im Werk Franz Kafkas* (Frankfurt, 1959). M. Susmann gives a different emphasis to the Jewish-Zionistic interpretation of Kafka in "Das Hiob-Problem bei Franz Kafka," in *Der Morgen,* vol. 5 (1929), pp. 31–49. Brod has included the Jewish-Zionistic views on Kafka and Job in his biography of Kafka, p. 214f.

⁹ H. Mayer, "Kafka und kein Ende," in *Ansichten zur Literatur* (Hamburg, 1962), p. 56.

¹⁰ H. J. Schoeps, "Theologische Motive in der Dichtung Franz Kafkas," in *Die Neue Rundschau* (1951), pp. 21, 32, 37. Literary critics rightly take issue with Schoeps for his identification of "castle" with "heaven" and "village" with "the world of men" in the novel *The Castle.* As early as 1934, G. Anders had spoken of Kafka's work as "theology without God." See G. Anders, *Kafka pro und contra,* 2nd ed. (Munich, 1963), p. 110. In an article "Bewusstsein und Dasein in Kafkas 'Prozess,'" in *Die Neue Rundschau* (1951), p. 32, Volkmann-Schluck speaks of the "hieroglyphics of a negative religion" in Kafka's writings. Maurice Blanchot points to a fundamentally anti-Zionist attitude in Kafka's diaries; see A. Flores and H. Swander, *Franz Kafka Today* (Madison, 1958), p. 206f.

¹¹ R. Rochefort, *Kafka ou l'Irréductible Espoir* (Paris, 1947); German translation: *Kafka oder die unzerstörbare Hoffnung* (Vienna, Munich, 1955), pp. 23, 25, 20. Rochefort, it seems to me, goes too far in interpreting Kafka's intention as a wish "for annihilation" and his personal life as a "systematic self-destruction" (p. 25). He pays too little attention to such problems as Kafka's inability to come to a decision, his ambivalence, his anxious self-preservation, his psychologically conditioned incapability of surrendering himself totally to another person (especially of the opposite sex), his "fear of being born," the problems of his split personality, his basic distrust of this world.

¹² Martin Buber, *Zwei Glaubensweisen* (Zürich, 1950); also in *Werke I, Schriften zur Philosophie* (Munich, Heidelberg, 1962), pp. 651–782; quotations, p. 777f. The racially and sociologically Jewish community in which

218

Kafka lived was only partially a religious one and could, therefore, be only partially a "concealing" one.

13 Brod, *Franz Kafka. Eine Biographie*, p. 208.

14 W. Grenzmann, *Deutsche Dichtung der Gegenwart*, 2nd ed. (Frankfurt, 1955), p. 339; W. Grenzmann, *Dichtung und Glaube*, 3rd ed. (Bonn, 1957), p. 16of.

15 Th. Adorno, "Aufzeichnungen zu Kafka," in *Die Neue Rundschau* (1953), pp. 325–353; quotation, p. 340.

16 G. Anders, *Kafka*, p. 108.

17 H. Pongs, *Franz Kafka. Dichter des Labyrinths* (Heidelberg, 1960), p. 58.

18 Buber, *Werke I, Schriften*, p. 777f. Cf. Kafka's notes in the series "Er" [He], 1920: "Original sin, the ancient injustice which man has committed, consists in the reproach that man makes and does not cease to make; that an injustice has been done him, that original sin has been committed against him" (*Beschreibungen eines Kampfes*, p. 295f.).

19 Brod, *Franz Kafkas Glauben und Lehre*, pp. 9, 54, 49.

20 R. Wilhelm in *Hochland* (1965), pp. 339–349; quotations, p. 348f. Wilhelm's positive quotations come, as might have been expected, from the diaries, but the title of his article speaks of the religious element in the "writings." Nor does he pursue the question of whether or not the "indestructible" element in Kafka's works is to be understood from a specifically religious point of view.

21 In this connection, see K. Rahner, "Ätiologie. Begriff und theologische Verwendung," in *Lexikon für Theologie und Kirche*, 2nd ed., vol. 1 (Freiburg, 1957), p. 1011ff.

22 W. Emrich, *Franz Kafka* (Bonn: Athenäum Press, 1958), p. 55. Emrich understands the word "transcendent" in the second part of the sentence as "that which transcends consciousness." From Kafka's statement: "One possible way of expressing this state of hiddenness is the belief in a personal God" (H 44), Emrich concludes: "By these words, Kafka unmistakably designates belief in a personal God as an unconscious obscuration of the original belief in the indestructible in man." Such an interpretation does not seem justified. W. Sokel, in his book *Franz Kafka—Tragik und Ironie* (Munich, Vienna, 1964), p. 267, also questions the existence of a "Jenseits" (a life after death) in the Jewish or Christian sense.

23 W. Muschg, *Tragische Literaturgeschichte*, 3rd ed. (Bern, 1957), p. 322.

24 Cf. W. Muschg, *Die Zerstörung der deutschen Literatur*, 3rd ed. (Bern, 1958), p. 205ff.; M. Goth, *F. Kafka et les lettres françaises* (Paris, 1956); J. Wahl, "Kafka et Kierkegaard," in *Petite histoire de l'existentialisme* (Paris, 1947).

25 Camus saw Kafka's works as the prefiguration of his own myth of Sisyphus and the anticipation of his proof for the existence of the absurd. But he felt, too, that Kafka had betrayed the notion of the absurd as it applied to God by embracing the God who devoured him. Cf. A. Camus, *Der Mythos von Sisyphos* (Hamburg, 1959), p. 110. It is clear that Camus interpreted Kafka very narrowly and from the single point of view of his own Sisyphus concept. "Kafka has renounced his gods very conditionally," writes Politzer in *Franz Kafka*, p. 474, "and then only negatively and, so to speak, clandestinely."

26 Adorno, "Aufzeichnungen zu Kafka," p. 325.

27 M. Bense, *Die Theorie Kafkas* (Cologne, Berlin, 1952), p. 90. There is no basic inquiry here into Kafka's relationship to reality. The distinction between "ideal and real factors and spheres" is omitted (pp. 19ff., 26ff.). Only the state of awareness is brought under consideration.

28 Emrich, *Franz Kafka*, pp. 59, 61.

29 K. Wagenbach, *Franz Kafka. In Selbstzeugnissen und Bilddokumenten* (Hamburg: Rowohlt, 1964), p. 17. This little volume offers an excellent first introduction to Kafka's person, world, and work.

30 G. Janouch, *Gespräche mit Kafka* (Frankfurt, 1951), p. 42. For Prague as the background of Kafka's works, the following are important: P. Eisner, *Franz Kafka and Prague* (New York, 1950); H. Politzer, "Prague and the Origins of R. M. Rilke, F. Kafka and F. Werfel," in *Modern Language Quarterly*, vol. 16, pp. 49–62; K. Hermsdorf, "Kafka und Prag," in *Roman und Weltbild* (Berlin-Ost, 1961), pp. 129–138.

31 Politzer, *Franz Kafka*, p. 247; K. Wagenbach, *Franz Kafka. Eine Biographie seiner Jugend* (Bern, 1958). Wagenbach has also published a *Kafka-Symposium* (Berlin, 1951) with valuable biographical and interpretational materials and a critical study of the dates of all the texts.

32 Emrich, *Franz Kafka*, p. 38. H is the symbol for the volume *Hochzeitsvorbereitungen auf dem Lande und andere Prosa aus dem Nachlass* (Frankfurt, 1953). Cf. also Kafka's letter to Brod, dated "end of March, 1917," "On Freud," in Kafka, *Briefe* (Frankfurt, 1958), p. 240. An undated fragment undoubtedly intended as depth psychology and probably also as critically ironic, reads, "We are digging the pit of Babylon" (H 387).

33 H. Kaiser, "Franz Kafkas Inferno," in *Imago* (Vienna, 1931), pp. 41–103; quotations, pp. 54ff. and 60. Kaiser's interpretation of "In der Strafkolonie" [In the Penal Colony] is even more extremely psychoanalytic.

34 Emrich, *Franz Kafka*, p. 38.

35 A. Kuhr, "Neurotische Aspekte bei Heidegger und Kafka," in *Zeitschrift für psychosomatische Medizin* (Göttingen, 1954–1955), pp. 217–227; quotations, p. 222ff. Methodologically, Kuhr puts too much emphasis on biography. He interprets Kafka himself in terms of his literary work and the literary work in terms of Kafka's personal life.

36 Emrich, *Franz Kafka*, p. 38.

37 Charles Neider, Paul Goodmann, Erich Fromm, Joachim H. Seypel, Angel and Kate Flores, and Michael Kowal might be mentioned here.

38 K. Weinberg, *Kafkas Dichtungen. Die Travestien des Mythos* (Bern, Munich, 1963). There is no question that Weinberg has produced a very independent work and has repeatedly discovered hidden relationships. But his work suffers from his one-sided and exaggerated interpretation of symbols as archetypal myths.

39 Pongs, *Franz Kafka*, p. 18. Even before Pongs, Werner Vordtriede had stressed Kafka's "ambivalence" in his contribution "Letters to Milena," in Angel Flores and Homer Swander, eds., *Franz Kafka Today* (Madison, 1958). Anders had already spoken of "ambiguity" (though not yet in the narrower psychological meaning of the word), p. 37ff. Sokel gives the whole second half of his book the heading "Die Tragik der Ambivalenz," p. 107ff.; see also pp. 251 and 541.

40 Adorno, "Aufzeichnungen zu Kafka," p. 332.

41 Politzer, *Franz Kafka*, p. 472.

[42] Emrich, *Franz Kafka*, p. 271.

[43] Hannah Arendt, "Franz Kafka, von neuem gewürdigt," in *Die Wandlung*, vol. 12 (Heidelberg, 1946), pp. 1050-1062; quotations, pp. 1052f., 1054f., 1058, 1062.

[44] Adorno, "Aufzeichnungen zu Kafka," pp. 343f., 332f., 347, 351. For a counterbalance to Adorno's too one-sidedly empirical conception of time and space in Kafka's works, see above (Ch. 2) under the heading "Considerations of Form and Structural Analysis," pp. 50-55.

[45] W. Emrich, "Franz Kafkas Bruch mit der Tradition und sein neues Gesetz," in *Protest und Verheissung* (Frankfurt, Bonn: Athenäum Press, 1960), pp. 248, 243ff.; W. Emrich, "Franz Kafka," in *Deutsche Literatur im 20. Jahrhundert*, eds. H. Friedmann and O. Mann, 3rd ed. (Heidelberg, 1959), p. 337; Emrich, *Franz Kafka*, pp. 25ff., 45ff., 53ff., 52, 72, 56.

[46] H. Richter, *Franz Kafka. Werk und Entwurf* (Berlin, 1962), pp. 13, 14, 25; F. Beissner, *Der Erzähler Franz Kafka* (Stuttgart, 1952), p. 28.

[47] P. Reimann, "Die gesellschaftliche Problematik in Kafkas Romanen," in *Weimarer Beiträge. Zeitschrift für deutsche Literaturgeschichte* (Weimar, 1957), pp. 598-618; quotations, pp. 600, 601, 603, 618; Richter, *Franz Kafka*, p. 29.

[48] Hermsdorf, "Kafka und Prag," pp. 19ff., 114ff., 99, 105ff.

[49] Richter, *Franz Kafka*, pp. 234, 285. Most Western critics doubt that Kafka's directive to destroy his literary remains could have been motivated by considerations of the "intrinsic value" of his message and by self-criticism of the "content." They doubt, and with reason, the unambiguous nature of his testamentary dispositions as such. In this connection, see Politzer's discussion of Kafka's "penultimate will," in *Franz Kafka*, pp. 416ff.

[50] What Hermsdorf calls "Kafkaesque irrationalism" and "latent fideism" is at the same time Kafka's premonition and knowledge of an objectivity that penetrated and surpassed everything and to which he was unable to put a name; a premonition, in fact, which even included within itself a lapse from that same objectivity, and which for that reason as much as for any other, could not be named, a part of the "original fall of man" (cf. Janouch, *Gespräche mit Kafka*, p. 73). It is well known that Kafka judged the Russian Revolution otherwise than did the Marxist critics of capitalism. Janouch reports Kafka's words: "The war, the revolution in Russia, the misery in the whole world, would seem to me to be like an inundation of evil. It is a deluge. The war has opened the sluice gates of chaos. The historical event is no longer borne by individuals, but only by the masses. We are being buffeted, driven, swept away. We are suffering history" (p. 72).

[51] G. Lukács, *Wider den missverstandenen Realismus* (Hamburg, 1958), pp. 87, 51, 33, 36. In *Zauber und Logik. Eine Kafka-Studie*, p. 13ff., Hasselblatt, under the heading "Kafka, ideologisch disqualifiziert," reports on the most recent Communist and Marxist interpretations in Eastern Europe that discuss Kafka from the standpoint of cultural politics. The book contains the lectures of the Communist Kafka-Symposium held in May, 1963 at Liblice Palace near Prague.

[52] Hasselblatt, *Zauber und Logik*, p. 28; H. Politzer, "Problematik und Probleme der Kafka-Forschung," in *Monatshefte für deutschen Unterricht* (Madison, Wisconsin, 1950), p. 279; also to be found in Politzer, *Franz Kafka*, p. 8; M. Walser, Nachwort in *Beschreibung einer Form* (Munich,

1961), p. 129; Emrich, in *Deutsche Literatur des 20. Jahrhunderts*, 3rd ed. (1959), p. 319.

53 Beissner's, and to some extent also Walser's, theory of the consistently unified and single narrative point of view from "within the soul of the main character" (F. Beissner, *Der Erzähler Franz Kafka*, Stuttgart, 1952) and the "congruence of the author with his medium, the hero" (Walser, *Beschreibung*, p. 22ff.) have been questioned by Sokel on the basis of broader textual scrutiny. Hillmann, too, recognizes a second narrative point of view, that of the "outer level": "not from the point of view of the hero with regard to the secondary characters, but directed toward the main character himself" (Hillmann, *Dichtungstheorie und Dichtungsgestalt* [Bonn, 1964], p. 137).

54 Cl. Heselhaus, "Kafkas Erzählformen," in *Deutsche Vierteljahrsschrift* (1952), pp. 353–376. "Kafka's anti-fairytale gives form to an experience of the world that emanates from the disappointment of a naïve soul and from indignation at the malicious and vile world. His representational technique aims at presenting a disillusioning caricature of the hostility of the world" (p. 358). "The anti-novel lacks the world context and the foreknowledge of the fairy tale" (p. 368). "The author of the anti-novel is not one who knows, but one who questions . . ." (p. 371). Heselhaus' concept of the anti-fairytale has been criticized by Sokel, *Franz Kafka*, p. 89, Hasselblatt, *Zauber und Logik*, p. 27, and Politzer, *Franz Kafka*, p. 126.

55 Emrich, *Franz Kafka*, pp. 74ff., 81; W. Emrich, "Die Bilderwelt Franz Kafkas," in *Akzente* (1960) and in *Protest und Verheissung*, pp. 249–263. "Similar tendencies appear in the surrealistic works of his contemporaries and in the novels of James Joyce, where the most varied elements of our empirical and mental spheres of reality are placed near and in one another without any explanatory comment; the sublime stands beside the trivial or changes into it without any change in its own status," (p. 253). "There no longer exists any such reciprocal relationship between the psyche and the empirical world of objects as existed in the Age of Goethe," (p. 254).

56 Politzer, *Franz Kafka*, pp. 43ff., 130ff., 45ff. The English title of this book is *Parable and Paradox* (New York, 1962).

57 W. Sokel, *Franz Kafka*. See the titles of the various parts of his work. The theme of Kafka's collected works appears in Sokel's interpretation "as the portrayal of a twofold struggle. This struggle is, first of all, a struggle of the ego with itself, a splitting of the 'I' of the stories into two opposed wills that struggle bitterly with one another. Second, it is a struggle of the ego with an overpowering force, a force which rules the reality of the stories because it is operative, while the conscious will of the 'I' remains, with very few exceptions, inoperative" (p. 28).

58 Hillmann, *Dichtungstheorie*, pp. 113–194.

59 Hasselblatt, *Zauber und Logik*, pp. 33ff., 54ff., 71ff., 87ff., 149ff., 171ff.

60 Cf. N. Frye, *Analyse der Literaturkritik* (Stuttgart, 1964), p. 74.

61 H. Mayer, "Kafka und kein Ende," p. 66. Kafka, H 100. W. H. Auden, in Flores and Swander, "Vorspruch zur Einleitung," in *Franz Kafka Today*.

Chapter 3

1 Aldous Huxley, *Literature and Science* (New York, 1963). Kurz uses

H. E. Herlitschka's German version of this work, *Literatur und Wissenschaft*. All quotations in the present English translation are, however, from Huxley's own text. [Translator's note.]

[2] Huxley, *Literature and Science*, p. 3.

[3] Ibid., p. 5.

[4] Ibid., p. 8.

[5] Ibid., pp. 7–8. Cf. also A. Brunner, *Erkenntnistheorie* (Cologne, 1948), p. 287ff.: "Die Naturwissenschaften."

[6] Huxley, *Literature and Science*, pp. 9–10.

[7] Huxley mentions, for instance, the scholarly findings of science and their antischolarly use for the organized manipulation of man into so-called mass murder.

[8] Huxley, *Literature and Science*, p. 82.

[9] Ibid., p. 77.

[10] Ibid., pp. 38–39. Literature as "a magical object endowed . . . with mysterious powers" (p. 38) must be understood correctly. It seems preferable not to seek its mystery and fascination in the realms of magic, fairy tale, or myth. Its fascination lies, in good measure, in the literary presentation and form itself.

[11] The famous line originates in Mallarmé's sonnet "On the Grave of E. A. Poe." The French word "tribu" is derived from the Latin "tribus." Its first reference is to a group of persons speaking the same language, then to the "plebs," the "masses." In the present context, not only the common language in general use but also the much-used language of daily life is meant.

[12] Werner Heisenberg, "Sprache und Wirklichkeit in der modernen Physik," in the lecture series *Wort und Wirklichkeit* (Munich, 1960), p. 37f.

[13] E. Grassi, "Das Naturbild der heutigen Physik," in *Rowohlts deutsche Enzyklopädie*, no. 8 (Hamburg, 1955), p. 133. Cf. also E. Grassi, *Von Ursprung und Grenzen der Geisteswissenschaften und Naturwissenschaften* (Munich, 1950).

[14] Since Heidegger, we have been aware that the question that must precede any attempt to distinguish between "nature" and "spirit," i.e., the question as to what supports and governs both, viz., being, has not been sufficiently discussed in Western philosophy. See W. Strolz, "Die Frage nach der ursprünglichen Einheit der Wissenschaften," in *Experiment und Erfahrung in Wissenschaft und Kunst*, ed. W. Strolz (Freiburg and Munich, 1963).

[15] Huxley, *Literature and Science*, p. 62.

[16] Ibid., pp. 60–61.

[17] H. Broch, *Gesammelte Werke* (Zürich, 1953ff.), vol. 2, p. 597 and vol. 6, pp. 69, 197. "For thirty years I have been tormented by the question of the 'observer in the field of observation,' a question that the theory of relativity aroused in me" (letter of Dec. 20, 1949 in vol. 8, p. 369).

[18] Novalis, *Werke, Briefe, Dokumente*, ed. E. Wasmuth (Heidelberg, 1953–1957), Fragmente 1442 and 1444.

[19] Beda Allemann, "Experiment und Erfahrung in der Gegenwartsliteratur," in *Experiment und Erfahrung in Wissenschaft und Kunst*, p. 271.

[20] Ibid., p. 268.

[21] Huxley, *Literature and Science*, p. 111.

[22] E. A. Bowring's translation of this poem appears in *The German Clas-*

sics, ed. Kuno Francke et al. (New York, 1913), vol. 1, pp. 27–28. The two stanzas quoted in the text read as follows:

> Bush and vale thou fill'st again
> With thy misty ray,
> And my spirit's heavy chain
> Casteth far away.
> Thou dost o'er my fields extend
> Thy sweet soothing eye,
> Watching like a gentle friend,
> O'er my destiny.

23 Huxley, *Literature and Science,* p. 116.
24 Ibid., p. 111. Cf. also L. Scheffczyk, "Der Sonnenuntergang des heiligen Franz von Assisi und die Hymne an die Materie des Teilhard de Chardin," in *Geist und Leben* (1962), p. 226.
25 Quoted by W. Clemens, *Das Wesen der Dichtung in der Sicht moderner englischer und amerikanischer Dichter* (Munich, 1961), p. 4.
26 Ibid., p. 5. Eliot's original statement in English, as it appears in this translation, has been quoted from Paul Valéry, *The Art of Poetry,* trans. from the French by Denise Folliot with an introduction by T. S. Eliot (New York, 1958), Introduction, pp. xviii–xx and passim [translator's note].
27 From Wordsworth's preface to the second edition of the *Lyrical Ballads,* quoted in Huxley, pp. 42–43.
28 Even in modern physics, the possibility of a verbal description of certain procedures and experiments has become a problem. See Heisenberg, *Wort und Wirklichkeit,* p. 40f.
29 See also A. Einstein, "Zur Erniedrigung des wissenschaftlichen Menschen," in *Mein Weltbild* (Berlin, 1964), p. 172f.
30 Quoted in Huxley, *Literature and Science,* p. 42.
31 Robert Musil, *Tagebücher, Aphorismen, Essays und Reden* (Hamburg, 1955), p. 755.
32 W. Jens in *Schwierigkeiten, heute die Wahrheit zu schreiben,* ed. H. Friedrich (Munich, 1964), p. 74.
33 Ibid., p. 75f.
34 Werner Heisenberg, *Das Naturbild der heutigen Physik* (Hamburg, 1955), p. 18.
35 H. Broch, *Gesammelte Werke,* vol. 9, p. 291.
36 Heisenberg, *Das Naturbild der heutigen Physik,* p. 18.

Chapter 4

1 Ernst Robert Curtius, *European Literature and the Latin Middle Ages,* trans. Willard R. Trask (New York, 1953), p. 214.
2 See Encyclical *Studiorum ducem,* June 29, 1923 (D 3665ff.).
3 "The Pastoral Constitution on the Church in the Modern World," in *The Documents of Vatican II,* ed. Walter M. Abbott, S.J. (New York, 1966), pp. 268–269, passim.
4 Helmut Heissenbüttel, "13 Hypothesen über Literatur und Wissenschaft als vergleichbare Tätigkeiten," in *Über Literatur* (Freiburg, 1966), p. 208.

[5] Under the heading "Der Literaturbegriff," in Jean Paul Sartre, "Was ist Literatur?" in *Rowohlts deutsche Enzyklopädie*, no. 65 (Hamburg, 1958), p. 176.

[6] Kurz makes a distinction, for which it is difficult to find English equivalents, between "*Dichtung*," here translated "poetical literature" (i.e., prose or poetry), and "*Literatur*," here translated "prosaic literature" (i.e., in the first meaning given by Webster: "of or pertaining to prose; now, usually characteristic of prose as distinguished from poetry"). Both terms refer, as Kurz makes clear in his statement about Hochhuth, to "a linguistic construct that is self-contained by virtue of its language," i.e., to belles-lettres. His last sentence, "*Erzeuger von Literatur heissen heutzutage Schriftsteller*," which I have not translated, distinguishes between "*Schriftsteller*," who write what I have called "prosaic literature," and "*Dichter*," who write "poetical literature." [Translator's note.]

[7] It was the sociologists and cultural critics, in particular, who tried to conceptualize this "today." One might mention, for instance, H. Freyer's *Theorie des gegenwärtigen Zeitalters* (Stuttgart, 1955) as well as the attempts of well-known scholars in the Deutsches Haus in Paris to determine the aspects of scientific and cultural life in the twentieth century (published as *Aspekte der Modernität*, ed. H. Steffen [Göttingen, 1965]), and many volumes in *Rowohlts deutsche Enzyklopädie*.

[8] "The Pastoral Constitution on the Church in the Modern World," pp. 268–270, passim.

[9] Heinrich Heine, *Sämtliche Werke*, ed. Ernst Elster (Leipzig and Vienna, 1887–1890), vol. 3, p. 304 and vol. 5, p. 220.

[10] Curtius, *European Literature*, p. 481, n. 3.

[11] Ibid., p. 224.

[12] Ibid., p. 469.

[13] Paul Hankamer, *Deutsche Gegenreformation und deutsches Barock*, 2nd ed. (Stuttgart, 1947), p. 110. This is an unchanged reprint from 1935.

[14] See the *Ultimistischer Almanach*, ed. K. M. Rarisch (Cologne, 1965).

[15] Ingeborg Bachmann in *Ingeborg Bachmann. Eine Einführung* (Munich, 1963), p. 19.

[16] Hamburg edition, vol. 9, p. 580.

[17] Heissenbüttel, *Über Literatur*, p. 206f.

[18] Bachmann, *Ingeborg Bachmann*, p. 19f.

[19] Gottfried Benn, *Gesammelte Werke*, ed. D. Wellershoff (Wiesbaden, 1959ff.), vol. 4, p. 165.

[20] See, for example, G. Thils, *Theologie der irdischen Wirklichkeiten* (Salzburg, 1954), p. 208ff. A typical example of such well-intentioned thinking and of the adoption of linguistic clichés is to be found in an article in *Der Gral* for April, 1920, which quotes a message from Pope Pius X to the Grail Society: "You rightly reject the notion that religion, which has produced our whole culture and, because it embraces all men, must also govern the whole life of man, is in a position of reciprocity with the Muses; or that the spirit of the poet can be hampered in its freedom of movement by the life-giving breath of religion, which presents to us the perfect ideal of beauty, unrestricted by any limitation—for, in reality, it is nourished and enflamed thereby. For as, in God, the beautiful is identical with the true and the good, so do you correctly insist that the beauty of art must be linked in Christian

poetry to the brilliance of truth and morality, indeed, that its role is to serve the true and the good . . ."

21 F. Muckermann in *Der Gral*, vol. 15 (1920–1921), pp. 194, 197.

22 For example, the poems "Der heilige Gral" and "Der Dichter" in *Der Gral*, vol. 14 (1920), p. 2.

23 Walter Höllerer, "Nach der Menschheitsdämmerung," in *Notizen zur zeitgenössischen Lyrik*, ed. R. Ibel, series 2 (Hamburg, 1955–1956), p. 144.

24 H. E. Bahr, *Poiesis. Theologische Untersuchung der Kunst* (Stuttgart, 1961), p. 232.

25 Bahr, *Poiesis*, p. 233.

26 Bachmann, *Ingeborg Bachmann*, p. 14.

27 "Declaration on Human Freedom," in *Documents of Vatican II*, p. 675.

28 J. B. Metz and Karl Rahner, "Grundstrukturen im heutigen Verhältnis der Kirche zur Welt," in *Handbuch der Pastoraltheologie*, ed. F. X. Arnold et al., (Freiburg and Basel, 1966), vol. 2, part 2, pp. 241, 245; J. B. Metz, "Weltverständnis im Glauben," in *Geist und Leben*, vol. 35 (1962), p. 166.

29 Cf. K. Riesenhuber, "Der anonyme Christ, nach K. Rahner," in *Zeitschrift für katholische Theologie*, vol. 86 (1964), pp. 276–303.

30 Herbert Vorgrimler expresses the opinion: "On the basis of Karl Rahner's theology, the fact will be accepted that there is a truly profane art." In Herbert Vorgrimler, ed., *Gott in Welt. Festgabe für Karl Rahner* (Freiburg, 1964), vol. 2, p. 683.

Chapter 5

1 Hermann Broch, *Gesammelte Werke*, 10 vols. (Zürich, 1953–1961), vol. 6, p. 208; cf. p. 204ff.

2 Broch, *Werke*, vol. 8, pp. 23, 47, 60 (letters); vol. 7, p. 86; vol. 6, p. 140.

3 Broch, *Werke*, vol. 2. Page references within the text refer to this volume. For an interpretation of *Die Schlafwandler*, see K. R. Mandelkow, *H. Brochs Romantrilogie "Die Schlafwandler"* (Heidelberg, 1962); R. Brinkmann, "Romanform und Werttheorie bei H. Broch. Strukturprobleme moderner Dichtung," in *Deutsche Vierteljahrsschrift*, vol. 31 (1957), pp. 169–197; Theodore Ziolkowski, "Zur Entstehung und Struktur von H. Brochs *Die Schlafwandler*," in *Deutsche Vierteljahrsschrift*, vol. 38 (1964), pp. 40–69; R. Geissler, "H. Broch. *Die Schlafwandler*," in *Möglichkeiten des modernen deutschen Romans*, ed R. Geissler (Frankfurt, 1962), pp. 102–160; H. Arntzen, "H. Broch. *Die Schlafwandler*," in H. Arntzen, *Der moderne deutsche Roman* (Heidelberg, 1962), pp. 58–75; E. Kahler, *Die Philosophie von Hermann Broch* (Tübingen, 1962).

4 Broch, *Werke*, vol. 8, p. 21f.

5 Ibid., vol. 8, p. 184; cf. p. 104. Hannah Arendt, "H. Broch und der moderne Roman," in *Der Monat*, vol. 1, no. 8/9 (1948–1949), p. 148.

6 Broch, *Werke*, vol. 8, p. 19.

7 Ibid., vol. 8, p. 45.

8 Ibid., vol. 10, p. 390, n. 51.

9 Letter of Immermann to his brother Ferdinand, April 1930, in Karl Leberecht Immermann, *Die Epigonen* (Düsseldorf, 1836), book 2, chap. 10.

[10] The word "metaphysical" is one of the basic concepts in Broch's vocabulary.

[11] As early as 1850–1851, in the foreword to *Die Ritter vom Geiste* (9 vols., 1850f.), Karl Ferdinand Gutzkow had outlined the norms of the novel of "juxtaposition" [*das Roman des Nebeneinander*] as opposed to the traditional novel, which depicts events in sequence [*das Roman des Nacheinander*].

[12] Gustave Flaubert presents a typically "romantic" person in *Madame Bovary*. Bertold Brecht used the epithet "romantic" in this sense in his early play *Trommeln in der Nacht* [Drums in the Night] (1919).

[13] Romantic characters belong to Broch's stock in trade. Cf. *Die Schuldlosen* [The Guiltless Ones] (1950) and Rosshaupt, Nazi leader of a volunteer corps, in the *Filsmann*-fragment.

[14] Broch, *Werke*, vol. 2, p. 204; cf. pp. 222, 306, 529. A striking likeness to this "flaw in the world" occurs a hundred years earlier in Heinrich Heine's *Reisebilder* [Travel Pictures] (4 vols., 1826–1831) book 3, chap. 4, where Heine speaks of the "Riss der Welt."

[15] Another basically anarchical character is Broch's "Marius" in *Der Versucher*.

[16] Like the romantic and anarchical man, the "objective" man is also to be found throughout Broch's work. The dying Vergil comments on a pair of fleeing murderers (Huguenau, too, is a murderer): "it is the fearfulness of the objective that is no longer concerned with man" (*Werke*, vol. 3, p. 126). The murder of Jews in the later concentration camps was also "objective."

[17] Broch, *Werke*, vol. 8, p. 51.

[18] Ibid., vol. 2, p. 684; cf. vol. 10, pp. 333, 389, n. 29.

[19] Ibid., vol. 10, p. 319.

[20] Ibid., and vol. 8, p. 61. In the present context, it is impossible to discuss the integration of the essays into the novel as a whole.

[21] Ibid., vol. 8, pp. 321, 115; cf. vol. 10, p. 319f. The beginning of Broch's thought about the philosophy of history revealed in the essays on the "Disintegration of Values" antedates the novel. Its incorporation into the novel belongs, in the history of its development, to the last stage (Ziolkowski, "Zur Entstehung," p. 54ff.).

[22] In criticizing their era, the Young Germans had opposed their "idea of the new time" to the "faded old feudal era." Their writings were a conglomeration of ideas drawn from the French Revolution and the Hegelian belief in progress, of sexual erotic efforts toward emancipation, and of utopian early socialism.

[23] Broch, *Werke*, vol. 8, p. 45.

[24] Cf. the view of Novalis in his essay "Die Christenheit oder Europa" (1798; printed 1826). Cf. also Sedlmayr's thesis about the "loss of the center" in his book of the same name: Hans Sedlmayr, *Verlust der Mitte* (Salzburg, 1948).

[25] Broch, *Werke*, vol. 7, p. 209f. These ideas were, it is true, first formulated in Broch's studies of "mass psychology," but, so far as content is concerned, the basic theme is already present in *Die Schlafwandler*.

[26] Ibid., vol. 2, pp. 477, 598; vol. 7, pp. 208–210; cf. vol. 4, pp. 70, 74; vol. 9, pp. 273, 282. This is a key word in Broch's thought.

[27] One might compare this contemporary criticism with the superficial sar-

casm in, for example, the third part of Günter Grass' *Die Hundejahre* (Neuwied, 1963).

28 Broch, *Werke*, vol. 8, p. 45. The title *Die Schlafwandler* occurs as early as 1929. Broch had at first thought of another title, which would either place one of the characters in the foreground (Bertrand, Huguenau, etc.), or would emphasize the genre ("historical novel") (vol. 8, p. 13).

29 Ibid., vol. 9, pp. 249, 277, 284; vol. 2, p. 609. In a letter of 1949, Broch uses the expression "increasing wakefulness" to describe the fruit of one's years of life (vol. 8, p. 345). Here, too, he criticizes "the romanticists"—in this case, even the literary romanticists—and "that twilight condition in which the happiness of younger men finds fulfillment" (ibid.).

30 Ibid., vol. 8, p. 17.

31 In speaking of "das Material für die rationale *Welt*formung," Kurz misquotes Broch, who speaks of "*Wert*formung": the formation of *values*. I have retained Kurz's word in translation, however, since it is basic to his discussion of the formation of values as one part of the formation of the world (see below). [Translator's note.]

32 Broch, *Werke*, vol. 6. p. 320.

33 Ibid., cf. vol. 8, pp. 13, 17, 27, 47, 57; vol. 6, pp. 57f., 324; vol. 7, p. 86.

34 Ibid., vol. 8, pp. 45, 17f., 47.

35 Ibid., vol. 10, p. 280f.

36 Ibid., vol. 8, p. 18.

37 Ibid.

38 Accounts of the genesis of the novel and the testimony of the novel itself make it clear that Bertrand II is not really identical with Bertrand I (Bertrand I commits suicide), as Mandelkow, *H. Brochs Romantrilogie*, sought to prove. Ziolkowski, too, on the basis of the "methodological prospectus" of the manuscript, disagrees expressly with Mandelkow's opinion; cf. Ziolkowski, *Zur Entstehung*, p. 51.

39 Cf. Broch, *Werke*, vol. 8, p. 18 and vol. 2, pp. 609, 595ff.

40 Ibid., vol. 10, p. 336; cf. also vol. 8, p. 140.

41 From this point of vantage, one can also understand the wish that issues repeatedly from the states of irrationality and sleepwalking to overcome and obliterate the era.

42 Broch, *Werke*, vol. 8, p. 140.

Chapter 6

1 Günter Grass, *Hundejahre* (Neuwied and Berlin, 1963).

2 Thus the *New York Times* characterized the novel *Die Blechtrommel*.

3 *Hundejahre*, p. 431.

4 G. Lukács, *Die Theorie des Romans*, 2nd edition (Neuwied and Berlin, 1963), p. 53.

5 Danzig-Langfuhr is Günter Grass' birthplace.

6 It is worthy of note that Grass, who uses every other possible association, does not use the Judas association. To do so, he would have had to mention the person of Christ as a positive figure, and this is apparently repugnant to him.

⁷ There was no previous mention of Harry's intellectual interest or thirst for knowledge. He appeared as a sensitive vegetative type.

⁸ To this must be added his technical knowledge, which, however, does not always seem to have been transformed into epic material and fused into the novel.

⁹ The person of the narrator disappears in novels that raise the interior monologue to a principle of presentation. Events, actions, and persons are almost totally lacking in Gottfried Benn's *Roman des Phänotyp* (Frankfurt am Main, 1961).

¹⁰ Cf. in this connection: "What was long forgotten comes . . . with the help of the Vistula back into memory" (p. 10). "Who wants to know . . . ?" (p. 36). "He, however, who stood at the foot of the hill . . ." (p. 47). "Who crouches there . . . ? Who . . . ? Who . . . ?" (p. 94), whispers the "spirit of the narrative."

¹¹ The "early stages" of National Socialism are not treated in the superpersonal historical novel, but this does not overly tax the "omniscience" that is later apparent in the author collective.

¹² In somewhat similar fashion, Jean Paul Richter's works [cf. Jean Paul Richter, *Werke*, 6 vols. (1960–1963)] contain chapters entitled "Hundpost-tage" [in *Hesperus oder 45 Hundposttage* (1795)], "Zettelkästen" [in *Leben des Quintus Fixlein aus fünfzehn Zettelkästen gezogen* (1796)], *Blumen-, Frucht-, und Dornenstücke* (1796-1797), "Jubelperioden" [=Jobelperioden; in *Titan* (1800–1803)], "Ruhestücke," "Summulae" [in *Dr. Katzenbergers Badereise* (1809)]; Adalbert von Chamisso had given the subtitle "Schieferta-feln" to parts 2, 3, and 4 of the poem "Salas y Gomez" (1829) [cf. Adalbert von Chamisso, *Werke*, 4 vols. (Berlin, 1880), vol. II, pp. 117–126]; Karl Lebercht Immermann had produced "Fensterscheiben" among his early narrative works; and Eduard Mörike had written *Wispeliaden* (1837) [cf. Eduard Mörike, *Sämtliche Werke*, 3 vols., 2nd edition (Stuttgart, 1959–1961), Vol. II, pp. 745-758].

¹³ By means of parentheses in the text, Kurz identifies the "twenty-nine potato years" as 1917–1946, that is, the years after and between World Wars I and II. In Germany, the term "potato years" is more commonly used to describe the years 1945-1948, that is, the "hunger years" *(Hungerjahre)* after World War II. [Translator's note.]

¹⁴ A comparison with other works of literature, such as Dante's "Inferno," Goethe's "Walpurgisnacht" scenes, and Sartre's *No Exit* would be rewarding.

¹⁵ The prophetic meal worms belong among the parodistic devices employed by the author for demonstrating his theme.

¹⁶ *Die Zeit*, Aug. 23, 1963, p. 11.

¹⁷ This undifferentiated atmosphere is not apparent in the part of the novel that might be designated the Danzig Saga.

¹⁸ The author makes it easy for Air Force Auxiliary Harry Liebenau when he lets him show his humanity by readily accepting a paternity for which he has no responsibility. In the very next moment, the author lets Tulla lose the two-month-old fetus by jumping from a moving streetcar, and Harry is deprived of all signs of nobility (pp. 382–386).

¹⁹ "Who believes not in God, but in Nothingness" (p. 375).

Chapter 7

1 T 293f. BM 214. The "wound" in "Das Urteil" signifies the growing awareness of struggle with the father. The abbreviations used here for the individual volumes of Kafka's works are the usual ones. B = *Briefe;* BK = *Beschreibung eines Kampfes;* BM = *Briefe an Milena;* E = *Erzählungen;* H = *Hochzeitsvorbereitungen auf dem Lande und andere Prosa aus dem Nachlass;* T = *Tagebücher.* All references are to Franz Kafka, *Gesammelte Werke,* ed. Max Brod, 11 vols. (S. Fischer Verlag, Frankfurt, 1950–1958).

2 E. A. Albrecht, "Zur Entstehungsgeschichte von Kafkas Landarzt," in *Monatshefte für deutschen Unterricht* (Madison, Wis., 1954), p. 212.

3 G. Janouch, *Gespräche mit Kafka* (Frankfurt, 1951), p. 27. The diaries report a surprising number of dreams. Dreamlike elements are to be found in most of Kafka's works. One of the best-known entries in the diaries reads as follows: "From the point of view of literature, my fate is very simple. The inclination to exhibit my dreamlike inner life has pushed everything else into second place, and it has become terribly stunted and does not cease to become more so. Nothing else can ever satisfy me" (T 420).

4 Kafka's uncle, Dr. Siegfried Löwy, was a country doctor and a bachelor. There are numerous entries about horses in Kafka's diaries. The diary mentions also a "coachman Joseph, whom no other master could have endured" (T 373). In July 1916, Kafka reported a sick call in which the doctor's inability to help and the patient's awareness of it meet in striking fashion (T 505). A verse entry of the same month (T 507) also apostrophizes the "lost generation."

5 M. Lüthi, *Märchen* (Stuttgart, 1962), p. 25.

6 C. Heselhaus, "Kafkas Erzählformen," in *Deutsche Vierteljahrsschrift* (1952), p. 355ff. Heselhaus' concept of the anti-fairy tale has not been without opposition. "W" in the Diary is the Swiss woman whom Kafka met in Riva. Janouch, *Gespräche,* p. 55.

7 M. Walser describes the critical moment with which Kafka's episodes begin as a "disorder" (*Beschreibung einer Form,* 2nd edition [Munich, 1963], p. 92).

8 On the figure of the bachelor, see T 17ff., 160f., 180f., 558. Politzer describes it as Kafka's basic character (H. Politzer, *Franz Kafka, der Künstler* [Frankfurt, 1965], pp. 45–80).

9 In Kafka's work, there is never a spiritual and personal relationship between man and woman nor one that is integrally sexual.

10 As opposed to this interpretation, Sokel is of the opinion that the doctor does not take his professional duties seriously. "The apathy, the insensitivity, the almost brutal conduct of the doctor, and above all his forgetfulness of duty, his superb indifference not only toward the boy, but also toward his 'district' are anti-utopian traits in his character" (W. H. Sokel, *Franz Kafka. Tragik und Ironie* [Munich and Vienna, 1964], p. 276). The dichotomy "utopian and anti-utopian" seems to me not to be especially suitable for an interpretation of this story. Emrich interprets correctly: "In an age that has lost the faith, then, the doctor is forced against his will to assume the task of the priest: the healing and saving of the human soul." "And a substitute for healing by the priest is not possible" (W. Emrich, *Franz Kafka* [Bonn, 1958], pp. 130, 136). It is in fact questionable if one can speak here of saving the "soul."

So far as I know, the word does not occur in Kafka's vocabulary and does not agree with the total existence that he intended. In contrast to Amfortas' wound in *Parzival*, for which one needed only to find the proper cure, the "great wound," which is a wound of existence, cannot be healed.

11 The metaphor of the charioteer and his horses Kafka knew from Plato's *Phaedrus*. With Max Brod, he had read Plato during his years at the university. He had in his library R. Kassner's translation of the *Phaedrus* (K. Wagenbach, *Franz Kafka. Eine Biographie seiner Jugend* [Bern, 1958], pp. 35, 259). But Kafka has changed, distorted, and alienated the basic references of the charioteer metaphor and made it grotesque. As charioteer, the doctor has nothing to guide.

12 Cf. Kafka, *Kleine Fabel* (BK 119).

13 Kafka made frequent use of the word "existence." Nevertheless, it would be unwise to speak without careful consideration, as has sometimes been done, of Kafka's "existential heroes." The possibility of freedom and of the determination to act at the existentially understood moment of time is largely lacking in Kafka's heroes. Insofar, however, as the liberation of the "hero" from self-deception and *"mauvaise foi,"* the violent experience of exposure, loneliness, and wretchedness, and the threat from forms of the collective are among the basic characteristics of a literary existentialism (which is not merely identical with philosophical existentialism), and since Kafka himself speaks again and again of "existence," it seems meaningful to apply the concept to his statement of the experience of existence (cf. W. Kudszus, "Erzählhaltung und Zeitverschiebung in Kafkas 'Prozess' und 'Schloss,'" in *Deutsche Vierteljahrsschrift*, 1964, p. 204ff.). "Doom," as "fateful doom," is primarily a romantic category. Cf. Rainer Grünter, "Beitrag zur Kafka-Deutung," *Merkur* IV (1950), no. 3 (March), p. 280ff. Kafka's "doom" seems to come not so much from outside as from within, necessitated by both inner and outer forces, to be not so much a fatal mechanism as an indication of a doomed existence. G. Anders believed that he had discovered in Kafka a parallel to the Calvinistic idea of predestination (*Kafka. Pro und Contra*, 2nd edition [Munich, 1963], p. 108ff.). But Kafka did not know such a direct causality of God.

14 B 164; cf. "Das Urteil" (E 53ff.); "Brief an den Vater" (H 162ff.).

Chapter 8

1 B. Allemann in *litterarium* 7 (Fall 1960) (house publication of the Walter Publishing Company, Olten/Freiburg); G. Böse, "Rechenschaftsbericht in Leinen. Rezension des 'Jahresring 59/60,'" in *Süddeutsche Zeitung*; Karl August Horst, "Helmut Heissenbüttels Textbuch 1," *Merkur* XV (1961), no. 158 (April), pp. 389–392; "Versuch einer Ortsbestimmung," ibid. XVI (1962), no. 169 (March), pp. 294–295; "Spekulationen über Helmut Heissenbüttels Texte," ibid. XVIII (1964), no. 199 (Sept.), pp. 885–888; D. Hasselblatt, *Lyrik heute. Kritische Abenteuer mit Gedichten* (Gütersloh o. J., 1963), p. 77; E. v. Kahler, "Form und Entformung II," *Merkur* XIX (1965), no. 206 (May), p. 424; H. Vormweg, "Material und Form. Zur Ästhetik der modernen Literatur," ibid., p. 434; H. Bienek, *Rückseite von Heissenbüttel, Textbuch 5;* K. Schwedhelm, "Das Gedicht in einer veränderten Wirklichkeit,"

Zeitalter des Fragments. Radio-Essays des Süddeutschen Rundfunks (Her-
renalb, 1964), p. 154; J. Becker, "Helmut Heissenbüttel," *Schriftsteller der
Gegenwart* (Olten/Freiburg, 1963), pp. 146, 148; K. Leonhard, *Moderne
Lyrik. Monolog und Manifest* (Bremen, 1963), p. 187; P. Hamm, "Die
Wiederentdeckung der Wirklichkeit," closing essay in *Aussichten. Junge
Lyriker des deutschen Sprachraums* (Munich: Biederstein, 1966), p. 328f.

2 K. Leonhard, *Moderne Lyrik*, p. 47. Cf. H. Heissenbüttel, *Über Literatur* (Olten/Freiburg, 1966), p. 236.

3 The following works of Heissenbüttel's have appeared to date: *Kombinationen* (Esslingen, 1954); *Topographien* (Esslingen, 1956); *Textbuch* 1,
2, 3, 4, 5, (Olten/Freiburg, 1960, 1961, 1962, 1964, 1965). "Das Sagbare sagen"
appeared in *Kombinationen* and was later included in *Textbuch* 1. The German text reads as follows.

> das Sagbare sagen
> das Erfahrbare erfahren
> das Entscheidbare entscheiden
> das Erreichbare erreichen
> das Wiederholbare wiederholen
> das Beendbare beenden.
>
> das nicht Sagbare
> das nicht Erfahrbare
> das nicht Entscheidbare
> das nicht Erreichbare
> das nicht Wiederholbare
> das nicht Beendbare
>
> das nicht Beendbare nicht beenden

4 In German, many of these directives use the infinitive form of the verb
as an imperative—e.g., "rechts gehen," "auf Vorfahrt achten"—and thus offer
a closer parallel to the infinitive construction in Heissenbüttel's poem. [Trans-
lator's note.]

5 The German text reads as follows.

> das nicht Sagbare nicht sagen
> das nicht Erfahrbare nicht erfahren
> das nicht Entscheidbare nicht entscheiden (usw.)
>
> or: das nicht Sagbare nicht beenden
> das nicht Erfahrbare nicht beenden
> das nicht Entscheidbare nicht beenden (usw.)

6 The German text reads as follows.

> einfache Sätze
> während ich stehe fällt der Schatten hin
> Morgensonne entwirft die erste Zeichnung
> Blühn ist ein tödliches Geschäft
> ich habe mich einverstanden erklärt
> ich lebe

7 It would be informative to compare the nature and form of consent in
Heissenbüttel's works with the lyrical texts of, for instance, Enzensberger,
Ingeborg Bachmann, Paul Celan, or even Nelly Sachs.

[8] *Frankfurter Allgemeine Zeitung*, Mar. 6, 1964.

[9] Ibid., Mar. 4, 1964.

[10] The German text reads as follows.

> ich erkläre mich einverstanden
> ich erkläre mich nicht einverstanden
> ich sage die Wahrheit
> ich sage nicht die Wahrheit

[11] On Wittgenstein's development, see W. Stegmüller, *Die Hauptströmungen der Gegenwartsphilosophie* (Stuttgart, 1965), pp. 526–696.

[12] The German text reads as follows.

Topographien

a
atemlos überqueren die Vögel der Weltgeschichte
  das ungedeckte Gelände
Irreparables Schocks schamlose Haut Verluste
Big Sid Catlett Art Tatum Fats Navarro
Rückerinnerung an den Untergrund meiner eigenen Landschaft
denn ich ein Roman von Gustav Freytag
einzelne weisse rasch über den sichtbaren Umriss
  wandernde Flecken
eine weisse Möve löst sich aus dem Profil des Flüchtenden
abgefallene Gesichter auf den Treppen der U-Bahnschächte
die Gesichter der Toten
in rasender Eile vermehren sich die Glühpunkte der Nacht
rostige Kastenformen schaukeln langsam verzweifelt
  unaufhaltsam in die stahlblaue Schutzschicht

b
Zeit
Vorzeit nimmt zu Zukunft ab
zwischen den rostgelben Oktoberbäumen bewegen sich die
  zitronengelben Autos
die schwärzliche Schönheit einer Hortensienmumie
der langsame Schritt der nichts Erwartenden
Zeitverlust
das Aufhören der Identität auf der Brücke
Spuren von Anis in der Luft
Türen von Anis
death is so permanent
die Messingstäbe des Zeitbewusstseins schlagen blind aneinander

c
unaufhörlich begegnen sich in den gegeneinander bewegten
  Strömen dieselben Gesichter
die Lautsprecher reden ununterbrechbar
das Klavierspiel der kleinen Mädchen gräbt einen Tunnel
  durch die Jahre
der Schrei der Möve der meinen Frühtraum zerschneidet ist
  immer noch meine Schwester

aus den Tunneln tauchen die beleuchteten Vorderflächen empor
Holzfeuerhimmel der hinten liegenden Gegenden
offenstehende Türen zu abgestellten Eisenbahnwaggons
    in der Novembersonne
flachgezogene Rauchgelände über Rangierbahnhöfen
aufgegitterte Spiegelbilder im Wellblech der Kanäle
in diesem Kanal und Brückengelände
die glitzernden Parallelen des vor mir liegenden Geländes

d
Tage abziehen Ärger zählen exakt funktionieren
interesselos an den Interessen der Interessierten
dass mit dem was erreicht werden kann weniger erreicht wird
    als wenn nichts erreicht wird
die Verführung zu immer derselben Sorte von Sätzen
Schlupfwinkel Benjamin Péret und Francis Picabia
stornierte Einfälle
überlebende Gedanken
alles ist anders als seine Hypothese
die Wahrheit ist mein Gedächtnis
ich sammle Passanten die vor sich hin reden
ich bedeute das Fehlen der Gedanken in den abgefallenen
    Gesichtern

e
inhaltlose Sätze im Nachtdrift
wirkliche nächtliche Strassenbahngesprächsfetzen
Stimmen über dem Eis
das menschenleere Gesicht das ich erkenne
ein Tag vor Weihnachten
Nachtland Nachtblau
geflügelte Peripetie der Nacht
die milchbraune Kreisform
jetzt
jetzt jetzt jetzt

13 Cf. the "Poem on the Practice of Dying" (*Textbuch* 3), in which Stuttgart-Heslach, Zürich, Alster-Hamburg, and Wilhelmshaven are placed next to each other.

14 Letter from Heissenbüttel to the author, May 27, 1966.

15 Cf. "The Remembrance of the Voice of Adolf Hitler on the Radio . . ." from the "Lehrgedicht über Geschichte 1954" in *Textbuch* 1, 7.

16 Heissenbüttel's letter of May 27, 1966. In view of the nature of the text, it may be well to give Heissenbüttel's commentary in the original German. "Ergänzt zu einem vollständigen Satz oder vielleicht besser zu einer ausgeführten Überlegung könnte das etwa so heissen: Denn, wenn ich so darüber nachdenke und mir überlege, wie die Hintergründe der Konvention aussehen, in die ich hineingekommen bin, bin ich (oder das, was da bei diesem Ich unten drunter liegt, das, was nachwirkt, nicht vielleicht so etwas wie) ein Roman von Gustav Freytag. . . ." [Translator's note.]

17 The quotation is part of the American slogan "Drive carefully, death is so permanent."

[18] Cf. V. Klotz, *Geschlossene und offene Form im Drama* (Munich, 1960).

[19] In 1953, E. Gomringer transferred the expression "concrete poetry" to literature, taking it from the realm of painting, where it meant reducing pictorial elements to point, line, surface, to geometric principles for dividing the pictorial surface, and to the relative values of the basic colors used. In both disciplines, it means reduction to rationally comprehensible basic elements. Cf. Heissenbüttel, *Über Literatur*, p. 71ff.

[20] Vormweg, "Material und Form," p. 435. *Topographie c* was interpreted by K. Leonhard, *Moderne Lyrik*, p. 31f.; *Topographie e* was interpreted by P. Horn in *Neue Deutsche Heimat*, no. 100 (July–August 1964), pp. 78–80. From the point of view of method, such a division is not permissible, since each individual topography is part of a larger whole.

[21] Nelly Sachs, *Fahrt ins Staublose* (Frankfurt, 1961), pp. 142, 93, 149, 380.

[22] H. Heissenbüttel, *Über Literatur*, p. 206ff.

Chapter 9

[1] M. Landmann, *Die absolute Dichtung* (Stuttgart, 1963), p. 20; H. M. Enzensberger, in *Nelly Sachs zu Ehren* (Frankfurt, 1961), p. 45; R. Italiaander, in *Der deutsche Buchhandel* (Mitteilungen für die Presse, 1965), no. 174.

[2] R. Thoursie, "Eine Schwester Kafkas," in *Nelly Sachs zu Ehren*, p. 68; G. L. Jost, "Eine Schwester Hiobs," in *Der deutsche Buchhandel*, no. 174.

[3] The German text reads as follows.

Hiob
O du Windrose der Qualen!
Von Urzeitstürmen
in immer andere Richtungen der Unwetter gerissen;
noch dein Süden heisst Einsamkeit.
Wo du stehst, ist der Nabel der Schmerzen.

Deine Augen sind tief in deinen Schädel gesunken
wie Höhlentauben in der Nacht
die der Jäger blind herausholt.
Deine Stimme ist stumm geworden,
denn sie hat zuviel *Warum* gefragt.

Zu den Würmern und Fischen ist deine Stimme eingegangen.
Hiob, du hast alle Nachtwachen durchweint
aber einmal wird das Sternbild deines Blutes
alle aufgehenden Sonnen erbleichen lassen (95).

The numbers in parentheses after the poems refer to the pages in Nelly Sachs' *Fahrt ins Staublose* (Frankfurt, 1961), the last collected edition of her poems to date. In strophe 2, Kurz has erroneously quoted *Höhlenstaub (cave dust)* for *Höhlentauben (cave doves)*. The correct reading has been used in this translation. [Translator's note.]

[4] *"Von Welle und Granit." Querschnitt durch die schwedische Lyrik des 20. Jahrhunderts* (Berlin, 1947); *"Aber auch diese Sonne ist heimatlos." Schwedische Lyrik der Gegenwart* (Darmstadt, 1957); J. Edfelt, *"Der Schatten-*

235

fischer." Gedichte (Darmstadt, 1959); G. Ekelöf, *"Poesie." Schwedisch und deutsch* (Frankfurt, 1962); E. Lindegren, *Gedichte* (Neuwied, 1963).

5 H. M. Enzensberger, "Nachwort," in Nelly Sachs, *Ausgewählte Gedichte* (Frankfurt, 1963).

6 Cf., for instance, I. Bachmann's invocation in the poem "Mein Vogel" [My Bird], or those of H. M. Enzensberger in the poem "mehrere elstern" [several magpies].

7 This version of the text from Job is from *The Anchor Bible: Job,* translated and with an introduction and notes by Marvin H. Pope (New York: Doubleday & Co., Inc., 1965), p. 129. A note in this translation comments: "The verse is notoriously difficult. The ancient versions all differ and no reliance can be placed in any of them" (p. 135). The translation of the same passage in *The Jerusalem Bible* (New York: Doubleday & Co., Inc., 1966) reads as follows: "After my awaking, he will set me close to him, and from my flesh I shall look on God" (p. 750). [Translator's note.] The German text of this poem reads as follows.

> *O die Schornsteine*
> Auf den sinnreich erdachten Wohnungen des Todes,
> Als Israels Leib zog aufgelöst in Rauch
> Durch die Luft—
> Als Essenkehrer ihn ein Stern empfing
> Der schwarz wurde
> Oder war es ein Sonnenstrahl?
>
> O die Schornsteine!
> Freiheitswege für Jeremias und Hiobs Staub—
> Wer erdachte euch und baute Stein auf Stein
> Den Weg für Flüchtlinge aus Rauch?
>
> O die Wohnungen des Todes,
> Einladend hergerichtet
> Für den Wirt des Hauses, der sonst Gast war—
> O ihr Finger,
> Die Eingangsschwelle legend
> Wie ein Messer zwischen Leben und Tod—
>
> O ihr Schornsteine,
> O ihr Finger,
> Und Israels Leib im Rauch durch die Luft!

8 Cf. M. L. Kaschnitz, "Dein Schweigen—Meine Stimme," now in *"Überallnie." Ausgewählte Gedichte* (Hamburg, 1965).

9 The German text reads as follows.

> *Vielleicht aber* braucht Gott die Sehnsucht,
> wo sollte sonst sie auch bleiben,
> Sie, die mit Küssen und Tränen und Seufzern
> füllt die geheimnisvollen Räume der Luft—
> Vielleicht ist sie das unsichtbare Erdreich,
> daraus die glühenden Wurzeln der Sterne treiben—
> Und die Strahlenstimme über die Felder der Trennung,
> die zum Wiedersehn ruft?
> O mein Geliebter, vielleicht hat unsere Liebe

in den Himmel der Sehnsucht schon Welten geboren—
Wie unser Atemzug, ein—und aus,
  baute eine Wiege für Leben und Tod?
Sandkörner wir beide, dunkel vor Abschied,
  und in das goldene Geheimnis der Geburten verloren,
Und vielleicht schon von kommenden Sternen,
  Monden und Sonnen umloht (25).

[10] A. Neher, *Jeremias* (Cologne, 1961), pp. 17ff., 20.
[11] The German text reads as follows.

  Klagemauer Nacht,
  Von dem Blitze eines Gebetes kannst du zertrümmert werden
  Und alle, die Gott verschlafen haben
  Wachen hinter deinen stürzenden Mauern
  Zu ihm auf (62).

[12] The German text reads as follows.
      Leget auf den Acker die Waffen der Rache
      Damit sie leise werden—
      Denn auch Eisen und Korn sind Geschwister
      Im Schosse der Erde— (68).

[13] The German text reads as follows.
        Aufgeflügelt sind seine Gebete
        aus täglichen Vernichtungen
        suchend die inneren Augenstrassen.
        Krater und Trockenmeere
        erfüllt von Tränen
        durch sternige Stationen reisend
        auf der Fahrt ins Staublose (331).

[14] *Widerspiel. Deutsche Lyrik seit 1945*, ed. Hans Bender (Munich, 1962),
pp. 124, 265.
[15] The German text reads as follows.
        Flucht aus den schwarzgebluteten Gestirnen
        des Abschieds,
        Flucht in die blitztapezierten
        Herbergen des Wahnsinns.
        Flucht, Flucht, Flucht
        in den Gnadenstoss der Flucht
        aus der zersprengten Blutbahn
        kurzer Haltestelle (164).

[16] The German text reads as follows.
        Wohin o wohin
        du Weltall der Sehnsucht
        das in der Raupe schon dunkel verzaubert
        die Flügel spannt,
        mit den Flossen der Fische
        immer den Anfang beschreibt
        in Wassertiefen, die

ein einziges Herz
ausmessen kann mit dem Senkblei
der Trauer.
Wohin o wohin
du Weltall der Sehnsucht
mit der Träume verlorenen Erdreichen
und der gesprengten Blutbahn des Leibes;
während die Seele zusammengefaltet wartet
auf ihre Neugeburt
unter dem Eis der Todesmaske (140).

17 Nelly Sachs mentioned the butterfly for the first time in the epitaph "Die Tänzerin" [The Dancer] (p. 37), but did not develop the image. The poetess had probably found the image in the Jewish Cabala. In the book "Sohar," to which many of her poems refer, reference is made in the first chapter to "the ray with which the 'beginning' sows the seed for its own glory, like the seed of the silkworm, which spins itself in and builds a palace around itself, for its own praise and as a blessing for the world" (*Die Geheimnisse der Schöpfung. Ein Kapitel aus dem Sohar,* trans. into German by G. Scholem [Berlin, 1936], p. 45).

18 In T. S. Eliot's remarks on poetic theory, the concept of the "objective correlative" (in German: "gegenständliche Entsprechung") plays an important role.

19 The German text reads as follows.

> *Schmetterling*
> *Welch* schönes Jenseits
> ist in deinen Staub gemalt.
> Durch den Flammenkern der Erde,
> durch ihre steinerne Schale
> wurdest du gereicht,
> Abschiedswebe in der Vergänglichkeiten Mass.
>
> Schmetterling
> aller Wesen gute Nacht!
> Die Gewichte von Leben und Tod
> senken sich mit deinen Flügeln
> auf die Rose nieder
> die mit dem heimwärts reifenden Licht welkt.
>
> Welch schönes Jenseits
> ist in deinen Staub gemalt.
> Welch Königszeichen
> im Geheimnis der Luft (148).

20 For example, in a mystic hymn, Moses ben Nachmann described the birth of the soul out of the depths of the divine sphere from which its life streamed forth. He says in part: "Out of nothing He called me, yet at the end of time / I am summoned again by the king." And "Down came the soul away from the woven ladder of descending steps / away from the pool of its mission into the garden of the king" (G. Scholem, *Die jüdische Mystik in ihren Hauptströmungen* [Frankfurt, 1957], p. 262. English ed., 1941).

21 The German text reads as follows.

In der Flucht
welch grosser Empfang
unterwegs—
Eingehüllt
in der Winde Tuch
Füsse im Gebet des Sandes
der niemals Amen sagen kann
denn er muss
von der Flosse in den Flügel
und weiter—
Der kranke Schmetterling
weiss bald wieder vom Meer—
Dieser Stein
mit der Inschrift der Fliege
hat sich mir in die Hand gegeben—
An Stelle von Heimat
halte ich die Verwandlungen der Welt— (262).

Index

Abenteuerliche Simplicissimus teutsch, Der. See *Simplicissimus* (Grimmelshausen)
Adorno, Theodor, 35, 39, 44, 45–46, 198–99
Adventurous Simplicissimus, The. See *Simplicissimus* (Grimmelshausen)
Albertus Magnus, Saint, 90
Allemann, Beda, 69, 173
Anders, Günther, 35–36
Andersch, Alfred, 69
Ansichten eines Clowns (Böll), 17, 25–26, 131
Antiquity, 8, 14, 63–64, 103
Arendt, Hannah, 44–45
Aristotle, 63, 64, 88, 91
Auden, W.H., 55, 73

Bachmann, Ingeborg, 194; quoted, 83–84, 85, 96–97, 102
Baroque era, 6, 7, 92–93, 209
Becker, Jürgen, 85, 174
Beissner, Friedrich, 47, 51
Benjamin, Walter, 85
Benn, Gottfried, 50, 66, 86, 98, 100, 106, 189, 205
Bense, Max 39

Bergengruen, Werner, 13
Bienek, Horst, 173
Bildungsroman, 9, 73. *See also* Novel
Blechtrommel, Die (Grass), 26, 101, 131, 132, 139, 147, 216 n.4
Böll, Heinrich, 17, 25–26, 85, 131
Böse, Georg, 173
Brecht, Bertolt, 30, 67, 85, 93, 205
Broch, Hermann, 13, 14, 21, 25, 66, 67, 69, 78–79, 105–30 passim; and author's "will to cognition," 105, 117; on ethical work of art, 105–6; on Kafka, quoted, 31; life of, 106; and Nietzche, 128; and phenomenon of time, 111; as phenotype of age, 105; philosophy of history of, 117–23; and theory of redemption, 124–30; and theory of values, 117, 118–20, 121–23, 128–29. *See also Schlafwandler, Die* (Broch)
Brod, Max, 32–33, 34, 36–37, 41, 169
Buber, Martin, 34–35, 36
Butor, Michel, 21

Castle, The. See *Schloss, Das* (Kafka)
Celan, Paul, 202

"Country Doctor, A." *See*
  "Landarzt, Ein" (Kafka)
Curtius, Ernst Robert, 90–91

Dante, 55, 80, 91, 203
Darwin, Charles Robert, 64–65
Declaration on Human Freedom,
  quoted, 103. *See also* Literature,
  and theology; Theology; Vatican
  Council II
Demetz, Peter, 40
Deputy, The. See *Stellvertreter,*
  Der (Hochhuth)
Déry, Tibor, 144–45
Döblin, Alfred, 30, 106
Donne, John, 64
Dritte Buch über Achim, Das
  (Johnson), 17, 68
Dürrenmatt, Friedrich, 67

Eich, Günther, 97
Eichendorff, Joseph von, 183
Elective Affinities. See
  Wahlverwandtschaften, Die
  (Goethe)
Eliot, T. S., 73, 182, 183
Emrich, Wilhelm, 37–38, 39–40,
  42–43, 46–47, 51–52, 55
Enlightenment, 6, 83, 93–95, 96;
  contemporary forms of, 94–95,
  96; as a continuing process, 93–95;
  of doubt, 94; and separation of
  reason and faith, 93–95
Enzensberger, Hans Magnus, 73, 85,
  194–95
Expressionismus, 30, 54, 70, 81, 86,
  99–100, 163, 165, 183, 185, 198

Fontane, Theodor, 13, 101, 107
Forster, Edward Morgan, 16, 19
Frankfurter Allgemeine Zeitung,
  180
Freud, Siegmund, 41–42, 44
Freytag, Gustav, 187
Frisch, Max, 17, 28, 85, 93, 180
"Fugue of Death." *See* "Todesfuge"
  (Celan)

Gellert, Johann Fürchtegott, 6

George, Stefan, 194
Goethe, Johann Wolfgang von, 4,
  5, 6, 7, 11, 13, 19, 51–52, 54, 55, 64,
  70, 93, 95, 98, 101, 155, 183, 192,
  208, 209. See also *Leiden*
  des jungen Werther, Die
  (Goethe); Novel, traditional;
  Wahlverwandtschaften, Die
  (Goethe)
Gottfried von Strassburg, 85, 90
Gottsched, Johann Christoph, 6
Gral, Der, 99–100
Grass, Günter, 7, 26, 101, 131–48
  passim; criticism of, as author,
  136, 140–41, 144, 145–48; purpose
  of, in *Hundejahre,* 145; in role of
  public nuisance, 145; subjectivity
  of, 145–46. See also *Blechtrommel,*
  Die (Grass); *Hundejahre* (Grass)
Grenzmann, Wilhelm, 35
Grimmelshausen, Jacob Christoffel
  von, 101
Group 47, 94
Gryphius, Andreas, 183
Guardini, Romano, 34

Halbzeit (Walser), 17, 20, 85
Hamm, Peter, 174
Hankamer, Paul, 92
Hartmann von Aue, 8, 85, 90
Hasselblatt, Dieter, 50, 52–53, 173
Hebel, Johann Peter, 55
Hegel, Georg Wilhelm **Friedrich**,
  18, 47
Heidegger, Martin, 37, 41; and
  Kafka, 39–40; parody of, in
  Hundejahre, 140, 143–44
Heine, Heinrich, 8, 89
Heisenberg, Walter: quoted, 63, 78,
  79
Heissenbüttel, Helmut, 83, 85, 96,
  173–93, 205; ambiguity in works of,
  177–78, 181–82, 187, 188; as critic
  of contemporary scene, 182; and
  critics, 173–74, 180–81, 191–92;
  "Einfache Sätze," 178–81;
  "Hypothesen über Literatur und
  Wissenschaften als vergleichbare
  Tätigkeiten," 83, 96, 193; "ich

erkläre mich einverstanden,"
181–82; language of, 173, 174, 176,
179, 180, 182, 192, 193; letter of,
to author, 186, 187, 234 n.16;
"Sagbare sagen, das," 175–78;
skepticism of, 182; *Topographies*
(See *Topographies* [separate
entry]); views of, on literature
and science, 83, 96, 193;
Wittgenstein's influence on,
175–76, 181–82, 187; works of,
as "texts," 175; works of, as total
criticism, 182; world view of, 181
Heller, Erich, 36
Herder, Johann Gottfried, 93
Hermsdorf, K., 48–49
Hero, 4–7, 13–17, 136; as anti-hero,
216 n.4; of *Bildungsroman*, 9;
and community, 8–11, 14;
demythologizing of, 15–17;
modern, 7, 9–10, 12, 15, 16,
17, 20, 26; and reader, 5, 14–15;
search of, for meaningfulness
of life, 8–11; traditional, 4–5,
9–10, 13–17, 29. *See also* Kafka,
Franz, characters of; Literature,
man as object of; Modern novel;
Narrator; Novel; *authors and
titles of individual works*
Heselhaus, Clemens, 51, 154, 222 n.54
Hesiod, 63
Hesse, Hermann, 30
Hochhuth, Rolf, 85, 131
Hofmannsthal, Hugo von, 187–88
Hölderlin, Friedrich, 30
Höllerer, Walter, 100, 205
Holz, Arno, 65
Horst, Karl August, 173
Hugh of St. Victor, 90
Humanism, 84, 91, 183
Hundejahre (Grass), 131–48;
alienation of reality in, 147–48;
author collective in, 136 (*See also*
narrator of); author as epic
persona in, 136–37; being and
time as motives in, 143–44; as
criticism of post World War II
era, 131–32, 138–40, 141, 144, 145;
deformation and revelation as

narrative principles in, 140,
141–44, 145; and Heidegger, 140,
143–44; and Hitler (*See* and Nazi
era); interaction of person and
world in, 132–33, 141, 144; language
of, 140, 143–44, 146–47; levels of
meaning in, 137, 141–44, 147; motif
of dog in, 135, 137, 138, 139, 141–43,
144, 146, 147; motif of scarecrow
in, 133, 140, 143–44, 146, 147;
narrator of, 135, 136–41, 142, 144,
145–46, 147; and Nazi era, 131–32,
133, 134, 135, 138–39, 141–42, 143,
147; nihilism in, 135, 146–47; parody
in, 137, 143–44, 229 n.15; plot of,
132–35; portrayal of living persons
in, 133, 139, 140; religion in, 132,
133, 134, 135, 139, 140, 143, 146–47,
228 n.6; revenge as motif in, 135,
138–40, 142, 144, 145–46; structural
flaws in, 138–41, 142, 143, 144,
145–48; tendentiousness of, 142,
147; world as hell in, 140, 141, 143,
145, 146
Huxley, Aldous, 56–72 passim;
quoted, 57, 57–58, 58–59, 59, 60,
61, 64–65, 65, 69–70, 71

Immermann, Karl, 111–12
Italiaander, Rolf, 195

Janouch, Gustav, 40–41, 152, 154
Jens, Walter, 21
Jerome, Saint, 80, 84
Johnson, Uwe, 4–5, 7, 17, 21, 27, 28,
68, 75
John XXIII (pope), 88
Joyce, James, 7, 14, 20, 25, 45, 50,
66, 105, 106, 110, 117
Jungdeutschland. See Young
Germany

Kafka-Bibliographies, 31–32
Kafka, Franz, 7, 14, 16, 28, 30–55, 65,
66, 67–68, 72, 91, 93, 105, 106,
149–72, 195; alienation in works of,
35–36, 45, 47, 49, 50, 55, 151–52;
ambivalence of, 35, 38, 44, 51–52,
55, 153; anti–fairy tales of, 51,

153–54, 222 n.54; appropriation of, by critics, 38, 39, 42, 48, 50, 51, 53–54; autobiographical elements in works of, 40–41, 45, 169–72, 230 n.4; bachelor in works of, 52 (*See also* "Landarzt, Ein," bachelor as hero of); biographies of, 40–41; and Calvinism, 35–36; and Camus, 219 n. 25; characters of, 16, 33, 36, 45, 51, 52, 155, 156, 163; and concept of being, 38, 39–40, 43, 46; as critic of contemporary scene, 30, 34, 45, 46, 47–50; diaries of, 32, 36, 37, 41, 149, 150, 165 166, 169, 171, 172, 230 n.3; and dreams, 39, 41, 43, 44, 55, 152–53, 169, 230 n.3; Existentialist interpretations of, 38–40, 231 n.13; and Expressionism, 30, 54, 163, 165; form in works of, 39, 50–55, 152–54; and Freud, 41–42, 44; and Gnosticism, 36; and Heidegger, 39–40; hero in works of (*See* characters of); and hope, 33, 34, 37, 48, 172; imagery of, 38, 39, 43–44, 51–52, 166 (*See also* "Landarzt, Ein," imagery of); irony in works of, 52 (*See also* "Landarzt, Ein," irony in); Jewish interpretations of, 33, 34–35; and Judaism, 31, 33, 34–35, 37, 40–41, 44, 218 n.8; and Kierkegaard, 33, 35; language of, 39–40, 50, 52, 55; last testament of, 31, 32, 49, 221 n.49; levels of meaning in works of, 36, 39, 52, 55; and Manichaeism, 36; Marxist interpretations of, 32, 45, 47–50, 54; as moralist, 46–47; narrative perspective in works of, 51, 52, 222 n.53; narrator in works of, 51, 154, 155, 158, 160, 164; negative religion of, 33–34; and Oedipus complex, 42; and original sin (*See* "wound of existence" in works of); pessimism of, 48; posthumous fame of, 30–32; psychoanalytical and psychological interpretations of, 36, 41–44; recent trends in criticism of, 50–55;

religious interpretations of, 32–38; and schizophrenia, 36, 43, 44, 52; sociological and cultural interpretations of, 44–47 (*See also* Marxist interpretations of); subjectivity in works of, 45, 48–49, 163, 166; works of, as parables, 51, 52, 55; "wound of existence" in works of, 43, 150–51, 153, 158, 159–63, 165, 166–69, 169–72, 219 n.18, 219 n.50. Works: "Bericht für eine Akademie, Ein" [Report for an Academy, A], 160; "Beschreibung eines Kampfes [Description of a Struggle], 67–68, 164; *Collected Works*, 31, 32, 149; "Er" [He], 149, 171; "Gibs Auf" [Give It Up], 52; "In der Strafkolonie" [In the Penal Colony], 165, 166; "Josefine, die Sängerin" [Josephine the Singer], 163; "Landarzt, Ein" [Country Doctor, A], 149–72; *Prozess, Der* [Trial, The], 16, 28, 41, 44, 48, 156, 158, 166; *Schloss, Das* [Castle, The], 16, 44–45; "Urteil, Das" [Judgment, The], 31, 149, 166; *Verschollene, Der* [Lost without Trace], 48; "Verwandlung, Die" [Metamorphosis, The], 42, 156, 159, 165; "Vor dem Gesetz" [Before the Law], 31. *See also* "Landarzt, Ein" (Kafka); *names of individual interpreters of Kafka*
Kahler, Erich von, 173
Kaiser, Hellmuth, 42, 43
Kalow, Gert, 180
Kierkegaard, Sören, 33, 35
Kipphardt, R., 67
Kleist, Heinrich von, 55
Klopstock, Friedrich Gottlob, 85
Klossowski, Pierre, 37
Kuhr, Alexander, 43

Lagerlöf, Selma, 196
"Landarzt, Ein" (Kafka), 149–72; alienating elements in, 151–52, 161, 162, 163, 166, 170; ambiguity in,

152–53, 157–58, 167; as anti-fairy tale, 154, antiworld in (*See* doomed existence as motif in); autobiographical elements in, 169–72; bachelor as hero of, 153, 156, 157, 158; dilemma in (*See* doomed existence as motif in); doomed existence as motif in, 151, 153, 154, 156, 157, 158, 164–65, 166–69, 170, 171, 172, 231 n.13; dream elements in, 152–53, 169; expressionistic elements in, 163, 165, 166; failure in (*See* helplessness as motif in), gods in (*See* doomed existence as motif in); guilt in, 153, 158, 166–68; helplessness as motif in, 153, 155, 156, 157–65, 168; imagery of, 151, 152, 153, 158, 160, 162–63, 164, 165–66; irony in, 156, 161, 165, 167, 170; isolation of hero in, 155, 156–57, 172; lack of motivation in, 151, 152; "law" as key word in, 155; metaphors in (*See* imagery of); as monologue, 154; "nakedness" as motif in, 153, 165; narrator of, 154, 155, 158, 160, 162, 164; peculiar logic of, 151–52; plot of, 150–51; reader and, 154, 155; rescue as motif in, 155, 157–65, 172; religious implications of, 150, 160–61, 162, 167; split personality of hero in, 158; space in, 152, 164, 165; "struggle" as key word in, 155; symbolism of (*See* imagery of); time in, 152, 154, 164, 165; "wound of existence" in, 150–51, 153, 158, 159–63, 165, 166–69, 169–72. *See also* Kafka, Franz

Landmann, Michael, 194
Leavis, Frank R., 56–57
Le Fort, Gertrud von, 13
Leiden des jungen Werther, Die (Goethe), 6, 23–24
Leonhard, Kurt, 174, 175
Literary artist: as guardian of human values, 75, 78–79, 144; and inspiration, 69–70, 74, 84; moral obligation of, 73, 102; and

observation of object, 13, 58–60, 67–68, 74, 146; and science, 56, 57, 64–69, 74–79; and theology, 81–83, 100, 101; and world, 10–11; 59, 60, 72, 101. *See also* Literature; "Today"; *names of individual authors*

Literature: Broch on, 105–6; difficulty of dialogue between, and theology, 81–83, 96–98, 101; as ethical work of art, 105–6; evaluation of, 8, 50, 53–55, 85, 90–91, 98, 146; as "experiment," 68–69, 74; and form, 50, 53–54, 84–85, 98, 100, 102; as "ideographic," 59; language of, 61–63, 74, 76; levels of meaning in, 55, 58, 62; man as object of, 13, 57–58, 59–60, 62, 77, 78, 86, 103, 104; and morality, 100, 102, 145; nature of, 53–54, 57–58, 73, 80–81, 83–86, 95; necessary ambiguity of, 62–63, 83; poetical vs. prosaic, 84–85, 225 n.6; and preconceptions of reader, 48, 53, 54, 98–100, 101; as protest, 94–95; as reflection of its age, 3, 6, 7–8, 9–13, 47, 57, 58–59, 59–60, 62, 73, 78, 81, 82, 86, 91, 95, 103, 111–12, 117, 131–32, 144–45; and science, 56–79, 96, 193 (*See also* Nature; Science; Two cultures); secularization of, 83, 89–95, 96, 100; techniques of, 3, 16, 17, 19, 20–21, 28, 61, 66, 68, 132; as theodicy, 60; and theology, 80–104 (*See also* Theology). *See also* Enlightenment; Literary artist; Modern novel; Narrator; Novel; "Today"

Lukács, Georg, 49–50
Luther, Martin, 85, 181

MacNeice, Louis, 73
Mann, Heinrich, 13
Mann, Klaus, 31
Mann ohne Eigenschaften, Der (Musil), 66, 106, 111, 112, 182

Mann, Thomas, 11, 13, 21, 30, 67, 106, 110, 112, 117, 146
Man without Qualities, The. See Mann ohne Eigenschaften, Der (Musil)
Mein Name sei Gantenbein (Frisch), 17, 28, 85, 180
Meun, Jean de, 90
Middle Ages, 9, 63–64, 87, 89–91, 92, 93, 126, 209
Modern novel, 3–29 passim; 105, 110; abstraction as technique of, 3, 16, 17, 72, 132; character of, 3, 4–5, 7–8, 10–11, 17, 18, 19, 20, 21, 68; evaluation of, 8, 29; experiment as technique of, 68–69; hero of (See Hero); inadequacy of designation "modern" for, 8; and modern world, 3, 9–13, 131–32; montage as technique of, 16, 17, 28, 132, 141, 142; and narrator (See Narrator); and preconceptions of reader, 3, 4, 5, 7–8, 15, 27; stream-of-consciousness technique of, 20, 21, 66, 110; time in, 25–26, 110. See also Literary artist; Literature; Novel; "Today"; authors and titles of individual works
Mörike, Eduard, 209
Muckermann, Friedrich, 99
Muschg, Walter, 38
Musil, Robert, 7, 21, 50, 66, 67, 75–76, 105, 106, 111, 112, 182
Mutmassungen über Jakob (Johnson) 4–5, 17, 27–28, 68
My Name Is Gantenbein. See Mein Name sei Gantenbein

Narrator, 7, 20, 22–25, 25–29, 136; and author, 22; collective, 136–41; first-person, 22, 23–24, 26, 154; and hero, 22, 23–24, 26; indispensable role of, in novel, 25; of modern novel, 4–5, 20, 24–25, 25–29, 68, 229 n.9; Olympian, 4, 22–25, 26–27, 28, 29, 76, 102; and plot, 22; perspective of, 4, 21, 22, 25, 26–28, 68; and reader, 4–6, 22, 23, 25;

traditional, 4–5, 22–24. See also Hero; Literary artist; Literature; Modern novel; Novel; authors and titles of individual works
National Socialism, 119–20. See also Hundejahre (Grass), and Nazi era; Sachs, Nelly, concentration camp in works of
Naturalism (literary), 65, 68–69
Nature: changing concept of, 75, 216 n.2; demythologizing of, 69–72; depoetizing of, 69–72; medieval concept of, 63–65; mythical concept of, 63, 70; Neo-Platonic concept of, 63. See also Literature; Science
Newton, Sir Isaac, 66, 69
Nietzsche, Friedrich, 128
Nonnenmann, Klaus, 194
Nouveau roman, 21, 68, 102, 185. See also Literature; Modern novel; Novel
Novel, 3–29; avant-grade (See Modern novel); and community, 8–11, 14; of contemporary criticism, 3, 6, 7–8, 9–13, 105–30, 131–48; crisis of, 18, 29, 136; and epic, 8–9; epistemological, 106; forms of narration in, 3, 19, 20–21, 25–29, 61, 66; naturalistic, 65, 68–69; plot of, 4, 5–6, 17–21, 217 n.7; and preconceptions of reader, 3, 4, 5, 6–7; as reflection of its age (See Literature, as reflection of its age); and search for meaningfulness of life, 8–11, 111; time in, 4–5, 25–26, 110, 112; traditional, 3–29 passim, 76, 110. See also Hero; Literary artist; Literature; Modern novel; Nouveau roman; authors and titles of individual works

Pastoral Constitution on the Church in the Modern World, The, quoted, 82, 88–89. See also Literature, and theology; Theology; Vatican Council II
phenotype, 14, 30, 86, 105

Plato, 71, 120, 123, 124, 126, 127, 129, 130
Politzer, Heinrich, 32, 50–51, 52, 55
Pongs, Hermann, 36, 44, 55
Pope, Alexander, 58
Proust, Marcel, 45, 50, 106 110, 187
Prozess Der (Kafka), 16, 28, 41, 44, 48, 156, 158, 166. *See also* Kafka, Franz

Reimann, Paul, 47–48
Renaissance, 14, 64, 67, 103, 118, 127, 183
Richter, Helmut, 47, 49
Rilke, Rainer Maria, 14, 66
Robbe-Grillet, Alain, 21
Rochefort, R. 33–34
Rococo era, 95
Romanticism, 66, 68, 89, 93, 99, 107, 113, 114–15, 118, 196

Sachs, Nelly, 85, 192–93, 194–215; and Bible, 195, 197, 199, 201, 205, 215; butterfly as image in works of, 208–15, 238 n.17; and Cabala, 199, 208, 211, 238 n.17; and Celan, 202; concentration camp in works of, 198–215 passim; and critics, 194–95; death in works of, 199–215 passim; "dust" as theme of, 201, 203, 206, 208, 210, 211, 213, 215; "flight" as theme of, 195, 205, 206–8, 211–215; and Hasidism, 199, 208; irony in works of, 200, 202, 212; Israel (=the Jewish people) as main theme of, 195–215 passim; and Job, 195, 199, 201; and Kafka, 195; life of, 196–98; "longing" as theme of, 203, 206; literary honors bestowed on, 198; "metamorphosis" as theme of, 201, 206, 208, 212–15; "midnight" in works of, 204; mysticism of, 203, 205, 210, 213; "objective correlative" in works of, 208, 209; on revenge, 205; "royalty" as theme of, 211; and suffering, 195–215 passim; and Sweden, 194, 196, 198; and Yahweh-God, 195, 199, 201, 207,

211, 215; works of, 196–98. Works translated in text: "Aufgeflügelt sind seine Gebete" [Upward from daily destruction], 206; "Flucht aus den schwarzgebluteten Gestirnen" [Flight from the black-bloodied constellation], 207; "Hiob" [Job], 195–96; "In der Flucht" [During the Flight], 212–15; "Klagemauer Nacht" [Wailing wall, night], 204–5; Leget auf den Acker die Waffen der Rache" [Lay upon the plowed fields your weapons of revenge], 205; "O die Schornsteine" (O the chimneys), 199–202; "Schmetterling" [Butterfly], 209; "Vielleicht aber braucht Gott die Sehnsucht" [But perhaps God needs longing], 203; "Wohin o wohin" [Whither o whither], 207–8
Sarraute, Nathalie, 21
Schaukal, Richard von, 99
Schiller, Friedrich, 85, 93, 179
Schlafwandler, Die (Broch), 14, 69, 105–30; anarchy as leading motif of, 107, 108, 113–14, 115–16, 117, 118–19, 122–23, 129; author as narrator in, 117–18; Broch on, 116–18, 125, 128; as criticism of contemporary scene, 106, 110–11, 112–14, 116–20, 130; disintegration of values as main theme of, 109, 110, 115, 117–23, 125–30; epilogue of, 109, 117, 119, 123, 127, 128–30; as epistemological novel, 117; essayistic comment in, 110, 115, 117, 118, 124, 125; form of, 106, 109, 110, 113, 114, 125, 130; honor as motif of, 107, 114, 118; irrationality as motif of, 111, 114, 115–16, 118–19, 120–23, 124, 129; Judaeo-Christian thought in, 126–28, 129–30; Messianic hope in, 129–30; National Socialism diagnosed in, 119–20; objectivity as leading motif of 107, 113–14, 116, 117, 118–19, 122, 125, 129;

order and disorder as motives of, 107, 108, 113, 114, 115, 124; Platonic thought in, 118, 120, 123, 126–28, 128, 129, 130; plot of, 106–10; redemption as motif of, 105, 108, 115, 120, 123, 123–30; rejection of established religions in, 125–28, 130; romanticism as leading motif of, 107, 113–14, 114–15, 116, 117, 118, 119, 122, 124, 129; sleepwalking as motif of, 108, 111, 120–23, 124, 130; time in, 107, 113, 115, 116. *See also* Broch, Hermann

Schlegel, August Wilhelm, 89
Schlegel, Friedrich, 8, 10–11
Schloss, Das (Kafka), 16, 44–45. *See also* Kafka, Franz
Schoeps, Hans Joachim, 33, 34
Scholasticism, 64, 90–91, 101
Schwedholm, Karl, 173
Science: definition of, 57; and demythologizing of world, 69–70; and drama, 66–67; and essay, 67; language of, 61, 62, 63; and lyric poetry, 64–66, 70–72, 74–75; nomothetic methods and goals of, 58–59; self-sufficiency of, 75. *See also* Literature, and science; Two cultures
Shakespeare, William, 8, 53, 55, 57, 145
Simplicissimus (Grimmelshausen), 7, 11, 13, 101
Sleepwalkers, The. See *Schlafwandler Die* (Broch)
Snow, Charles P., 56–57
Socrates, 10–11, 63
Sokel, Walter, 44, 52, 55
Sorrows of Young Werther, The. See *Leiden des jungen Werther, Die* (Goethe)
Speculations about Jacob. See *Mutmassungen über Jakob* (Johnson)
Stellvertreter, Der (Hochhuth), 85, 131
Stifter, Adalbert, 11, 12, 13

Tennyson, Alfred, 64

Theology: attitude of, to literature, 81, 82–83, 90–91, 100; difficulty of dialogue between, and literature, 81–83, 91, 96–98; as reflection of its age, 81–82, 86–89; and secularization of world view, 89–95, 103, 104; of today, 86–89, 102. *See also* Literature, and theology; Renaissance
Third Book about Achim, The. See *Dritte Buch über Achim, Das* (Johnson)
Thomas Aquinas, Saint, 82, 90
Tin Drum, The. See *Blechtrommel, Die* (Grass)
"Today": literature of, 71–74, 83, 86, 174; man of, 10, 12–13, 76, 78; meaning of word, 85–86; science of, 65, 75; theology of, 86–89, 102; world of, 11–12, 15, 60, 70, 78, 87, 101, 103–4. *See also* Literature; Modern novel; Science; Theology
"Todesfuge" (Celan), 202
Topographies (Heissenbüttel): analysis of, 182–93; aphorisms and illustrations in, 186; association as technique in, 187, 188; description as literary device in, 185, 190; exemplary landscape of, 185–86; isolation in, 190, 191; memory in, 187, 190; open structure of, 191; polarity of, 186; textual "I" of, 186, 189, 190, 191; time in, 187–88, 190–91; traffic images in, 188; world view in, 189, 191–92
Tractatus logico-philosophus (Wittgenstein), 175–76, 181–82
Trial, The. See *Prozess, Der* (Kafka)
Tucholsky, Kurt, 30
Two cultures: evolution of, 63–64; increasing proximity of, 69, 72; theory of, 56–57. *See also* Literature, and science
Two Views. See *Zwei Ansichten* (Johnson)

Vatican Council II, 82, 88, 94, 103; as historical caesura, 88
Views of a Clown. See *Ansichten*

eines Clowns (Böll)
Vormweg, Heinrich, 173, 191

Wagenbach, Klaus, 41, 53
Wahlverwandtschaften, Die
(Goethe), 4–7, 11, 64; hero of,
4–5; narrator of, 4–5, 22–23; plot
of, 5–6, 18–19; time and place in,
4–5
Walser, Martin, 7, 17, 20, 51, 85
Walter, Otto F., 21
Walther von der Vogelweide, 85,
89–90
Weidlé, Wladimir, 17–18

Weinberg, Kurt, 43–44
Weiss, Peter, 21, 85
Wittgenstein, Ludwig, 175–76,
181–82, 187
Wolfram von Eschenbach, 8, 90
Woolf, Virginia, 20, 66, 106, 110
Wordsworth, William, 66, 71, 74–75;
quoted 74–75

Young Germany, 112

Zola, Émile, 68–69
Zwei Ansichten (Johnson), 85
Zweig, Stefan, 196